THE
ONE POT
COOK

D1100437

Hattie Ellis is an award-winning food writer and has appeared on programmes such as *Breakfast Time*, *Woman's Hour* and *The Food Programme*. She won the Guild of Food Writer's Food Book of the Year in 2013 for *What to Eat?* and was shortlisted for the 2014 André Simon Food and Drink Awards and the Guild of Food Writer's Cookery Book of the Year for her book *Spoonfuls of Honey*. She lives in West London.

HEAD
of ZEUS

HATTIE ELLIS

With illustrations by Emily Faccini

THE
ONE POT
COOK

150 recipes for feeding
family & friends

First published in 2015 by
Head of Zeus Ltd

1 3 5 7 9 10 8 6 4 2

A catalogue record for this book is
available from the British Library.

ISBN
(HB) 9781781851265
(E) 9781781853108

Book designed by Zoë Bather

Illustrations by Emily Faccini

Printed and bound in China
by 1010 Printing Internationl Ltd

Head of Zeus Ltd
Clerkenwell House
45–47 Clerkenwell Green
London EC1R 0HT

WWW.HEADOFZEUS.COM

For Tim, Rupert,
Theo & Brodie

MEAT

FISH

VEG

PUD

001 **SOUP**

035 **SIMPLE SUPPERS**

073 WINTER WARMERS

153 EXPLORE THE WORLD

197 EASY PUDS

THIS BOOK

IS A SUMMARY

OF MY ONE POT

DISCOVERIES

THE ONE POT COOK

Most of us start out as One Pot cooks. Our first kitchens are often the smallest and least well equipped. There may well be just the one large pot. Yet this is also a sociable time of burgeoning friendships and relationships, and that pot feeds many tablefuls, usually on a budget and with unpredictable numbers.

What is true for your first kitchen turns out to be relevant to the rest of your cooking life. I went back to being a One Pot cook due to nothing less than a revolution in circumstances. In my early 40s I met and married Tim, and found myself in an ever-shifting household of three ravenous teenage boys and a man who works nights as a news producer. Ours is a 24-hour household, not least because the habits and appetites of growing teens do not arrive like the hands of the clock to the appointed hour.

So this is how I cook. Alongside day-to-day assemblies, my food pivots on a couple of precious spare hours each week that can be devoted to the batch preparation of One Pots, generally on a spare weekday evening, a Saturday afternoon, or a Sunday morning. The stove and hob fill up with a stew, a thick soup, some stock for quick lunchtime broths, and a pudding. These are either eaten straight away, or cooled to go in the fridge for the coming days. You could call this a production line of homemade ready meals; they just need heating up in portions, whenever suits whomever. This book is a summary of my discoveries.

A One Pot boils down to this: put well-chosen
ingredients in a single receptacle – be it a
casserole, sauté pan, roasting tray, saucepan,
wok, tagine or cowboy cauldron – apply
heat, and let the dish come together. With
the odd stir and other small interventions –
an adjustment of seasoning, a finishing scatter
of herbs – the flavours are left to work their
magic. You might add a salad; you might have
vegetables alongside rather than in the pot –
it's easy enough to throw a few spuds in the
oven, or to steam some greens. What matters
most is that the heart of the dish comes
together in one place.

The classic One Pot is a meal-in-a-bowl.
Versatile and economical, this is homely, easy
food. But your One Pot is a capacious container
and One Pot cooking is more gloriously varied
and wide-ranging than its simple image
initially suggests.

The following recipes span the whole range
of One Pot dishes: from casseroles and
tagines to pies and gratins; from fruit salads
to steamed puddings. Six chapters arrange
the One Pots by type: Soup; Simple Suppers;
Winter Warmers; Summer Spreads; Explore the
World; and, last but not least, Easy Puds.

You don't need many pots to make these
recipes. One single casserole or a large saucepan
with a lid will do for most. The dishes fit into
the rest of life and leave minimal washing-up.

Most are very simple – shopping and chopping, with the occasional stir between other tasks – but even the more complex ones can be made in advance to suit your timing.

Making delicious food need not be difficult or require gadgets, but it can take a little time and preparation. This is time worth taking for several reasons. Firstly, you know that you are providing good food for everyone, not least yourself. Secondly, I believe in what Rabbi Lionel Blue called 'the sanity of small tasks'. Stand rooted by a chopping board and your mind is free as your hands work. This is a precious, still space in the midst of the world's swirl. And then, finally, something else happens as we chop, simmer and stir. Time helps to make food part of a household; it brings with it companionship and love, rather than a quick trick. The tempting scent of supper diffuses through the evening. Along with the sounds of a kitchen and the anticipation of tucking in, it helps turn the kitchen into 'the most comforting and comfortable room in the house', as Elizabeth David writes in *French Country Cooking*.

Originally, we were all One Pot cooks. Before stoves became common in the Industrial Revolution, a sturdy three-legged pot would sit over or near the embers. Into this went thick soups called pottage, pieces of simmered meat and cloth-wrapped puddings. There are visible remnants of this tradition in the fireplace of my cottage in Hastings, linking me to the cooks of the past who would have used this hearth daily.

The longevity of One Pots subtly influenced my attitude towards this type of food. One Pots can be seen as chuck-it-in's: cheap and cheerful but perhaps a bit ordinary. I am now much more respectful of their evolved nature. Lancashire Hot Pot, to take just one example, is a brilliant concept that makes the most of all parts of a chop – meat, fat, bone – in order to flavour and enrich an entire dish. The recipe has passed through the lives and kitchens of innumerable cooks and households, all nourished and made happy by its charms.

Looking back over the centuries has also renewed my sense of the communality of cooking and eating. Far more than today, we made food together and we ate food together. One Pots are one of the best way to do this now, as then. The One Pot is a portable contribution taken to Pot Luck suppers. Pop-up restaurants and supper clubs often use such dishes because they are good to feed a crowd. One Pots are part of the recent growth of community kitchens, be it people batch cooking to save money, or meals that bring people together. This is sharing food.

My one overarching rule for eating well is to eat home-cooked, fresh food as much as possible. I'd take this further and say that home cooking is the front line for all of us who care about food, not least how it relates to health. This is the line we must hold, defend and advance with our hearts, souls and wooden spoons. One Pots help you to do this for one simple reason: they make the task of cooking from scratch much easier.

Straightforward home-cooked food can, alas, get pushed to one side, overshadowed by the whole circus of 'foodyism'. Elaborate cheffy concoctions turn the image of food into something that is impossible for the home cook to achieve. TV programmes, naturally enough, concentrate on competitive cooking rather than the straightforward task of feeding a tableful at home. You hear new cooks talk of how they want to 'step up to the next level' and 'create an original dish'; notions that have nothing to do with real everyday eating.

At a time of processed food, flashy and trashy ubiquitous eateries, time pressures and diet faddery, One Pots restore much common sense to food. Let's celebrate and continue the goodness of the shared pie and the nourishing stew. Reach for the One Pot.

SOUP

FOR ALL

ITS TIDY

DOMESTICITY,

SOUP IS

FAR FROM

MEAN

Soup is the purest form of One Pot food. Everything goes together into the pan to bubble away and develop. Despite the simplicity, each soup explores flavours and every soup cook makes happy discoveries through the serendipity of using up ingredients and imagining new combinations.

Supremely warming in winter, soup is also refreshing, cooling and fragrant in summer. You can keep it light and fresh, or brew a rich and dark potful. It can be a sophisticated starter or sturdy fodder: bright, limpid, tangy or comforting – or have all of these qualities at once, as in an Asian broth.

This chapter has recipes for classic soups from around the world, comforting bowlfuls that use seasonal vegetables, quick recipes for last-minute lunches and substantial One Pots that are more than enough for a meal.

Always taste soup at the end and adjust the seasoning. Remember that the flavours will continue to develop if you make it in advance, so taste again just before serving. Salt, a spoonful of cream, lemon juice, a little soy sauce or a dot of chilli sauce can all make a difference. Final flourishes such as a swirl of good olive oil or cream, or a scatter of bright, chopped herbs turn a plain bowlful into a good meal.

Soup is economical, making the most of inexpensive foods and leftovers, but for all its tidy domesticity, soup is far from mean. Take a little care over the small yet crucial details, and your soup will be transformed.

BEEF
& BARLEY
SOUP

SERVES **8**

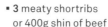

- **3** meaty shortribs or 400g shin of beef
- **80g** pearl barley
- **4 cloves** garlic, *finely chopped*
- **3** leeks, green & white part, *cleaned & chopped*
- **2** onions, *finely chopped*
- **100g** mushrooms, *roughly chopped*
- **1 tbsp** five spice powder
- **1.8 litres** beef stock (instant is fine)
- Japanese soy sauce, to serve (optional)
- **2 tbsp** *finely chopped* flat-leaf parsley

I like the dark density and nourishing nature of this soup. It's the sort of stuff that medieval peasants would have spooned up to sustain them through yet another day in the cold fields. If you are heading off to your computer keyboard after lunch, you need just a small bowlful to keep you going all afternoon. The recipe is adapted from one in Laurie Colwin's *Home Cooking*, a book that celebrates the joys and foibles of the real home kitchen and is one of my all-time favourites.

Beef shortribs are found in butchers and some supermarkets and are terrific value for money.

Barley sucks up moisture, so this soup gets thicker when left overnight. Don't be tempted to add more than this amount of grains or the dish becomes a touch stodgy.

The fat will rise if you leave this overnight to cool. You can remove it, though I leave about half so it gleams on top and adds richness and flavour.

I make a large potful of this so it can be served at several meals, adding different vegetables to each serving.

1. Put everything into a big pot, apart from the soy sauce and the herbs. Bring to the boil, turn down the heat and leave to simmer, covered, for 3 hours.

2. If using ribs, take them out of the pot. Cut the meat off the bone, removing any sinewy bits, and chop into small pieces. Put the meat back in the soup and discard the bone. If using shin, use a spoon to break up the pieces – it should be soft enough to do this. Taste the soup and season with salt or Japanese soy sauce, if necessary. Reheat until piping hot.

3. Serve the soup with green herbs scattered over the top, a grind of pepper and crusty bread alongside.

CRAB & SWEETCORN CHOWDER

SERVES 5–6

- **a big knob** of butter
- **a dash** of olive or vegetable oil
- **100g** smoked bacon, *chopped into 2cm pieces*
- **1** onion, *finely chopped*
- **1 stalk** celery, *finely chopped*
- **¼ bulb** fennel, *finely chopped* (optional but good)
- **2** sweetcorn cobs, *kernels cut off the cob*
- **1 large** potato, *scrubbed or peeled & cut into 3cm dice*
- **1–2 tsp** smoked or unsmoked paprika
- **100ml** white wine
- **200ml** water
- **500ml** whole milk
- **1** bay leaf
- **juice of ½** lemon
- **250g** prepared crab, brown & white meat
- **2–3 tbsp** *finely chopped* flat-leaf parsley

Western pots and Native American ingredients come together in chowder. The soup's name is thought to originate from a *chaudière*, the iron cookware taken by early French settlers to what is now Canada. Before Europeans arrived, Native Americans cooked their clams in bark bowls with water heated by rocks that had been put in the fire. Iron pots placed over heat made life easier and the dish evolved into a thick and tasty New England soup that is a mix of seafood and potatoes. This meal-soup has many variations and here's mine. Dressed crab, with the meat all picked and packed into the shell, is a delicious and easy-to-use ingredient and adds a richness that is balanced by the freshness of fennel and lemon.

For a smarter presentation, mix the white crab meat with half the parsley and scatter this over the bowl before serving.

To prepare the sweetcorn, remove any leaves and whiskers from the cobs, stand each one on its end and run a sharp knife down the sides to remove the kernels.

1. Melt the butter and oil in a large pan over a medium-low heat. Cook the bacon for 3–4 minutes, stirring occasionally. Add the chopped onion, celery and fennel to the pot, turn down the heat and fry gently for 10 minutes to soften and sweeten, stirring occasionally.

2. Add the sweetcorn and potato with the paprika, a small scatter of flaky sea salt and several generous grinds of pepper. Give the potful a stir. Pour in the wine and bring the soup up to the boil. Add the water, milk and bay leaf and bring back to the boil. Cover the pot, turn down the heat and simmer for 10 minutes or so, until the potato is cooked.

3. Stir in the lemon juice, crab meat and parsley and simmer until they are heated through. Taste and adjust the seasoning if necessary. The Americans serve chowder with crackers, or you could serve it with chunks of bread – you may find it enough of a meal in itself.

END-OF-VEG-BOX
SOUP

SERVES **4–5**

- **2 tbsp** olive or vegetable oil
- **1** onion, *finely chopped*
- **2 stalks** celery, *finely chopped*
- **1 clove** garlic, *finely chopped*
- **100g** cooking chorizo or bacon, *cut into 2cm dice or slices*

- **350g** root vegetables or squash – eg potato, sweet potato, swede, parsnip, *peeled & cut into medium dice*
- **1 x 400g** tin chopped tomatoes
- **150ml** cider or 1 apple, *peeled, cored & finely chopped*
- **800–900ml** stock (instant is fine)
- **a squeeze** of lemon juice (optional)

My cooking is partly based on a weekly veg box. Like most people, I generally eat everything apart from the root veg and squash. Here's how to use them up, plus other kitchen odds and sods.

1. Pour the oil into a medium-large pan and sweat the onion, celery and garlic with the chorizo or bacon for 10 minutes over a medium-low heat, stirring occasionally.

2. Add the diced roots to the pan, season with a little salt and plenty of pepper, stir everything well and continue to cook for another 5 minutes, stirring occasionally.

3. Pour in the tomatoes, cider (or add the apple) and stock. Stir everything together. Cover with a lid, turn up the heat and bring to the boil, then lower the heat and simmer for 30-40 minutes, until the roots are tender.

4. Leave to cool slightly or completely, then whizz up using a stick blender. Thin the mixture with a little water if you want. Check the seasoning and add a little lemon juice if slightly too salty, or to add a bright edge.

A chopped apple helps most root vegetable soups, or else a glass of cider – or a small glass of wine, if you have a bottle open – is also excellent.

BRETON ONION SOUP WITH TARRAGON & CIDER

SERVES **4–6**

- **a big knob** of butter
- **½ tbsp** olive or other vegetable oil
- **6** onions, *finely sliced*
- **2 leafy stalks** tarragon
- **1 litre** vegetable or chicken stock (fresh is best here)
- **200ml** dry cider

French onion soup is a real warmer that manages to be light yet filling. This Breton version has cider to add another layer of flavour to the stock. This can be made with good instant stock, but onions have a delicate flavour and the soup benefits from homemade (see pages 28–33).

You can top the soup in the classic fashion with small rounds of bread: toast on one side and rub with a little garlic, then cover the other side with grated cheese and grill until melty.

Add salt to slow-cooking onions to help stop them burning.

1. Put the butter and oil in a large saucepan and heat to melt the butter. Add the sliced onions and give them a good stir around with a large pinch of salt. At this point it seems like a lot of onions in the pan but they will melt down over time. Season with pepper and stir in the tarragon, with the leaves still on the stalks.

2. Cook the onions on a medium-high heat for 10 minutes to get them going, stirring occasionally. Then add another pinch of salt and turn the heat right down to cook the onions long and slow, stirring occasionally, until they are soft, sweet and golden. Ideally this should take about 1 hour, but you can turn the heat up slightly and do it in 30 minutes or so, keeping an eye out for burning (use your ears and nose to sense this too).

3. Add the chicken stock and cider and season with pepper. Bring to the boil and simmer for 20 minutes, covered. Fish out the tarragon stalks – don't worry if some leaves remain in the soup – and ladle into bowls.

FISH SOUP WITH SAFFRON-GARLIC CROUTONS

SERVES **8**

- **200g** shell-on cooked prawns (not tiger prawns)
- **2 tbsp** olive oil
- **1** onion, *finely chopped*
- **1** carrot, *finely chopped*
- **1** leek, *finely chopped*
- **1 stalk** celery, *finely chopped*
- **2 cloves** garlic, *finely chopped*
- **½** fennel bulb, *finely chopped*
- **1** red pepper, *finely chopped*
- **150ml** white wine
- **a small splash** of brandy (optional but good)
- **225g** fish fillet, with skin (see note)
- **300g** fresh tomatoes, *finely chopped* (or 1 x 400g tin)

A bowlful of this terracotta-red soup, with its saffron-and-garlic croûtons and flecks of melted cheese, turns a light lunch into a special meal. Many ingredients from sunny, southern countries go into this dish resulting in a soup full of Mediterranean flavours. The recipe has several stages and lots of ingredients, but is worth the effort and can conveniently be made in advance and finished at the last minute.

1. Remove the shells from the prawns. Pour the oil into a large, deep pan and sweat the prawn shells (heads and all), onion, carrot, leek, celery and garlic over a medium-low heat for 10 minutes, stirring occasionally, until they soften. Add the fennel and pepper to the pan and continue to cook slowly for another 3 minutes or so.

2. Pour in the wine and brandy, if using. Turn up the heat and let the soup bubble away for a minute to burn off the alcohol. Add the fish fillet, tomatoes, orange peel and juice, bay leaf, stock and saffron. Season with ½ tsp flaky sea salt and a good grind of pepper. Cover and bring to the boil. Turn down the heat and simmer, covered, for 40 minutes.

3. Meanwhile, make the saffron-garlic mayonnaise by stirring the soaked saffron into the mayonnaise. Add the garlic, then mix together thoroughly, pushing down on the saffron so it releases its glorious sunshine-yellow into the mayonnaise. Put in the fridge, covered, until needed.

- **2 large strips** of orange peel
- **juice of 1** orange
- **1** bay leaf
- **1.5 litres** fish stock (see page 32)
- **a large pinch** of saffron, *crushed*
- **a good squeeze** of lemon juice

saffron-garlic croûtons:
- **a small pinch** of saffron, *crushed & soaked in a little warm water for 20 minutes*
- **3 tbsp** mayonnaise
- **¼ clove** garlic, *finely chopped*
- **8 thin slices** of baguette, *cut in half*
- **3 tbsp** *finely grated* cheese (gruyère for preference)

4. Allow the soup to cool slightly or completely. Take out the bay leaf (I leave the orange peel in, but remove if you don't like a strong orange taste). Whizz up the soup with a stick blender or in batches in a liquidiser. Sieve the soup back into the pan and add the shelled prawns. Reheat, then taste, adding lemon juice and more salt if necessary.

5. Lightly toast the bread. Put a dollop of the saffron-garlic mayonnaise on each piece of toast. Ladle the soup into bowls and float two croutons on top. Sprinkle with the grated cheese and serve immediately.

Use whatever fish looks best when you shop. I like, if possible, to get the fishmonger to fillet a gurnard and use the flesh for the soup and the bones and head for an extra tasty stock. I tend to make the stock at the same time as sweating the vegetables to keep it fresh (see page 32).

If you want to make this more of a meal add extra pieces of fish fillet and some scallops along with the peeled prawns at the end.

Instead of saffron croutons I often rub a cut clove of garlic onto sourdough bread, tear it up into smallish pieces and float these on the soup to give it substance and a garlic kick.

POTATO & 'NDUJA SOUP

SERVES 6

- **2 tbsp** olive oil
- **1** onion, *finely chopped*
- **1** carrot, *finely chopped*
- **2 cloves** garlic, *finely chopped*
- **1 stalk** celery, *finely chopped*
- **700g** firm-textured potatoes (eg Charlotte), *peeled & cut into 2cm dice*
- **1 litre** water or chicken or beef stock (instant is fine)
- **1 tsp** Marmite (optional)
- **2–4 tsp** 'nduja
- **a squeeze** of lemon juice, to taste

Spuds make a soup more of a meal, and I've experimented a fair amount to find potato soups that are flavourful and avoid the gloop factor. I found a great contrasting partner for the comforting blandness of potatoes in 'nduja, a spicy, spreadable Southern Italian sausage that's available in good delis. The flavour is strong as well as chilli hot and you can add as much or as little as you want.

1. Pour the olive oil into a pot over a medium-low heat. Add the onion, carrot, garlic and celery and season with a little salt. Cook for 10 minutes, stirring occasionally, until soft.

2. Add the potatoes to the pan and stir them around with the other ingredients. Pour in the water or stock and add the Marmite, if using (I do if not using stock). Spoon in the 'nduja, according to taste. About 2 tsp is good to start with.

3. Bring the soup to the boil, turn down the heat, cover and simmer for 15 minutes, or until the potato is soft. Stir in a little lemon juice to brighten the flavour. Taste and adjust the seasoning and also the spiciness by adding more 'nduja, if desired.

Serve the soup as it is, then let chilli-lovers stir extra 'nduja into their portion.

If you can't find 'nduja, substitute 100g finely chopped spicy chorizo, added with the potatoes.

CULLEN
SKINK

SERVES **4**

- **1 tbsp** olive or vegetable oil
- **1 onion**, *finely chopped*
- **1 stalk** celery, *finely sliced*
- **1 clove** garlic, *finely chopped*
- **1 medium** firm-textured potato (eg Charlotte), *peeled & cut into small dice*
- **300ml** milk
- **200ml** water
- **2** bay leaves
- **1** lemon
- **250g** smoked haddock
- **2 tbsp** *finely chopped* flat-leaf parsley
- **a squeeze** of lemon juice (optional)

Even served without bread, this Scottish soup is enough to make a satisfying small meal that balances the saltiness of smoked fish with mild milk and mealy potatoes. Cullen is a town in north-east Scotland on the Moray Firth, an area rich in fishing traditions, and 'skink' is an old Scottish term for soup, originally meaning the shin, knuckle or hough (hock) of beef that were the base of many a soup.

The cooking smell of smoked fish is familiar to me, but some may feel less keen. Open the doors and windows and hope for a strong Scottish breeze, or else cook the second part of your cullen skink – from when you add the fish – in the microwave in a covered dish.

1. Pour the oil into a medium pan over a medium-low heat. Add the onion, celery and garlic and cook, stirring occasionally, until soft (about 10 minutes). Add the potato, stir in and cook for a couple more minutes.

2. Pour in the milk and water and add the bay leaves. Use a vegetable peeler to get 3 or 4 long strips of rind from the lemon and add those to the pot. Give everything a good stir.

3. Cut the haddock into 2 or 3 large pieces and put in the pot, skin-side up. Bring the mixture almost to the boil, then turn down the heat, cover and leave to simmer for 10 minutes.

4. Check that the haddock is cooked and the potatoes are tender. Using a knife and fork, carefully remove the skin from the haddock, then gently flake the fish up and stir through the soup along with the chopped herbs. Take out the bay leaf and lemon rind. If you like, stir in some lemon juice to add extra seasoning and serve.

ROASTED CARROT, ORANGE & ALMOND MILK SOUP

SERVES **4**

- **500g** carrots, *cut into large chunks*
- **2 tbsp** olive or vegetable oil
- **1 large** onion, *roughly chopped*
- **1 clove** garlic, *finely chopped*
- **1 stalk** celery, *roughly chopped*
- **400ml** almond milk (or chicken or vegetable stock)
- **2 tbsp** *chopped* herbs such as coriander leaves, parsley or chives, plus extra to serve
- **juice of 1** orange
- **1 tbsp** Japanese soy sauce
- **a small handful** of toasted flaked almonds (optional)

Almond milk comes and goes in my household according to whether someone is in a vegan or dairy-free phase. In the meantime, I've experimented with it as an instant stock and been pleasantly surprised. I recently learnt that medieval cooks used almond milk instead of dairy produce during Lent and other periods of fasting so feel that I'm hooking into a long tradition of healthy, nourishing cooking with this thick, satisfying soup.

Fresh carrots can be used, but I like the depth of flavour of roasted. If using fresh, finely chop the carrots and cook with the other vegetables, adding another ½ tbsp olive oil, and simmer the soup for 40 minutes.

1. Toss the carrots in 1 tbsp oil and put in a hot oven (200°C/Gas 6) until they are browning at the edges and soft (about 45 minutes). Leave to cool then roughly chop.

2. Heat 1 tbsp of oil in a large pan over a medium-low heat and add the onion, garlic and celery. Season with ¼ tsp flaky sea salt and plenty of black pepper. Cook over a medium-low heat for 15 minutes, stirring occasionally, until soft.

3. Add the carrots, almond milk and 400ml water, bring to the boil, then turn down the heat and simmer for 20 minutes, covered. Add the herbs, then whizz up with a stick blender or in a food processor.

4. Add the orange juice and soy sauce. Taste and adjust the seasoning if necessary.

5. Serve with some extra herbs scattered on top and, if you like, some toasted flaked almonds.

AFGHANI
TEAPOT SOUP

SERVES **6**

- **2 onions**, *finely sliced*
- **400g** scrag end of lamb, *in pieces on the bone*
- **100g** split peas
- **1 litre** water
- **6 tbsp** *chopped* coriander leaf

I discovered this excellent simple, soup in Helen Saberi's *Noshe Djan: Afghan Food and Cookery*, which is full of culinary knowledge Helen picked up over years spent in Afghanistan. The name of the dish comes from it being cooked in improvised cooking vessels made from mended broken teapots. The pot is nestled in embers, or on top of a brazier, to cook for hours and the soup is then poured over a naan as simple nourishment. I've adapted the quantities to suit a saucepan.

To make this more of a meal, serve with naan and perhaps a side salad of onions dressed in little white wine vinegar or tomato wedges.

Scrag end of lamb is the top part of the neck and is a real bargain, with lots of flavour especially if on the bone. Butchers sometimes sell scrag chopped up into chunks that are ideal for this soup. The cut is also worth buying for thrifty, slow-cooked stews.

1. Put all the ingredients except the coriander into a pot. Season with ¼ tsp flaky sea salt. Slowly bring to boil and skim off any scum that rises.

2. Turn the heat down, cover and simmer for 1½–2 hours, or until the lamb is tender.

3. Stir in the coriander and adjust the seasoning.

SEASONAL

HARIRA

SERVES **8**

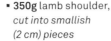

- **350g** lamb shoulder, *cut into smallish (2 cm) pieces*
- **2** onions, *grated*
- **2 stalks** celery, *finely chopped*
- **4 medium-large** waxy potatoes, *scrubbed & cut into chunks*
- **3 types** of seasonal veg (about 1kg total weight): eg: 300g squash, *peeled*; 3 large carrots, *cut into chunks* & 2 leeks, *sliced*
- **7–8 tbsp** *finely chopped* coriander stalks
- **50g** red lentils
- **1 x 420g** tin chickpeas, *drained*, or 225g home-cooked
- **2 tbsp** tomato purée
- **1.5 litres** water or chicken or lamb stock (instant is fine)

spice mixture:
- **1 tsp** ground ginger
- **2 tsp** turmeric
- **½ tsp** ground cinnamon
- **1 tsp** *grated* nutmeg
- **1 tsp** *freshly ground* black pepper
- **1 tbsp** coriander seed, *roughly crushed*

to finish:
- **3 tbsp** fine semolina
- **juice of 1** lemon
- **2 tbsp** *roughly chopped* flat leaf parsley
- **1 tbsp** *roughly chopped* coriander leaf

This North African soup sustains Muslims through the fasting days of Ramadan, when it is traditionally served with dates and honey cakes to break the day-long fast at sunset.

The mix of lamb and chickpeas is enlivened by a fragrant, peppery spice mix and refreshing lemon juice. As Ramadan moves throughout the year, different kinds of vegetables are added and I've found the soup works with whatever is in season. Don't be put off by the number of ingredients. This is an easy dish to make as you put almost everything in the pot in one go and let the soup bubble away for an hour.

1. Put everything for the soup in a large cooking pot. Stir together the spice mixture and add to the pot. Bring to the boil, then turn down the heat and simmer, covered, for 1 hour.

2. Scoop a ladleful of stock from the pot – about 100ml – and put it in a small bowl with the semolina. Mix together, then stir back into the pot with the lemon juice. Leave to simmer for 2 minutes. Stir in the chopped herbs and serve. Some will want bread with this and others find it is filling enough already.

Vegetables are heaped into the soup, making the dish both healthy and cheap. I once added up the weight of vegetables that I'd used and reckon just one serving sorts half of the advised 'five-a-day' quota, which is generally calculated as 500g veg and fruit a day in total, with the emphasis on veg.

The amount of meat is variable. You can use 500g lamb shoulder if your household is meat-loving but 350g of this tasty cut is enough.

COCONUT

DHAL

SERVES **6**

- **1 x 400ml** tin coconut milk
- **1** red onion, *finely chopped*
- **3 cloves** garlic, *finely chopped*
- **1 thumb** root ginger, *peeled & finely chopped*
- **2** tomatoes, *roughly chopped*
- **1–2 tsp** garam masala (a trusted brand or homemade)
- **1 tsp** turmeric
- plenty of black pepper
- **½–1** green or red chilli, *deseeded & finely chopped*
- **a bunch** of coriander, *stalks & leaves separated & finely chopped*
- **1 large handful** rocket leaves, *roughly chopped*
- **juice of ½** lemon
- plain yoghurt, to serve

Dhal is so versatile and economical that it's become a staple in my household. Make more than you need as the dish improves in flavour over time. You can have it on standby as a lunchtime soup or as a saucy vegetable accompaniment to a piece of fish or meat. Any number of vegetables can be added to dhal (see below), making it even more healthy and adaptable.

Add any veg that you have or need to eat up. Chop roots into medium-small pieces and add at the start. Add green veg, such as broccoli florets, frozen peas and sliced green beans, for the last 5 minutes of cooking.

1. Put all the ingredients in a medium-large pan, apart from the coriander leaves, rocket and lemon juice. Use the coconut milk tin to measure out 1½–2 tinfuls of water, depending on how thick you want the dhal. Season with ½ tsp flaky sea salt.

2. Bring the dhal to the boil, turn the heat down, cover with a lid and simmer for 40 minutes, stirring occasionally towards the end to stop the bottom catching.

3. Stir in the coriander and rocket leaves and the lemon juice. Adjust the seasoning, if necessary, and serve with a blob of yoghurt added to each helping.

SOUPE
AU PISTOU

SERVES **4**

- **1 tbsp** olive oil
- **2 medium** shallots, *finely chopped*
- **3 medium** waxy potatoes, *peeled & cut into 2cm dice*
- **a large handful each** of 3 types of greenery: eg pointed cabbage, *finely chopped*; broad beans, *with skin on or off, as desired*; courgettes, *cut into 2cm dice*
- **2 medium** carrots, *peeled & cut into 2cm dice*
- **10** cherry tomatoes, *halved*
- **a squeeze** of lemon juice, to taste
- **a drizzle** of good olive oil, to dress

for the pistou:
- **4 tsp** good-quality pesto

or make your own:
- **1 small clove** garlic
- **a large or double handful** of basil
- **½ tbsp** pine kernels
- **1 tbsp** good olive oil
- **2 tbsp** *finely grated* hard & flavourful cheese (eg parmesan/pecorino/strong cheddar)

Provençal cooks find this classic soup a great way to celebrate the tastes and colours of summer vegetables. The recipe is adaptable to whatever is fresh and good in the kitchen or garden.

Three elements make a difference to this soup: vibrant veg, good olive oil and good pesto. Use the best that you can.

To make this more substantial, add soaked rice noodles towards the end. Food writer Patience Gray throws in a handful of rice at the start which is good too.

1. Heat the olive oil in a medium pot over a medium-low heat and add all the vegetables. Cook for 10 minutes to soften, stirring occasionally. Pour in 1 litre water, add a pinch of salt, cover and bring to the boil. Turn the heat down and simmer for 10 minutes.

2. Meanwhile, make the pesto by putting all the ingredients apart from the cheese into a small food processor or a pestle and mortar and blend or pound to amalgamate to a green paste. Place in a small bowl and stir in the cheese. Taste and add a little salt if desired.

3. Taste the soup and add lemon juice for seasoning. Serve in bowls with a dollop of the pesto and a drizzle of good oil in the centre for each person to stir in.

ADAPTABLE QUICK
MISO SOUP

SERVES **4**

- **1 litre** water or dashi stock (instant or homemade; see note)
- **1 tsp** *finely grated root ginger*
- **4–6 tbsp** assorted *chopped or finely sliced* vegetables, (see note)
- **4 tbsp** miso
- **1** spring onion, *finely chopped, including the green part*

Tasty, light and satisfying, this dish is one of the most useful and speedy of my One Pot recipes, with as many variations as there are days. Traditional miso soup is a simple broth enriched with Japanese miso paste, often with some finely chopped spring onions on top. The soup forms part of a meal, be it breakfast, lunch or supper. This recipe makes the dish go further by westernising it through the addition of whatever vegetables are around.

1. Put the water or stock in a saucepan, adding 2 tsp dashi powder to the hot water if making an instant Japanese stock. Add the grated ginger and chopped vegetables.

2. Bring the soup to the boil, then turn down the heat and simmer for 5 minutes, or until the vegetables are cooked.

3. Stir in the miso, one spoonful at a time, and mix gently until dissolved. Heat until the soup is almost boiling.

4. Serve in bowls topped with the finely sliced spring onions.

ONE OF THE MOST USEFUL AND SPEEDY DISHES OF ONE POT COOKING

Dashi is the basic Japanese stock. If buying instant dashi from a Japanese specialist, try to get one without monosodium glutamate. Or make your own dashi (see page 33).

Cut the vegetables into pieces that will cook in roughly the same time. A good mix might be: 1 finely sliced carrot, 4 sliced mushrooms (shiitake for preference) and a few florets of broccoli, plus perhaps a turnip or a smaller piece of Japanese radish (mooli) peeled and cut into thin semi-circles.

Miso is a richly nutritious (14% protein) and useful ingredient to have for soups and dressings. Keep in the fridge once opened. This salty, savoury paste is made with fermented soya beans and a grain, most commonly rice but also barley or rye. It varies in colour according to grain and age, the light pastes being sweeter and less intense in flavour than the darker, saltier versions.

To make more of a meal of this soup, cut 200g firm tofu into 3cm dice and add to the soup with the vegetables.

Toasted sesame seeds are a useful Japanese storecupboard ingredient, handy for adding to noodles and salads as well as soup. Scatter 1 tsp over the top of each bowlful of miso soup.

SPEEDY
SPINACH SOUP

SERVES **4**

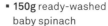

- **150g** ready-washed baby spinach
- **150ml** double cream
- **500ml** chicken or veg stock (instant is fine; fresh preferable)
- ½ lemon, *juice & finely grated zest*
- **¼ tsp** *freshly grated* nutmeg
- **1 small clove** garlic, *crushed*

This fresh, quick dish can be pulled together in 10 minutes, tops. It's a useful soup to make as a last-minute lunch for friends, or can be prepared the night before and kept in the fridge to serve hot or cold.

1. Put all the ingredients in a pot and season with ¼ tsp flaky sea salt and a good grind of pepper. Bring to the boil.

2. Liquidise, then pour it back into the pan. Heat up until boiling. Turn off the heat, taste and adjust the seasoning as necessary.

Snipped chives work well on top, with perhaps an extra swirl of cream.

Lemon is a strong flavour in this soup. If you have a taste for tart, as I do, then it'll be just fine; if you prefer sweetness, use half the lemon juice initially and then add more, to taste.

QUICK
BORSCHT

SERVES **6**

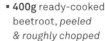

- **400g** ready-cooked beetroot, *peeled & roughly chopped*
- **1 large**, tart apple (eg Cox or Braeburn), *quartered, cored & roughly chopped (leave the skin on)*
- **¼–½ tsp** caraway seeds, to taste
- **1 litre** veg, beef or chicken stock (instant is fine)
- **1–2 tsp** balsamic vinegar, to taste
- **1–2 tsp** Dijon mustard, to taste
- **100ml** full-fat plain yoghurt or sour cream

Here's a short-cut way to enjoy this tangy Eastern European classic. If there's time I will sweat onions, garlic and celery as the base for building up the flavours. But there are occasions when you need a quick recipe using what is in the storecupboard and whatever fresh produce is around. Borscht is such a tasty and beautiful soup that sometimes I want to make it last minute, when soup just feels like a good idea.

Dill or a small amount of tarragon are good additions to this soup, both in the stock and scattered over the top, if you have such herbs to hand. If I have a mild tarragon mustard, I use that instead of the Dijon here.

Ready-cooked beetroot is often sold by greengrocers and supermarkets. Watch out it isn't the kind that is soaked in vinegar. If you use fresh, simmer the soup for 20 minutes longer.

The flavours develop in this tangy soup if you leave it overnight so reign back on the yoghurt and mustard if not eating straight away and taste and adjust those seasonings just before serving.

1. Put the beetroot, apple and caraway seeds in a medium pan with the stock.

2. Cover, bring to the boil and simmer for 20 minutes.

3. Whizz up using a stick blender or a liquidiser. Stir in the balsamic vinegar and mustard, to taste. Season with salt if necessary (instant stock can be salty).

4. Whizz in the yoghurt or sour cream to give the soup another sharp edge and to make it a beautiful bright pink.

SOPA DI LIMA

SERVES **6**

- **1 tbsp** good lard or olive oil
- **1** red onion, *finely chopped*
- **1 clove** garlic, *crushed*
- **1** green pepper, *cut into thin slivers*
- **½** green chilli, *deseeded & finely chopped*
- **½ tsp** dried oregano
- **1.2 litres** chicken stock (must be fresh)
- **2** chicken breasts, *thinly sliced* (optional)
- **3** ripe tomatoes, *cubed*
- **juice of 1½** limes, to taste

garnish:
- **12–18** corn tortillas, *roughly crumbled*
- **a handful** of *chopped* coriander leaf

This is one of my favourite soups to make with chicken stock; it has style and plenty of flavour. The Yucatan in Mexico has peppers that are so hot they are referred to as 'dog's nose' chillies because of the way they make your nose run. Sopa di lima hails from this region and can have a mighty kick. I've toned it down to make a dish that adds fragrance and some heat to your best chicken stock.

1. Heat the lard or oil in a saucepan over a medium-low heat. Add the onion, garlic, pepper and ¾ tsp flaky sea salt and cook gently for 10 minutes, stirring occasionally. Add the chilli and oregano and cook for another minute or so.

2. Pour in the stock and add the chicken, if using. Bring to the boil, then turn down the heat and simmer for 10 minutes. Add the tomatoes and lime juice and continue to simmer for another minute. Taste and adjust seasoning, remembering that the tortillas you serve this with will be salty.

3. Pour into bowls and garnish with the tortillas and coriander.

Limes can be helped to yield their juice by rolling them around on the work surface for a minute or so; a good job to give to a child.

COCK-A-LEEKIE

SERVES **6–8**

- **2 large** leeks, *cleaned*
- **2 litres** water
- **2 medium** carrots, *peeled & quartered*
- **6** chicken thighs or drumsticks on the bone
- **1kg** stewing beef, eg brisket, *ideally in one piece, tied up*
- **2 bushy sprigs** thyme
- **14** prunes, *7 whole, 7 pitted & cut into quarters*
- **1 medium** swede, *peeled & cut into 1–2cm chunks*

Some of the most delicious broths combine clear flavours and textures rather than being whizzed up together. This Scottish classic is one such dish. Yotam Ottolenghi has a tip of putting prunes into vegetarian stocks to add more flavour. It's a good trick and one already traditionally used in the chicken broth for cock-a-leekie.

Use the leftover meat in dishes such as hash (see note, page 99).

Prunes have been rebranded from their pallid, stewed days of school dinners to seem like 'sun-dried plums'. Their rich, fruity flavour is great in sweet and savoury dishes, as well as for snacking.

1. Thickly slice the green tops of the leeks and put in a large pot, reserving the whites for later. Put all the rest of the ingredients, apart from the quartered prunes and the swede, into the pot along with 1 tsp of flaky sea salt. Bring to the boil then turn down the heat and simmer, covered, for 2 hours.

2. Strain the liquid into a bowl. Remove the chicken thighs and put to one side to cool slightly. Discard the carrots, prunes and thyme.

3. Pour the stock back into the pot. Slice the whites of the leeks into 2cm pieces and add to the pot with the prunes quarters and swede. Bring to the boil and simmer for 15 minutes, or until the vegetables are tender.

4. Meanwhile, remove the skin and bones from the chicken and cut the flesh into medium chunks. Cut about a quarter of the beef into slivers. Add the meat to the pot of stock, heat through and serve.

TUSCAN CHICKPEA & ROSEMARY SOUP

SERVES **6**

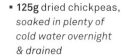

- **125g** dried chickpeas, *soaked in plenty of cold water overnight & drained*
- **2 tbsp** best olive oil
- **1** onion, *finely chopped*
- **1 stalk** celery, *finely chopped*
- **1** carrot, *finely chopped*
- **2 cloves** garlic, *finely chopped*
- **100ml** white wine
- **1.2 litres** chicken or chickpea stock (see right and below)
- parmesan rind, if you have one
- **1 sprig** rosemary
- **2 thick strips** lemon rind

to finish:
- lemon juice
- parmesan, *finely grated*
- best olive oil, to taste

stock for cooking chickpeas:
- **1.5 litres** water or chicken stock
- **1** onion, *halved, one piece with a clove stuck in*
- **2 stalks** celery, *cut into big chunks*
- **2** carrots, *peeled & quartered*
- **1 bulb** garlic, *cut in half, minus 2 cloves for the soup*
- **2 sprigs** rosemary

Chickpeas are more than just plain fare. One of the beauties of Tuscan food is the way such apparently humble ingredients are elevated and appreciated. The key to this dish is to use the best possible olive oil; it really makes a difference. This is perfect post-Christmas food, when you make good stock from poultry bones and crave clean-tasting, wholesome meals, although I love it at all times of year.

1. First cook the soaked chickpeas. Put the pulses in a pot, add all the stock ingredients and 1 tsp flaky sea salt. Cover, bring just to the boil then immediately turn down the heat and scoop off any froth that rises. Cook, partially covered, for 1 hour. Drain, reserving the liquid. Discard the vegetables.

2. Pour the olive oil into a pot over a medium heat and add the onion, celery, carrot and garlic. Season with ½ tsp flaky sea salt and a good grind of pepper. Cook for a couple of minutes, then turn down the heat and sweat gently for 15 minutes, until soft, stirring occasionally.

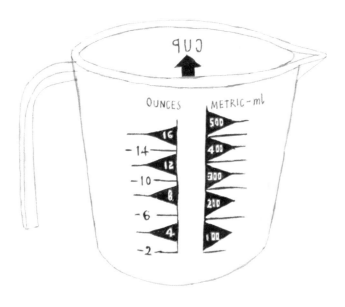

3. Turn the heat up slightly, tip in the wine and let it bubble up. Pour in the chickpea or chicken stock and add the chickpeas, parmesan rind if you have one in the fridge (cut it off the hunk of parmesan), and also the rosemary and lemon rind.

4. Cover, bring to the boil, then turn down the heat and simmer for 45 minutes. Fish out the rosemary, lemon rind and parmesan rind. Taste and add more seasoning and a squeeze of lemon juice, if necessary.

5. Ladle into bowls and top with a scatter of grated parmesan and a drizzle of your best olive oil – this last step makes a huge difference to the soup.

To get the very best flavour, I like to cook the chickpeas in good chicken stock.

Add leafy greens such as kale or savoy cabbage, finely chopped, for the last 10 minutes of cooking to give another dimension of the soup.

Strips of parma ham, or other air-cured ham, are good to scatter on top of the final soup.

LENTIL &
CHESTNUT SOUP

SERVES **6**

- **1½ tbsp** good olive oil, plus more to drizzle on top
- **1 medium** carrot, *finely chopped*
- **1 stalk** celery, *finely chopped*
- **2** banana shallots, *finely chopped*
- **½** fennel bulb, *finely chopped*
- **2 cloves** garlic, *finely chopped*
- **2** bay leaves
- **1 tsp** fennel seeds
- **1 tbsp** tomato purée

- **1 tsp** fresh thyme leaves or ½ tsp dried
- **a small pinch** of chilli flakes (optional)
- **150ml** white wine
- **200g** green lentils
- **1.4 litres** vegetable or chicken stock (fresh is best; or else use good instant & add more herbs to boost the flavour)
- **200g** chestnuts, *roughly chopped*
- **3** tomatoes, *diced*

Lentils and chestnuts are both nourishing ingredients that absorb and set off other flavours. This recipe is informed by the considerable kitchen wisdom of Deborah Madison, in particular her book *Vegetable Soups*. The title may be plain, but the world of flavour within the pages will last you a lifetime. Her tips about softening vegetables and loading flavour into stocks make a difference, as does adding wine (see page 31).

Chopped parsley is good to sprinkle on top of the soup at the end.

The lentils can be used as both a soup and a side dish. For a side dish, use a ladle to scoop out mostly lentils with just a little bit of broth, heat in a microwave or pan and serve alongside fish, meat or a baked potato.

1. Pour the olive oil into a large pan over a medium-low heat. Stir in the chopped carrot, celery, shallots, fennel and garlic. Season with 1 tsp flaky sea salt and a good grind of pepper. Cook gently for 15 minutes, stirring occasionally.

2. Add the bay leaves, fennel seeds, tomato purée and thyme leaves, plus the chilli flakes if using. Continue to stir over a medium-low heat for a minute. Pour in the wine and let it bubble up. Add the lentils and stir around well.

3. Pour in the stock, turn the heat up and bring to the boil. Reduce the heat and simmer, covered, for 20–25 minutes, or until the lentils are tender. Add the chestnuts and tomatoes and continue to cook, still covered, for another 10 minutes. Taste and adjust the seasoning if necessary. Serve in bowls with a swirl of good oil on top.

CHICKEN-FAT
DUMPLINGS

MAKES **16** SMALL DUMPLINGS

- **75g** self-raising flour
- **25g** fine white breadcrumbs
- **½ tsp** *finely grated* lemon rind (optional)
- **20g** (2 tbsp) chicken or goose fat (see note)
- **1** medium egg white

Treats are all the more treaty for being unexpected. I sat down at Rochelle Canteen in East London one January lunchtime when cash-flow and cold took me straight to the wholesome chicken broth on the menu. The scraps of dark kale were invigorating; the broth rich and good. But it was the small silky dumplings that turned the dish into a delight. Their secret? Chicken fat.

Goose fat is an alternative to the chicken fat and can be bought in pots.

Chicken fat is easy to make at home. Buy chicken thighs with the skin and bone and use each part separately. The meat goes into pies, stews and salads. The bones make stock. Put the skins in a single layer on a roasting tray in a 200°C/Gas 6 oven for 15 minutes or so, until the skins crisp up and brown and the fat has melted off.
    Salt the skins and serve them with a pre-supper drink, or crackle them over a salad. Keep the fat in the fridge, covered, for these dumplings or for sautéing potatoes.

1. Put the flour and breadcrumbs in a mixing bowl and stir in a pinch of salt and a good grind of black pepper along with the lemon zest, if using.

2. Use a spoon to stir in the chicken fat and egg to form a firm dough that leaves the sides of the bowl clean, then use your hands to lightly knead the mixture into a dough.

3. Divide the dough into 4 pieces and then each of these into 4 and roll each piece into a dumpling slightly larger than a marble.

4. Put the dumplings into your hot soup, cover, and simmer for around 15 minutes, then roll them over carefully and continue to cook for another 15 minutes.

GENERAL TIPS FOR
MAKING STOCK

Roasting your main ingredient – bones and also vegetables – first will add depth of flavour to meat stocks. Gently frying chopped vegetables will help release their flavours into fish and vegetable stocks in particular.

Vary the flavour of the stock according to the dish. For an East Asian dish use a kaffir lime leaf instead of bay; for a Mexican broth add oregano and some allspice berries; for a French or Jamaican recipe add thyme; for an Indian dish add some cumin and coriander seeds. Look at the aromatics in your final recipe and reinforce the flavours by adding them to the stock too.

Season your stock with sea salt or leave the seasoning to the end dish, which makes saltiness easier to control.

Reducing your stock will add intensity to its flavour. Leave it light and subtle, or boil it down to darken and enrich its impact on your final dish.

Store your stock, covered, in the fridge for up to 5 days (2 days for fish stock), or freeze it to ensure a longer life – ice cube trays are great for storing reduced-down stock cubes.

Expand what you think can go into the stock. There is plenty of flavour in clean peelings – some restaurants make soup for their staff entirely from trimmings. But don't just hurl in the herbs or it starts to be a touch composty, watch out for stale walnuts and brassicas such as swedes are too strong.

Certain vegetables with strong flavours are useful to boost the flavour of appropriate dishes, for instance dried mushrooms add a depth to soups (especially veg ones) while asparagus trimmings are part of the best stock for an asparagus risotto.

CHICKEN
STOCK

MAKES ABOUT **1.5** LITRES

Nourishing chicken stock boosts the flavour and goodness of any number of soups and other dishes. I'm always glad when I have chicken stock on the bubble as part of a batch-cooking session. To make my stock, I either use the carcass of a roast chicken, get some fresh bones from the butcher or an inexpensive pack of free-range chicken wings. What you are doing is dissolving the flavours and proteins from the chicken bones. Larger, more mature free-range birds have better bones and make the best stock of all.

Boost flavour by chopping up the vegetables more finely and cooking them over a medium-low heat in 1 tbsp olive oil for 15 minutes before adding the chicken and other ingredients.

Other bird carcasses make fabulous stocks, not least duck, pheasant and grouse, with 1 tsp lightly crushed juniper berries a good addition to the stock.

Always boil up chicken stock before eating, to avoid the risk of food poisoning. After 4 days, smell the pot and chuck if it smells sour. You can extend the shelf life of good stock (not sour) by boiling up and cooling it again.

- **1–2** cooked or fresh chicken carcasses, or 10–15 fresh wings (the more the merrier)
- **1** onion, *unpeeled, cut in quarters*
- **2 stalks** celery, *roughly chopped*
- **1** carrot, *roughly chopped*
- **2** bay leaves
- **½ tsp** peppercorns
- **1.8 litres** water

other good flavourings:
- green parts of **2–3** leeks, *roughly chopped*
- stalks from **a small bunch** of parsley
- **2–3** tomatoes, *roughly chopped*
- **a bushy sprig** of thyme
- **3** juniper berries, *lightly crushed*
- **100ml** white wine

1. Put all the ingredients in a large pot, along with any extra flavourings you want. Bring to the boil and skim off any scum that rises.

2. Turn the heat down and simmer, uncovered, for at least 1 hour. Some prefer chicken stock left fresh like this; others prefer to cook it for longer, at least 2 or 3 hours. When I have a large poultry carcass, such as a big free-range chicken, a capon or turkey, then I certainly leave it for 3 hours to extract all the goodness from the bones.

3. Strain off the gubbins. You can put the stock back in the pot, bring to the boil and let it bubble away to make it more intense. I often reduce it by about half to make it easier to store.

BEEF
STOCK

MAKES **1.5** LITRES

- **1 kg** beef bones, or beef shanks cut into large pieces
- **1 tbsp** olive or vegetable oil
- **2** onions, *unpeeled, cut in quarters*
- **2** carrots, *cut into large chunks*
- **3 stalks** celery, *cut into large chunks*
- **2** leeks, green part, *roughly chopped*
- **2** bay leaves
- **1 bushy sprig** thyme
- **1 tsp** peppercorns
- **2 litres** water

Some other good flavours:
- **2–3 large** mushrooms (eg Portobello), *finely chopped*
- **3** tomatoes, *roughly chopped*
- **1 tsp** juniper berries, *roughly crushed*
- **½ piece** star anise
- **100–200ml** red wine

Dark, rich beef stock adds oomph and body to soups and a whole other dimension to stews: beef cooked in beef stock is superb.

Veal bones produce wonderful stock with a gelatinous quality that adds body to dishes and is the chef's top stock. British rose veal doesn't have the welfare issues of traditional veal and it is worth asking a butcher for the bones of such animals.

1. Preheat the oven to 220°C/Gas 7. Put the beef bones or shanks into a roasting tray and roll them around in the oil. Roast for 30 minutes, until nicely brown. You can also add the onions, carrots and celery, with ½ tbsp extra oil, and roast them at the same time for extra flavour.

2. Put all the ingredients in a large pot, along with any extra flavourings, and deglaze the roasting tray with 200ml of the water. Bring just to the boil then turn down the heat. Skim off any froth that rises then leave to simmer slowly for 3–4 hours.

3. Strain off the gubbins. Pour back into the pan and ladle off some of the fat on top. Boil to reduce: slightly for a light stock, or right down to around 300ml for a richer taste.

VEGETABLE
STOCK

MAKES ABOUT **1.5** LITRES

- **a knob of** butter or 1 tbsp olive oil
- **1** onion, *roughly chopped*
- **1 small** carrot, *roughly chopped*
- **1** leek, *roughly chopped*
- **1 stalk** celery, *roughly chopped*
- **100ml** white wine
- **a small bunch of** parsley, stalks only
- **1 tsp** peppercorns
- **2** bay leaves
- **1.6 litres** water
- **a good squeeze of** lemon juice

Other good flavours (the more the merrier):
- **2** tomatoes, *roughly chopped*
- **1 small** bulb fennel, *roughly chopped*
- **3** mushrooms, *roughly chopped*
- **1** red pepper, *roughly chopped*
- **3** garlic cloves
- **1 tsp** coriander seeds, *roughly crushed*
- **1 tbsp** lentils
- **2** chard stems, *roughly chopped*
- **a small handful of** walnuts or almonds
- **a bushy sprig of** thyme
- **1** apple, *cored & roughly chopped*
- **5** prunes
- **2** corn cobs (with or without the corn), *chopped into 3 pieces*

This fresh, aromatic stock adds much to dishes such as risottos and braises, as well as soup. Vegetables release their flavours into water in the same way that tea leaves are brewed. The key is to keep it fresh and avoid over-stewing the stock. Use a large amount of vegetables; it may feel wasteful, but they should ideally half-fill the pot. Consider using other ingredients such as lentils and nuts to add depth, but take care; manky peel and old flavours taint the potful. Only use what you'd like to eat in the first place.

1. Melt the butter or heat the oil in a large pan on a medium-low heat. Add the roughly chopped vegetables and cook them slowly for 15 minutes, stirring occasionally.

2. Turn up the heat, pour in the wine and let it bubble up and evaporate slightly. Add the rest of the ingredients, apart from the lemon juice, plus any extra flavourings you want to use. Bring to the boil then turn down the heat and simmer for 30 minutes.

3. Strain off the gubbins and return the liquid to the pan. At this point, you can boil the stock hard to reduce it by about one quarter to slightly concentrate the flavour. Either way, add the lemon juice at the end. You can season with about ¼ – ½ tsp sea salt or leave the seasoning to the end dish.

FISH
STOCK

MAKES ABOUT **1.5** LITRES

- **½ tbsp** olive oil
- **1** onion, *peeled & finely chopped*
- **1** leek, *finely chopped*
- **3 stalks** celery, finely chopped
- **1** carrot, *finely chopped*
- **100ml** white wine
- **plenty of** fresh fish bones eg skeletons of 3–5 flat fish such as sole (see note)
- **2** bay leaves
- **1 clove** garlic, *halved*
- **a small bunch** of parsley, stalks only
- **½ tsp** peppercorns
- **1.6 litres** water

some other good flavours:
- **1 tsp** coriander seeds, *lightly crushed*
- **½** red pepper, *roughly chopped*
- **3** tomatoes, *roughly chopped*

Freshness is key to fish stock, both in terms of the ingredients and when the stock is made. It's best made on the day of eating or the day before.

In contrast to meat stock, you simmer fish stock for no more than 30 minutes. In order to get the most flavour from the vegetables in this short time, it is best to chop them up finely and soften them gently first to help release their flavours.

1. Pour the oil into a pot over a medium-low heat and in it cook the onion, leek, celery and carrot for 15 minutes, stirring occasionally. Turn up the heat, pour in the wine and let it bubble up.

2. Briefly rinse the fish bones and make sure there's no blood on the carcasses. Add to the pot along with the rest of the ingredients, plus any extra flavourings you want to use. Bring just to the boil. Turn down the heat and skim off any scum that rises. Simmer on a low heat, uncovered, for 30 minutes.

3. Strain off the gubbins. If you like, you can boil up the strained stock to reduce it by a quarter to a half to concentrate the flavour. You can also add a little salt (about ¼ tsp flaky sea salt), or leave the seasoning for the final dish.

FRESHNESS IS KEY TO FISH STOCK

The shells of prawns, crabs, lobsters and langoustines make superb stock. For the best taste of all, toast the shells. Bash the larger shells into large pieces using a sturdy plastic bag and rolling pin. Put in a pan with ½ tbsp olive oil over a medium heat and cook until you can smell a beautiful seafood scent. Remove, sweat the vegetables and then return the shells with the water and fish bones.

Bones from different fish are excellent but, steer clear of those from oily fish such as mackerel or salmon.

Japanese dashi is a wonderful alternative to fish stock. To make fresh dashi, put 1.6 litres water in a pan with a 10cm piece of dried kombu seaweed. Bring up to the boil, then immediately turn down the heat and add 10g katsuobushi (dried bonito) flakes. Simmer for 10 minutes, then strain. Best used immediately, dashi also keeps in the fridge for up to 3 days and adds a wonderful savoury richness to western as well as eastern soups, stews and dipping sauces.

SIMPLE

SUPPERS

SUPPERS

ARE WHAT

MAKE THE

KITCHEN

THE HEART OF

THE HOME

Supper is the bedrock of home cooking, and One Pots make the task simple by concentrating the work down to a chopping board and a pot, cutting out much of the faff and mountains of washing up.

Every home needs a roster of such tried-and-trusted daily dishes that can be thrown together almost without thinking. These recipes soon slide into the evening routine. Supper? Solved.

Some of these supper dishes are suitable for batch cooking, to be made in advance when you have a spare hour, then deployed during the week. Others are speedy concoctions that can be thrown together. Then there are dishes that take very little preparation and can be left in the oven, or on the hob, while you sort the other needs of domestic life. Most of these recipes are inexpensive and adaptable to the vegetables and other ingredients you have to hand.

Beyond sustenance, weekday suppers are what make the kitchen the heart of the home. Meals flow in and out like tidal turns and we are drawn to them with an instinctive and sensory tug. The sound of sizzling, the smell of baked potatoes, the crisp crunch of the side salad and the warmth of a plateful mean we come to the table, even in the midweek rush, and feel restored and contented.

CHICKEN
THIGHS
WITH SHERRY
& RICE

SERVES 4

Sherry works brilliantly with food, both as a drink and as an ingredient. A bottle of fino is a happy addition to a One Pot kitchen. You can use fresh red peppers in this; the long thin Spanish ones are best (eg romano), but any kind works well. I've also used the ready-roasted peppers you find in delis and supermarkets; a useful and tasty storecupboard ingredient.

To tart this up a bit more, add a large pinch of saffron with the chicken stock. First crumble the saffron and soak it for 20 minutes in warm water. This dissolves the wax coating of the stamens, helping release the colour and flavour.

Spanish short-grain rice, sometimes called 'paella rice' or named by variety such as bomba or calasparra, absorbs a large amount of liquid (3 times its volume) and is the ideal choice here. Other types of short-grain rice, such as arborio or risotto rice also work fine. Otherwise, use standard long-grain and cut down the liquid by 150ml.

- **2 tbsp** olive or other vegetable oil
- **8** chicken thighs, with skin & bone
- **2 stalks** celery, *finely chopped*
- **2** onions, *finely chopped*
- **3** leeks, *cleaned & sliced into 2cm rings*
- **5 cloves** garlic, *finely chopped*
- **250g** Spanish paella rice
- **100ml** sherry (medium or dry)
- **3** red peppers, *cut into thick strips*
- **700ml** chicken stock (instant is fine)
- **2–3 tbsp** *finely chopped* flat leaf parsley or chives (optional but good)

1. Preheat the oven to 200°C/Gas 6. Pour the oil into a large pan, ideally a wide-bottomed sauté pan with a lid. Brown the chicken on both sides over a medium-high heat. Remove from the pan and put to one side.

2. Lower the heat to medium. Soften the celery, onions, leeks and garlic in the pan, stirring occasionally (about 10 minutes).

3. Add the rice to the pan and stir it around to mix with the other ingredients and coat the grains in oil. Pour in the sherry and let it bubble up for 30 seconds or so.

4. Nestle the chicken into the rice, skin-side up, and add the peppers. Pour over the stock. Cover with a lid and turn up the heat to bring the liquid to the boil, then place in the oven for around 40 minutes, or until the rice has absorbed the liquid and the chicken is cooked to the bone. Stir the ingredients around halfway through the cooking time.

5. If you like, add some more colour at the end by scattering over some finely chopped parsley or chives. Serve hot or warm with a green salad.

LAURIE COLWIN'S VEGETABLES & BUTTER-POACHED EGGS

SERVES **1, 2** OR MORE

Follow this recipe once and you'll forever have an unhurried and easy supper at your fingertips using any veg that you have around and a box of eggs.

The vegetables should be cut so they cook at a roughly even rate. This is a sample selection but mangetout, carrots (cut into thin batons), broccoli, asparagus and any number of veg can be cooked in this dish. A mix of colours is good.

The idea of steam-frying vegetables and eggs in buttery juices is taken from Laurie Colwin's wonderful *Home Cooking*. In a typically truthful piece called 'The Low-Tech Person's Batterie de Cuisine', she writes about how pots and pans are like sweaters. However many you amass in the kitchen, you find yourself using two or three over and over again.

Colwin advises that while the civilized will arrange the veg on a plate and place the egg on top, you can also eat everything straight out of the pot – and scrape some cheese on top with a knife if you wish.

- **20g** butter (a bit more if cooking for more than 2)
- **a splash** of olive oil
- **½–1 clove** garlic, *crushed*
- **a wide selection** of veg (about 250g per person) eg for one: 1 small courgette, *cut into thin batons*; ½ leek, *sliced*; ½ red pepper, *cut into small chunks*; 2 spears purple-sprouting broccoli, *stem roughly chopped*; 1 small red onion, *finely sliced*
- **1–2** eggs per person
- **a squeeze** of lemon juice
- parmesan or other strong cheese (optional)

1. Melt 15g of the butter in a small sauté pan or saucepan on a medium heat. You want the pan to be big enough so the veg lie more or less in a single layer, but aren't too spaced out. Add the olive oil and garlic. Season with a pinch of flaky sea salt and plenty of black pepper. Stir the garlic around for 10 seconds or so to flavour the fat.

2. Add the chopped veg to the pan, turn the heat down and cook slowly, with a lid on, stirring occasionally, until the veg are mostly tender. This will take about 15 minutes.

3. Remove the lid. Push the veg into a wide ring around the edge of the pan with a dip in the middle, like a nest. Melt the rest of the butter in the central gap and let it mix with the juices that have come out of the veg, then break the eggs into the centre of your nest. Cover and cook until the eggs are cooked to your liking, steam-poached in the butter and vegetable juices. For some reason that Freud could doubtless unravel, I'm not too keen on runny egg yolk and leave my eggs for about 5–6 minutes, until firm. If you like softer yolks, cook them for more like 3–4 minutes.

4. A last minute seasoning of the eggs and a squeeze of lemon over the veg are both good ideas, and perhaps a sprinkling of salty cheese.

HOLE-&-SOME-
TOAD

SERVES **4**

• **for the hole:**
• **200g** plain flour
• **450ml** liquid (half milk; half water)
• **2 large** eggs

for the toad:
• **4 tbsp** dripping or olive oil
• **8** sausages

This recipe evolved when I noticed that teenagers often request plenty of 'hole' rather than being overly interested in the 'toad', as you might think. I tend to cook a few additional sausages, just in case of hunger (leftover bangers in the fridge are always useful) but cook these separately, on a baking tray in the oven, to allow lots of space in the dish itself for more batter. The trick to any kind of toad-in-the-hole is to have plenty of tasty fat, dripping for preference, to stop the batter sticking to the bottom of the dish. For a long time I used 3 tbsp, then I upped it to 4 and this makes all the difference. The result is, unashamedly, a layer of almost fried batter – and very good it is too.

1. First make the batter. Put the flour in a large bowl and make a slight dip in the centre. Measure out the liquid in a jug and crack in the eggs. Whisk lightly to amalgamate. Pour the eggy liquid into the centre of the flour and use a whisk or wooden spoon to mix it gradually into the flour, trying to avoid lumps. If lumps do occur, give the mixture a good, hard whisking at the end. Season with a little salt – sausages are nearly salty enough to season the dish – and plenty of black pepper. Ideally, leave the batter in the fridge, covered, for at least 30 minutes, but if you don't have time to do this, don't worry; it's not essential.

LEFTOVER BANGERS IN THE FRIDGE ARE ALWAYS USEFUL

2. Preheat the oven to 220°C/Gas 7. Put half the dripping or oil in a large, shallow casserole or ovenproof sauté pan about 30cm in diameter over a high heat. Brown the sausages all over in the hot fat.

3. Add the rest of the dripping and get it really hot. Pour the batter onto the hot fat around the sausages. Place in the preheated oven for 30 minutes, or until nicely browned. This isn't a high-rise batter so don't worry if it doesn't puff up.

4. Serve with a salad, green veg or veg roasted in the oven at the same time.

To make an onion gravy whilst the toad is cooking, put 4–5 sliced onions (sprinkled with a little salt to stop them browning) in a frying pan with 1 tbsp olive oil. Fry over a high heat for 5 minutes, stirring occasionally, then turn the heat down to low and cook for another 20 minutes, stirring from time to time. Stir in 1 tbsp plain flour and cook out for a few minutes before adding 500ml hot instant chicken or beef stock. Simmer for 5 minutes. Season with a squeeze of lemon juice and perhaps a little Marmite, if necessary, to adjust the flavours.

Beef dripping can be easily bought in butchers and supermarkets. The best I've ever had was from a farmer's market and it made every dish special, not least roast potatoes. The texture of the dripping in the pot feels hard but is easy enough to scrape out with a sturdy spoon and a tubful keeps for ages in the fridge.

LAMB WITH YOGHURT & SPICES

SERVES **5–6**

- **300g** full-fat Greek yoghurt (must be full-fat)
- **2–3 tsp** garam masala (good quality bought or homemade)
- **½ shoulder** of lamb (approx. 1.3kg, shank end is best)
- **3** red peppers, *deseeded, cut into 8 chunks each*
- **3 large** red onions, *cut into 6–8 wedges each*
- **slug of** olive oil
- **2 tbsp** *finely chopped* mint and/or coriander leaf, to finish
- lime quarters, to serve

Here's an easy Indian-inspired recipe for a weekend when you're at home and want to warm both hearth and heart with an ovenful of fragrant food. The dish couldn't be quicker to put together, then can be left in the oven while you get on with something else. Lamb shoulder is one of the meat lover's favourite cuts. Cheap and sweet, it can be found whole or in half sections. If the latter, go for the half with the foreleg bone in order to enjoy the sweet nuggets of meat near the bone. This dish isn't a looker, but it's tasty. It looks best if you pull the meat off the bone and mix it with the sauce to serve as a form of stew.

The marinade given here is at its simplest. I also like to add 2 finely chopped cloves of garlic and a finely chopped thumb of root ginger. You could also add herbs or vary the spicing as you like, or make your own garam masala.

1. In a pot large enough to take the lamb, mix together the yoghurt, garam masala and 1 tsp flaky sea-salt.

2. Slash the lamb at its thickest parts – about three times on the top and bottom and twice on the shank, or end of the leg. Put in the marinade. You can do this the night before to add to the flavour and leave the meat, covered, in the fridge for up to 48 hours (this dish is also fine if you don't have time).

3. Preheat the oven to 200°C/Gas 6. Put the peppers and onions in the bottom of a large pot, sprinkle with salt, the olive oil and 100ml water. Put the lamb on top, scooping over any spare marinade. Put a lid on and cook for about 3 hours, or until tender, adding more water if the vegetables look dry.

4. Take the lamb out of the pot and put on a carving board (covered with foil and a clean tea towel to keep it warm if you aren't eating immediately). Mix the herbs into the vegetables in the pot, along with a squeeze of lime juice. Taste and adjust the seasoning if necessary.

5. Serve the lamb with the sauce and naan bread (or rice or potatoes). Put a lime wedge on the side of each plate for squeezing.

SLIGHTLY CHEATY THAI GREEN CURRY

SERVES **4–6**

Sweet potatoes have an affinity with Thai flavours and form the base of a delicious and quick curry. This version can be entirely vegetarian, but if there are some omnivores at the table I would stir some fish sauce into the pot for a final seasoning, after serving any vegetarians.

- **50g** ready-made green Thai curry paste
- **1 x 400ml** tin coconut milk
- **2 large** sweet potatoes (approx 500g, peeled weight), *cut into 3–4cm chunks*
- **4 large** mushrooms, *cut into halves or quarters depending on size*
- **300–400ml** water or stock
- **2** lime leaves (optional but good)
- **1 stalk** lemongrass (optional but good)
- **200g** frozen peas
- **a small handful** of basil leaves, *roughly torn*
- **juice of ½–1** lime, to taste
- **½–1 tbsp** fish sauce, to taste (optional)

1. Place the curry paste and coconut milk in a medium-sized pan and stir together over a low heat to combine. Add the potatoes and mushrooms along with enough water or stock to cover. I prefer to have a bit of fresh, aromatic flavour so also add lime leaves and a stalk of lemongrass, bashed a bit to release its flavour.

2. Put a lid on the pot, bring to the boil then turn down and simmer for 20 minutes, or until the sweet potatoes are cooked, adding the frozen peas after 15 minutes.

3. Stir in the basil leaves. Taste the sauce and add some lime juice and fish sauce, if using, to balance the flavours.

4. You can serve this with rice or noodles, or eat on its own for a lighter dish.

If you want to include meat, cut 4 or 5 chicken thighs (skinned and boned) or 2–3 chicken breasts into strips. Add the thighs to the pot at the same time as the potatoes. If using breasts, add just before the peas so they cook for about 10-12 minutes.

If you want to include fish, add 200g tiger prawns or firm-fleshed fish about 5 minutes before the end of cooking and stir in carefully.

MORE-IS-MORE
MINCE

SERVES **8**

- **1 tbsp** olive or other vegetable oil
- **2 onions**, *finely chopped*
- **2 stalks** celery, *finely chopped*
- **2 carrots**, *finely chopped*
- **2 cloves** garlic, *finely chopped*
- **4 rashers** smoked streaky bacon, *chopped into 2cm slices*
- **¼ medium** butternut squash (about 200g), *cut into 1.5–2cm dice* (optional)
- **100g** mushrooms, *cut into 1.5–2cm dice*
- **500g** beef mince
- **100g** red lentils
- **1 tsp** thyme leaves
- **1 x 60g** tin anchovies, drained of oil
- **2 x 400g** tins chopped tomatoes
- **2 tbsp** tomato purée
- **2 tbsp** tomato ketchup
- **100ml** red or white wine
- **500ml** stock (can be instant but watch the salt levels)
- **30g** rolled porridge oats

For me, there are two modes of mince. First is the 'less-is-more' version cooked by my mother and based on her Scottish roots. She uses lots of onions and a certain amount of pepper, but overall lets good mince speak for itself. I find this dish deeply nostalgic, especially when served with triangles of bread called sippets (my English father likes them fried), or plain boiled potatoes with a dab of butter. For a dish as bare as this to work, the mince must be good (as it tends to be in Scottish butchers). Mince isn't always so good, however. I now veer towards the 'more-is-more' direction. Plenty of vegetables replace some of the mince, partly because of the standard tactic of smuggling extra veg onto a teenager's, or child's, plate (or an adult's for that matter), and partly to make the meat go further. Mostly, though, it's because I like the variety of colours, textures and tastes of vegetables.

1. Pour the oil into a large, reasonably deep, pan and gently fry the chopped onions, celery, carrots, garlic and bacon for about 10 minutes, or until softened, stirring occasionally.

2. Add the chopped butternut squash, if using, and mushrooms and fry for another 3–4 minutes, stirring occasionally. Then add the mince, lentils, thyme, anchovies, tomatoes, tomato purée and ketchup. Stir everything thoroughly so it is well combined, and season with salt and pepper.

3. Pour in the wine and stock, increase the heat and bring the mixture to the boil, then turn down the heat and simmer for 15 minutes, stirring occasionally. Stir in the oats and continue to cook for another 30–45 minutes, or until the liquid has reduced and thickened.

4. Taste and adjust the seasoning if necessary. A few dashes of Worcestershire sauce or soy sauce can work wonders, or perhaps a blob more ketchup.

This makes 8 portions that can be spread over several meals, for example as a meal for 2 people or a family supper served with jacket potatoes and then leftovers to go in the fridge or freezer to be used as a sauce for tagliatelle or as the base for a cottage pie.

The use of mince is economical in this dish. The meat is made to go further, not just with the veg, but also by adding lentils and oats – the latter a trick my mother uses in her less-is-more mince, partly to soak up any fat.

This dish is One Pot batch cooking at its best. I often make a panful at the weekend and deploy it at various meals during the busy week.

CHEESY BAKED POTATOES WITH HORSERADISH

SERVES **4**

- **4 large** baking potatoes

filling:
- **150ml** sour cream
- **4** spring onions, *finely chopped*
- **1–2 tbsp** horseradish sauce
- **150g** *grated* strong cheddar

Have you forgotten how good these are? I had. But they were a staple of my childhood; a dish I looked forward to from the smell of the roasting skin to the taste and texture of the soft, buttery insides. No wonder some chefs think the best mash of all is made from the insides of baked potatoes. I rediscovered the idea in *Simone's Kitchen Secrets*, by Simone Cunliffe. The book is full of excellent, easy recipes, partly inspired by her years spent living in Japan, and is sold in aid of the Huntingdon's Disease Association (www.hda.org.uk). It is one of those collections of recipes that you know come from a real kitchen, as well as from a good cook, and such books provide plenty of inspiration.

1. Preheat the oven to 190°C/Gas 5. Pierce the potatoes with a skewer or fork and put on a baking sheet in the oven for about 1 hour, or until cooked.

2. While the potatoes are cooking, prepare the filling. In a large bowl, mix together the sour cream, chopped spring onions, 1 tbsp of the horseradish sauce and 100g of the cheddar. Season with plenty of black pepper.

3. Take the potatoes out of the oven and cut in half to help them cool. When the spud halves are cool enough to handle, scoop out the flesh, leaving the skins intact with ½–1cm flesh inside.

4. Mix the scooped-out flesh into the rest of the ingredients, using a fork to break up the potato and combine it with the rest of the filling. Taste and add more horseradish sauce if you want a little more poke (some horseradish sauces are very strong, others lack firepower).

5. Spoon the mixture back into the skins. Scatter over the rest of the cheese. Either wrap well in clingfilm and freeze to reheat another day, or put back in a 180°C/Gas 4 oven and reheat for about 20 minutes, until the mixture is hot all the way through and the cheese on top is melty and brown. Serve with a salad.

One half of a large potato is enough for one person if served either with a large green salad, or to accompany another dish, such as cheaty chicken & mushroom pie (see page 78). Stuffed spuds make your main meat go much further.

Cheesy baked potatoes can feed a crowd. In any case, it's always worth making more than you need and freezing some. They reheat well from frozen.

Vary the filling as you wish; the possibilities are as endless as sandwiches. Good tuna with little capers; chicken with a little French mustard instead of the horseradish; ham and gruyère: all these can go alongside the sour cream and spring onions in the mixture.

MUSSELS WITH LEEKS, BACON & CIDER

SERVES **2** AS A MAIN COURSE; **4** AS STARTER

- **1 tbsp** olive oil
- **3 rashers** back bacon (smoked or not), *finely sliced*
- **1 stalk** celery, *finely sliced*
- **2 leeks**, *finely sliced*
- **1 clove** garlic, *finely chopped*
- **1kg** mussels
- **100ml** cider
- **100ml** double cream

With their rich sweetness, high zinc and iron and omega-3s, mussels are healthy as well as delicious. Cleaning mussels does take a little bit of time, but is a task you can do whilst listening to the radio, having a think or unobtrusively monitoring the homework being done at the kitchen table. Mussels take a while to eat and this makes supper more leisurely and pleasurable – as well as less fattening.

Mussels vary in terms of quality, especially in supermarkets. Occasionally I've had to throw out half of them, though usually it is only a couple. The beauty of all mussel recipes is that the shellfish also flavour the sauce so the dish is still tasty, even if you hit a duff batch.

1. Pour the oil into a large, wide pan with a lid and heat. Add the chopped bacon, celery, leeks and garlic and fry over a medium heat for 5–10 minutes, stirring often, until cooked. Season with a good grinding of black pepper. You don't need any salt as the mussels and their liquor are already quite salty.

2. Meanwhile, prepare the mussels by rinsing them with cold, running water then pulling off the beard, or straggle of fibres. Look at each one to check it isn't cracked or broken. If the mussel is open, tap it on the side of the sink and check that it closes. Discard any that don't.

3. Tip the prepared mussels into the pan followed immediately by the cider. Cover with a lid and cook over a medium heat for 3 minutes or so, until the mussels are open. Throw away any that remain shut tight.

4. Pour the cream into the pan and bring to the boil to thicken slightly. Serve with bread to mop up the delicious juices.

CART DRIVERS' PASTA

SERVES **4**

- **2 cloves** garlic, *finely chopped*
- **20** basil leaves, *finely chopped*
- **10** mint leaves, *finely chopped*
- **2 tbsp** *finely chopped* chives
- **500g** ripe tomatoes, *roughly chopped*
- **4 tbsp** extra virgin olive oil (as good as possible)
- **a pinch** of caster sugar
- **300–400g** pasta, depending on appetite (spaghetti or linguine are authentic)
- **50g** parmesan or pecorino, *grated*
- **1 x 50g** tin anchovies in oil, *drained & roughly chopped*

This recipe is an adaptation of one in Giorgio Locatelli's *Made in Sicily*, a book that brilliantly explores the special food of the island. The name of the recipe in Italian, *pasta alla carrettiera* (cart drivers' pasta), is thought to refer to the uncooked sauce that cart drivers would quickly mix together by the side of a road to eat with pasta cooked in a pot over an improvised fire. It then became a staple of simple truckers' cafes. This recipe is simple and adaptable. Baked beans and a fried slice, it ain't.

Italians have a useful two-layer pasta pot with a perforated container that sits inside the pot. This is then lifted up to drain the pasta, retaining the cooking water – tasty, starchy liquid that can be used as part of the sauce. It also means you don't have to lug a heavy, hot panful of pasta and water to the sink.

1. Put the garlic, herbs, tomatoes and olive oil in a bowl. Season with the sugar, salt and pepper. Stir everything together. If you have time, leave to infuse for an hour.

2. Cook the pasta in plenty of boiling, well-salted water according to packet instructions until al dente (this should take about 10–12 minutes). Drain briefly, quickly putting the colander of pasta back over the cooking pot so that a good few tablespoonfuls of the cooking water are saved.

3. Add the cheese, anchovies, if using, and herby tomato mixture to the pot, followed by the pasta and stir well.

4. Serve in big bowls, perhaps with a squeeze of lemon on top and definitely a final grind of black pepper.

ARTICHOKE, PANCETTA & ANCHOVY PASTA

SERVES **2**

- **150–200g** penne, according to appetite
- **1 tbsp** olive oil (or olive oil from the artichoke hearts, if available)
- **50–100g** pancetta, *cut into small cubes*
- **1–2 cloves** garlic, *finely chopped*
- **8** anchovies, *roughly chopped*, plus ½ tbsp of oil from the jar or tin
- **1 x 400g** (260g drained weight) tin artichoke hearts, *drained & roughly chopped*
- **juice of ½** lemon

Jars of good ingredients are ever-ready for moments when you are too knackered to prepare much fresh food. Trish, the owner of Penbuckles – the excellent deli near me in Hastings – suggested this particularly delicious and useful combination one day when I was too tired to even think of what to eat. Add a couple of chopped shallots to the pancetta and some herbs or rocket at the end, if they come to hand, but the dish is also delicious as it stands.

Pancetta is Italian cured pork belly, the equivalent of streaky bacon. You can buy it in rashers, cubes, or in one piece. Keep in the fridge, wrapped loosely in clingfilm or in a small, sealed box. It's a useful ingredient to pick up in a good deli.

Artichoke hearts are sold in jars or loose, stored in oil, but I also tend to buy the cheaper ones in tins. Either use the whole drained tin or store any remaining hearts in olive oil in a small covered bowl in the fridge.

If you have some double cream in the fridge, then bubble some up with the rest of the sauce for a richer dish. To make it even richer, add some parmesan.

1. Bring a large pot of water to the boil, add 1 tsp salt and then the pasta. Stir and cook, according to packet instructions, until al dente.

2. Meanwhile, pour the olive oil into a frying pan and cook the pancetta over a medium heat, stirring occasionally, for 5 minutes or so, until browned.

3. Add the garlic and continue to fry for another minute or so.

4. Add the anchovies with their oil and stir so they dissolve into the other ingredients, then add the artichoke hearts and mix with the other ingredients.

5. Squeeze in the lemon juice and season with plenty of black pepper. Turn off the heat.

6. When the pasta is ready, drain, but leave a little of the cooking water in the pan. Tip the pasta back into the pot. Add the sauce and mix together well. Taste and add a little more pepper if necessary.

QUICK
SPAGHETTI
CARBONARA

SERVES **2**

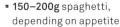

- **150–200g** spaghetti, depending on appetite
- **1** leek, *finely sliced*
- **150ml** double cream
- **½ clove** garlic, *crushed*
- **50g** parmesan, *finely grated*
- **100g** air-dried ham, such as parma, serrano or a British kind, *cut into 2cm strips*
- **2 tbsp** *finely chopped* chives and/or flat leaf parsley
- **juice of** ½ lemon
- **2 eggs**

This is an extra-speedy version of spaghetti carbonara using fridge ingredients thrown together in one pot. There are different schools of thought as to whether you should have onion in a carbonara. Naturally, each Italian has an opinion on the only way it should and shouldn't be done. If you do add onions, they are generally softened first in a frying pan with chopped pancetta or bacon. I like onions, but don't always have the time or patience to soften them first. This One Pot uses the short-cut of cooking the leeks with the pasta, then adding some chopped chives and a little garlic to the sauce, so your allium element is done in double-quick time. Air-cured ham replaces bacon and requires no cooking.

Other green vegetables such as broccoli, kale or chard can be steamed above the spaghetti. Add any extra veg after the herbs and eggs have been stirred through as too much greenery means the egg doesn't cook so well.

1. Cook the spaghetti, according to packet instructions, in well-salted water until al dente (about 10–12 minutes), adding the sliced leeks to the pot towards the end so that they cook for around 3 minutes.

2. Briefly drain the pasta and leeks, leaving about 2 tbsp of cooking water in the pan. Add the cream and garlic to the pan and bring to the boil. Season well with black pepper. Stir in the parmesan and 75g of the ham.

3. Tip the spaghetti and leeks back into the pan. Add the chopped herbs, squeeze in the lemon, crack in the eggs and quickly stir everything together thoroughly. Divide between 2 bowls and lay the last strips of ham on top. Grind on a little more pepper and serve.

QUICK BUT CLASSY MACARONI CHEESE

SERVES 4–6

- **750ml** vegetable or chicken stock (instant is fine)
- **25g** dried mushrooms
- **1 tbsp** olive oil
- **1 red onion**, *finely chopped*
- **2 cloves** garlic, *finely chopped*
- **300g** macaroni
- **1 x 250g** tub mascarpone
- **40g** parmesan or strong cheddar, *finely grated*
- **2 tbsp** *finely chopped* parsley or chives
- **60g** air-cured ham, eg parma, serrano or a British kind, *cut into thin strips* (optional but good)

Macaroni cheese used to have the sniff of mean economy, but has recently been given a new lease of life as trendy 'mac and cheese'. This recipe adds a few extra ingredients to turn an old standby into a meal that you will be more than happy to serve to friends and family. I tend to make more than I need in order to have leftovers for quick comfort suppers in front of the telly, or even a mid-morning breakfast after a stint at my desk.

Other additions to mac-and-cheese include sunblush tomatoes, halved cherry tomatoes, 2 tbsp drained capers or a drained tin of anchovies, roughly chopped.

If you like a bit of extra texture (I do), make some breadcrumbs whilst the macaroni is cooking. Melt about 1 tbsp butter in a frying pan and add 6 tbsp breadcrumbs. Cook over a medium heat, stirring quite often, until brown and crunchy. Scatter over the finished dish or each portion.

1. Mix up the stock with boiling water and add the dried mushrooms. Leave them to soak and add flavour to the stock while you get on with the rest of the recipe.

2. Put the olive oil in a large pan. Add the finely chopped onion and garlic and cook over a medium heat for 5 minutes, undisturbed. Cook for a further 5 minutes, until soft, stirring occasionally.

3. Add the stock, mushrooms and macaroni to the pot. Bring to the boil and leave to bubble away for a minute or so. Lower the heat, cover and simmer quite fast for around 12 minutes, stirring occasionally. Remove the lid and simmer for another 3 minutes or until cooked, adding a little more water if necessary. Cover and leave for another couple of minutes, with the heat off, to make the pasta softer.

4. Stir in the mascarpone, the parmesan or cheddar, chopped herbs and strips of ham, if using. Season with plenty of black pepper and more salt if necessary. Serve with a sharply dressed green salad.

ROASTED CAULIFLOWER CHEESE

SERVES **4** AS A MAIN DISH;
6–8 AS A SIDE DISH

- **1** cauliflower, *broken into florets*
- **3 tbsp** olive oil
- **1 tsp** *freshly grated* nutmeg
- **a pinch** of chilli flakes (optional)
- **16** cherry tomatoes, *halved*
- **4** spring onions, *roughly chopped*
- **500ml** ready-made cheese sauce
- **1 tbsp** Dijon or grainy mustard
- **30g** strong cheddar, *grated*

There is something supremely comforting about cauliflower cheese, not least one as easy to make as this. The dish is a tasty spin on an old favourite, using ready-made, shop-bought cheese sauce that is whooped up with extras. Roasting is the way to go with cauliflower, intensifying the vegetable's sweetness and avoiding any sogginess. For spices, nutmeg has an affinity with cauliflower and I like a bit of chilli heat in there, plus some mustard. Play around with the flavours according to your tastes and spice rack.

If you want to add meat to the dish, cut about 60g ham into thick strips and stir in with the cheese sauce before putting in the oven.

Spices go well with cauli. Get kids to eat this beautiful and healthy brassica by rebranding it as 'smokey bacon cauli', roasted with Spanish smoked paprika, or 'salt 'n' vinegar cauli', with sea salt and then balsamic vinegar added towards the end.

A quick recipe for cheese sauce is given on page 95. Up the quantity slightly for this (500ml milk; 30g butter; 30g flour and 3 tbsp grated parmesan).

1. Preheat the oven to 200°C/Gas 6. Place the cauliflower in a gratin dish big enough for the florets to lie in a single layer (eg. 25cm square and 8cm deep). Pour over the olive oil, grind over a decent amount of pepper, grate over the nutmeg and scatter over the chilli flakes, if using. Mix everything together well and put in the oven.

2. Roast the cauliflower for around 15 minutes, then mix in the halved cherry tomatoes and continue to cook in the hot oven for a further 15 minutes.

3. Add the chopped spring onions and pour over the cheese sauce. Dollop on the mustard and mix everything together so it is well combined and coats the cauliflower and tomatoes. Scatter over the grated cheddar and put the dish back in the oven for another 25–30 minutes, or until the cheese is browning and the dish is bubbling hot.

4. Serve with crusty bread and, if you like, a sharply dressed salad. This is also good alongside meat or fish.

HONEY-MUSTARD GLAZED SAUSAGES & 'SMOKY BACON' CAULIFLOWER

SERVES **4–6**

- **4–6 medium-large** potatoes, *cut into 5cm thick wedges*
- **1** cauliflower, *cut into florets*
- **12** good-quality sausages

- **3 tbsp** olive or other vegetable oil
- **1 tsp** smoked paprika
- **2 tbsp** honey
- **1 tbsp** Dijon mustard
- **a big squeeze** of lemon juice

Sausages are a great staple supper and here are given a tasty glaze that lifts the dish into a supper to serve to friends. The preparation is quick and easy, then it can be cooked and kept warm in a low oven until you are ready to eat.

Alternative spices that go well with the roasted cauliflower include 1 tsp ground cumin or ½ tsp nutmeg or ¼–½ tsp chilli flakes; or a combination of all three.

1. Preheat the oven to 200°C/Gas 6. Place the potato wedges on one side of a large baking tray and the cauliflower florets, made roughly the same size as the wedges, on the other side. Don't waste the stalk, cut it into large chunks and mix it in with the florets.

2. Arrange the sausages on a smaller baking tray. Drizzle over a small amount of the oil and turn the sausages over so they are lightly coated.

A GREAT STAPLE LIFTED INTO SUPPER FOR FRIENDS

3. Drizzle the rest of the oil over the potatoes and cauliflower. Dust the cauliflower with the smoked paprika, then season both veg with a scatter of salt and plenty of black pepper. Turn the vegtables over so they mix with their seasonings.

4. Put the sausages and veg trays in the oven; veg on a shelf above the sausages. Cook for 30 minutes, or until the cauliflower is starting to go crispy brown on some edges and the wedges are tender and golden.

5. Pour the honey over the sausages and dollop on the mustard, then use two spoons to turn them in their melting glaze. Turn the cauliflower and the potatoes over. Put back in the oven, turn off the heat and leave for 10 minutes.

6. Squeeze the lemon over the cauliflower. Coat the sausages once more in their sticky glaze, which will have thickened slightly. Serve with greenery if wanted.

FISH WITH BALSAMIC TOMATO SAUCE

SERVES **6**

- **800g** tomatoes, *cut in half*
- **1 small** bulb fennel (about 170g trimmed), *cut into 6 chunks*
- **3 cloves** garlic, *roughly chopped*
- **2** red onions, *cut in quarters*
- **1–1½ tsp** caster sugar
- **1 tbsp** balsamic vinegar
- **3 tbsp** olive oil
- **2 handfuls** basil leaves, *roughly torn*
- **a handful** of black olives, *stoned & roughly chopped*
- **6 fillets** of fish

There are so many kinds of fish in the sea, it is useful to have one recipe that accommodates any of them. This simple Mediterranean supper dish is adaptable to whatever looks best on the day on a fishmonger's slab or supermarket shelf (or what you have in your freezer ready to defrost). The recipe benefits from delicious ripe tomatoes, but also improves sadder specimens.

Make this One Pot more substantial by cooking small potatoes with the vegetables, adding a little water if necessary to make it more saucy.

1. Preheat the oven to 220°C/Gas 7. Put the tomatoes, fennel, garlic and onions in a shallow dish so they lie roughly in one layer.

2. Sprinkle over the sugar and balsamic vinegar and season well with salt and pepper. Drizzle over the oil, add half the roughly torn basil and the chopped olives and stir well. Cover with foil and bake in the preheated oven for 45 minutes.

3. Remove the foil and stir the ingredients around to combine loosely into a sauce. Put the fish fillets on top, season lightly with salt and pepper and a drizzle of oil. Cook for 10–15 minutes, uncovered, until the flesh of the fish is opaque at its thickest part.

4. Serve the fish with the sauce and the rest of the torn basil on top. This is excellent with potato wedges or baked potatoes cooked in the oven at the same time, or just plain boiled rice.

SPANISH CHORIZO & POTATOES

SERVES **4**

- **1–2 tbsp** olive oil
- **2 medium** onions, *sliced*
- **2 large cloves** garlic, *chopped*
- **275g** cooking chorizo, *sliced into 1cm pieces*
- **750g** firm-textured potatoes, eg Charlotte, *peeled or not, chopped into large chunks*
- **1** red pepper, *deseeded & cut into large chunks*
- **1** green pepper, *deseeded & cut into large chunks*
- **2 large** tomatoes, *roughly chopped*
- **1–2 tsp** Spanish smoked paprika
- **600ml** water
- **2–3 tbsp** *finely chopped* coriander leaf, to finish
- **a squeeze** of lemon juice, to taste

Chorizo is a handy, well-flavoured ingredient to have on standby for quick and easy suppers. Ideally use a sauté pan that's wide enough for the ingredients to cook evenly in one layer. You can also make this in a deeper casserole dish, but make sure you stir it around a bit.

Cooking chorizo is softer than standard chorizo, but use either.

Spanish smoked paprika, or pimentón, gives the dish an extra dimension, but it will be in the chorizo if you don't have a tin of the spice to hand.

1. Pour the olive oil into a sauté pan or casserole. Add the sliced onions and cook for 10–15 minutes over a medium-low heat, stirring occasionally, until softened. Add the garlic and chorizo and stir them into the onions. Let this mixture cook for 5 minutes, stirring occasionally, so the chorizo starts to release its fat.

2. Add the potatoes, peppers, tomatoes, smoked paprika and water to the pan with a little salt (not too much as the chorizo will be salty; you can add more at the end). Stir everything together and leave to cook on a medium heat for around 45 minutes to 1 hour, or until the potatoes have cooked through and the sauce has reduced down and thickened a bit.

3. Taste and add more salt if necessary. Scatter over the coriander and brighten the dish up with a squeeze of lemon. Serve in big bowls, followed by a salad.

SURF'N'TURF
'N'FIELD

SERVES **4**

- **2 tbsp** olive oil, plus extra for a final drizzle
- **2 sprigs** rosemary
- **3** shallots, *finely chopped*
- **1 clove** garlic, *finely chopped*
- **80g** ham, *cut into 2cm slices* (air-cured is best eg parma, serrano or a British kind)
- **a slosh** of whatever booze comes to hand, ideally white wine
- **2 x 400g** tins cannelleni beans or chickpeas
- **300g** peeled, raw king prawns or 8 scallops, *cut if half across (ie 2 discs) if large*
- **300g** ready-washed baby spinach
- **1½ tbsp** lemon juice

The combination of shellfish, salty ham and beans soaked with tasty juices is a winner, as well as being nutritious. Add a handy bag of baby spinach leaves and you have a classic One Pot.

The surf, turf and field elements of this can all be altered. Use whatever you like or have to hand. What matters is the mixture of textures, tastes and colours.

1. Over a medium heat, warm the olive oil with the rosemary in a sauté pan, deep frying pan or large saucepan with a lid. Add the shallots, garlic and ham and cook for 3 minutes, stirring occasionally. Add the white wine, or whatever else you have open – a vermouth such as Noilly Prat is useful at such times.

2. Drain one of the tins of beans and add to the pot along with the other tin and it's liquor. Cook for 2 minutes, stirring occasionally. Add the prawns or scallops, the baby spinach and lemon juice and stir into the beans.

3. Cook, with a lid on, for 2–3 minutes, or until the seafood is nearly cooked and the spinach has wilted down. Take the lid off and boil away any excess juices – 30 seconds or so.

4. Season with salt, pepper and more lemon juice, if needed. Top with a final drizzle of olive oil and serve with crusty bread to mop up the juices.

TANDOORI CHICKEN

SERVES **6**

- **12** chicken thighs, without skin, on the bone (or use 2–3 drumsticks per person)
- **225g** plain full-fat yoghurt (must be full-fat & not Greek)
- **2 tbsp** tandoori powder
- **2 cloves** garlic, *crushed*
- **juice of 1** lemon

Many households have a standby supper that uses packets of chicken thighs or drumsticks. This is ours. The dish comes from a Simon Hopkinson recipe in *The Good Cook*. His tandoori chicken is done with the usual attention to detail. As it became a standard in our home, the method got slightly simplified, not to say 'dumbed down'. The end result is still delicious, if not quite so perfect.

If I have a busy week ahead, I mix the chicken with the marinade in a covered dish at the weekend and leave it in the fridge to be on hand to cook early in the week.

You can easily scale the recipe up or down and do more chicken pieces, either for a crowd or to have extra to eat cold from the fridge. This is a generous amount of well-seasoned marinade and you'll need to add just a bit more yoghurt and spice if adding more chicken.

1. Slash each skinless chicken piece through to the bone in three places. Mix the rest of the ingredients together with 1 tsp flaky sea salt in a shallow container that will hold the chicken in a single layer, or thereabouts. Mix the chicken into this tandoori marinade, massaging it into the cuts. Cover the dish and put in the fridge to marinate for anything from 20 minutes to three days.

2. Preheat the oven to 180°C/Gas 4. Line a baking tray with tin foil. Cook the chicken in its marinade for 40 minutes or so, turning over once, until the meat is cooked through to the bone and the juices run clear when you poke a knife through the thickest part – the outside should be patched with brown.

3. Serve with naan bread warmed in the oven for the last 5 minutes or so of cooking, or else with plain boiled rice and chutney.

CARIBBEAN CHICKEN WITH IRISH POTATOES

SERVES **4**

- **4 medium** baking or sweet potatoes
- **1½ tbsp** olive or other vegetable oil
- **2 cloves** garlic, *finely chopped*
- **1** red onion, *sliced*
- **2** red, yellow or orange peppers, *deseeded & finely sliced* (a mix looks good)
- **½** red chilli, *deseeded & finely chopped* (Scotch bonnet is authentic & is hot so only use ¼)
- **4 large** chicken thighs, with skin & bone
- **1 x 400ml** tin full-fat coconut milk
- **a big squeeze** of lime juice
- **4 tbsp** *roughly chopped* coriander leaf

This tasty and colourful dish cooks in the oven along with baked potatoes, either sweet ones or what Caribbean cooks sometimes call 'Irish' potatoes – our standard potatoes (a staple food of the Irish) as opposed to the sweet ones more commonly cooked on the Islands.

You can cook the chicken on the hob for the same amount of time and serve it with rice, noodles or boiled potatoes instead.

Use full-fat coconut milk. The reduced fat kind doesn't work so well in this dish.

Chicken thighs are a budget way to eat high welfare meat. If using ones without skin and off the bone, they won't brown so well and will cook more quickly.

1. Preheat the oven to 200°C/Gas 6. Scrub the potatoes and cut out any damaged bits. Put in the oven on a baking tray for 1 hour for standard potatoes and 40 minutes for sweet potatoes, until tender all the way through.

2. While the potatoes are cooking, make the chicken. Heat 1 tbsp of the the oil in a casserole dish with a lid. Add the chopped vegetables. Cook over a medium high heat for 5 minutes, or until softened, stirring occasionally.

3. Remove the vegetables from the pan and put on a plate whilst you brown the chicken. Put another ½ tbsp of oil in the pot, and turn the heat up to high. Lay the chicken thighs in the pan, skin-side down, and leave to cook until golden. Turn the thighs and leave to colour on the other side.

4. Add the coconut milk and stir to scrape up any tasty, gooey bits of chicken that have got stuck to the bottom of the pot. Let the coconut milk bubble up for a minute or so to slightly thicken. Turn off the heat. Stir the vegetables back into the pot. Stir in a pinch of salt to season the dish. Squeeze over the lime juice.

5. Place the lid on the pot and put in the hot oven to cook alongside the potatoes for about 30 minutes. To check if the chicken is cooked, use a knife to cut down into one thigh, right to the bone. If the juices run clear, and the meat comes away from the bone quite easily, the chicken is cooked. If not, put it back in the oven for another 10 minutes.

6. Scatter the chopped coriander over the chicken and serve with the baked potatoes, putting a few chunks of butter in each potato. This is good with a green salad dressed with a little olive oil and a squeeze of lemon or lime juice.

HOLIDAY COTTAGE
HEAVEN & EARTH

SERVES **4—6**,
DEPENDING ON SAUSAGE-HUNGER
(ADD MORE FOR HUNGRY MALES)

- **1 tbsp** vegetable oil
- **12** sausages
- **a bowlful** of assorted alliums: eg. 2 onions, *sliced*; 2 leeks, *cut into 2cm slices*; 2 cloves garlic, *finely chopped*
- **a slosh** of booze, if you have some open
- **750g** firm-textured (eg salad) potatoes, *cut into chunks*
- **2** eating apples, *quartered, cored, & cut into thick slices*
- any strong herbs around (eg rosemary, bay leaves or thyme) and/or a piece of kombu or other seaweed
- **1 litre** water
- **a few generous handfuls** of green veg: eg *sliced* cabbage, frozen peas, bag of baby spinach
- **a touch** of something acid to balance the flavours: eg a squeeze of lemon juice or 1 tbsp of grainy mustard

Many homes have a sausage dish that is useful for mid-week feeding. My childhood diet included something called 'sausage gunge' which doesn't sound appealing, but hit the spot – especially on our camper-van holidays. Such food isn't about looks, but all about taste, ease and sustenance. My adult version is based on the German *himmel und erde* (heaven and earth), a witty name describing the combination of apples and potatoes. It is an especially useful dish for any form of self-catering holiday, when you might want to try the meat in a local butcher's, but don't have much to hand in terms of pots and other kitchen kit.

1. Pour the oil into a large pot and brown the sausages over a medium-high heat, turning them over three or four times (or just twice if you are feeling lazy). Turn the heat down, push the sausages to the side of the pot if it's large, or remove and put to one side. Add the onions, leeks and garlic to the pan. Stir them around in the fat and cook over a medium-low heat for about 10 minutes, to soften, stirring occasionally.

2. If you have a bottle of wine, beer, cider or sherry open then add a slosh of this to the pot, let it bubble up then stir it into the veg. Add the potatoes, apples and any herbs you have around – a bay leaf or two, a sprig of rosemary or a couple of sprigs of thyme. If you have some kombu, add this now too, plus a seasoning of salt and pepper. Return the sausages to the pot if you have taken them out.

SUCH DISHES ARE ALL ABOUT TASTE, EASE AND SUSTENANCE

3. Pour over the water and stir everything together. Put a lid on the pot and bring to the boil, then turn down the heat and simmer for 30 minutes, or until the potatoes are tender and the sausages cooked through.

4. Add the greens and continue to cook until they are done (3–5 minutes).

5. Add a squirt of lemon juice or, even better, some grainy mustard to balance out the sweetness of the apples. Taste and adjust the seasoning if necessary.

For self-catering holidays, I tend to pack a small box of flavours and, having learnt the trick of using a piece of seaweed in a stew (see page 182), often take along a bit of kombu to enhance the umami savouriness of dishes such as this. Knowledgeable foragers will find a substitute on a clean beach.

HOT-SMOKED
SALMON OMELETTE

SERVES 2, 3 OR 4,
DEPENDING ON APPETITE

- **100g** hot-smoked salmon
- **2 tbsp** *roughly chopped* dill
- **6 medium** eggs
- **a large knob** of butter (about ½ tbsp)
- **4 tbsp** double cream
- **4 tbsp** *grated* parmesan

The combination of smoked fish, eggs and fresh dill is especially delicious and makes a good supper dish for friends. The recipe is based on omelette Arnold Bennett, a meal created for the author whilst staying at The Savoy. To make the cooking simpler, I've used hot-smoked salmon as it requires no pre-cooking unlike Bennett's smoked haddock. The cream is important in order to make the filling richly soft; please don't be tempted to leave it out.

A small tortilla pan means you can make two smaller omelettes to feed 2 hungry people, keeping the first warm on a covered plate, in a low oven or below the grill pan, while you make the second.

1. Heat the grill to high. Flake the hot-smoked salmon and mix it gently with the chopped dill.

2. Crack the eggs into a bowl and whisk with a fork. Melt the butter in a small frying pan with a heat-proof handle (and ideally sloping sides to make it easier to serve) over a medium heat. When the butter is frothing, pour in the eggs.

3. Leave to cook for a minute or so, until the bottom has set. Use a spatula or palette knife to gently pull part of the set base towards the centre, then tip the pan so the runny egg goes into the gap. Do this a couple of times around the omelette so that it cooks in an even layer.

4. When the omelette is nearly cooked, with shallow puddles of liquid egg on top, spread over the salmon and dill, spoon over the cream and sprinkle over the parmesan.

5. Put the omelette under the grill for about a minute, until the cheese has melted and the egg cooked. Season with black pepper.

6. Serve half or quarter per person, depending on appetite, with a salad and crusty bread.

LAMB MEATBALLS WITH GRAINS

SERVES **4**

- **1 tbsp** olive oil
- **1** onion, *finely chopped*
- **3 cloves** garlic, *finely chopped*
- **150g** freekeh or pearled spelt or barley
- **550g** butternut squash, *peeled & seeds removed, cut into 3cm pieces*
- **1 tsp** sumac, plus a sprinkling for the top
- **500ml** chicken stock (instant is fine)
- **1 tbsp** tomato purée
- **2** preserved lemon, *pithy centres removed, skin finely chopped*
- **3 tbsp** *finely chopped* flat-leaf parsley

meatballs:
- **500g** lamb mince
- **2 cloves** garlic, *finely chopped*
- **1 tsp** coriander seeds, *roughly or finely ground*

Interesting grains make a great accompaniment to meatballs. I particularly like to make this with freekeh, the roasted green wheat used in the Middle East. Happily, it is becoming more popular and available in health food shops, delis, good supermarkets and online, but if you can't find any this dish is also great with pearled barley or spelt.

Sumac is a tart and fruity spice made from ground-up berries. It is one of the ingredients from Iranian cooking that is worth getting hold of and exploring. In general, sumac is used as a substitute for (or in addition to) lemon juice. Sprinkle some over a dish at the end to show off its beautiful red colour.

1. Mix together all the ingredients for the meatballs. Roll into 16 firm balls about the same size as a walnut in its shell. Heat the oil in a large, shallow pan. Brown the meatballs on two sides over a medium-high heat and remove from the pan.

2. Add the onion and garlic to the same pan and cook over a medium-low heat for 10–15 minutes, stirring occasionally. Add the grains, butternut squash and sumac and stir well. Add the chicken stock, tomato purée and preserved lemon. Season with salt and pepper, if necessary (stock can be salty, especially instant).

3. Return the meatballs to the pan. Bring to the boil, then turn down the heat. Cook, covered, for around 40 minutes, or until the liquid has been absorbed.

4. Taste for seasoning. Scatter with the finely chopped parsley and a final light dusting of sumac before serving.

KITCHEN

PAELLA

SERVES **5–6**

- **1 tbsp** olive oil
- **4–5** skinless chicken thigh fillets, *cut into 3 chunks each*
- **2 thick rashers** of smoked bacon (about 100g), *roughly chopped*
- **1** onion, *finely chopped*
- **2 cloves** garlic, *finely chopped*
- **1 large** red pepper or 2 romano peppers, *deseeded & cut into thin strips*
- **300g** Spanish paella rice
- **a large pinch** of saffron, *crumbled & soaked in 2 tbsp warm water for 20 minutes*
- **900ml** hot well-flavoured stock
- **140–200g** peeled, raw king prawns
- **100g** trimmed green beans, *cut in half*, or frozen peas
- **2–3 tbsp** *roughly chopped* flat-leaf parsley
- **1** lemon, *cut into 8 wedges*

An authentic paella is made in a wide, shallow pan placed over a broad heat source, traditionally a wood fire outdoors, so that the rice cooks evenly. The rice isn't stirred, and by the end of cooking you get the delectable crust on the base that is one of the most prized parts of the dish. This trick is far harder to achieve in a standard kitchen. Usually, you risk getting a mixture of cooked and slightly chalky grains. One way to avoid this is to finish the cooking of the paella in an oven, as it has a more even heat. This rough-and-ready 'kitchen paella' doesn't bother too much with the bottom crust, but is still full of flavour and can handily be eaten with just a fork for a party or sofa supper.

Increase the quantities to feed 8–10 or so by adding 100g more rice and about a third more of everything else. You'll need a big pan (if you don't have one, use 2 smaller ones), and it will probably get a bit of a crust as it's harder to move all the ingredients around. Be proud to be authentic rather than ashamed to have 'burnt' the bottom.

1. Pour the olive oil into a sauté or large frying pan and fry the chunks of chicken for 5–7 minutes, stirring occasionally. Remove from the pan and set aside.

2. Add the chopped bacon, onion, garlic, and pepper to the pan. Cook for 10 minutes over a medium heat, stirring occasionally. Put the chicken back in the pan and add the rice. Stir well so that all the grains of rice are mixed into the other ingredients. Add the saffron and hot stock.

3. Cook the paella over a medium heat for 10 minutes, stirring the rice from the outside into the centre every 2 minutes to ensure it cooks evenly. Taste and add salt if needed.

4. Stir in the prawns and green beans or frozen peas and continue to cook for another 8 minutes, covered with a lid – stirring the rice around a few more times. Give the paella one final mix and leave, lid on, for 5 minutes, for the rice to finish cooking. Scatter over the chopped parsley and serve with lemon wedges.

RED CABBAGE STIR-FRY

SERVES 4

- **1 tbsp** olive or vegetable oil
- **1 small** red onion, *finely sliced*
- **2 cloves** garlic, *finely chopped*
- **1 small thumb** root ginger, *finely chopped*
- **½ medium** red cabbage (about 450g), *trimmed & finely sliced*
- **100g** unroasted cashews
- **150g medium** egg noodles, *cooked* *according to packet instructions & drained*
- **3 tbsp** *roughly chopped* coriander leaf
- **juice of ½** lime

sauce:
- **a small glass** dry sherry or white wine
- **3 tbsp** Japanese soy sauce
- **2 tsp** brown sugar
- **½ tbsp** rice vinegar
- **1 tsp** sesame or vegetable oil

Necessity is the mother of kitchen invention. Red cabbage tends to hang around in the bottom of my fridge and this dish was a 'using up' supper when there was nothing else in the house. It is now a favourite option for this colourful cabbage.

To add meat, cut 3 medium boned and skinned chicken thighs (about 300g) into 1cm. Stir-fry these first for 2 minutes in ½ tbsp extra oil and remove from the pan. Add the chicken back to the pan after the cabbage has gone in and cook until done (about 10 minutes). Turn up the heat and continue as usual.

Stem ginger syrup is good in this dish. Substitute 1 tbsp for 1 tsp of the sugar, plus 1 tsp more rice vinegar as a counterbalance. You can also use ½ bulb of preserved ginger, finely chopped, instead of the fresh ginger.

Kecap manis is a delicious, thick Indonesian sauce that is somewhat addictive (in some cases, no doubt, because of its monosodium glutamate). You can stir in 2–4 tbsp at the end for extra flavour.

1. Mix all the ingredients for the sauce together and leave to one side.

2. Pour the oil into a wok over a high heat and stir-fry the red onion, garlic and ginger for about 2 minutes, until the onion has softened. Add the red cabbage and cashews and stir fry for another 2 minutes.

3. Pour the sauce into the pan, stir, turn the heat down and leave to steam-cook, covered, for 8–10 minutes, stirring occasionally until the cabbage is almost soft.

4. Turn the heat up to high and cook, uncovered, for another 2 minutes, stirring occasionally. Toss the cooked noodles into the rest of the ingredients and finish by stirring in the coriander and lime juice. Serve immediately.

MEATLOAF

SERVES **6**

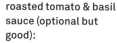

- **1kg** mince (I like a mixture of 500g lamb & 500g pork)
- **1 tsp** ground spices (to your preference; I tend to use 1 tsp five spice or 1 tsp ground cumin & a pinch of cinnamon)
- **3 cloves** garlic, *finely chopped*
- **a large handful** (about 10g) fresh basil or other herbs
- **1 medium** egg
- **a little** olive oil
- **100–200g** feta
- **1kg** small or new potatoes

roasted tomato & basil sauce (optional but good):
- **12** tomatoes
- **2 tbsp** olive oil
- **1 tsp** *chopped* chilli or ½ tsp chilli flakes (optional)
- **juice of ½** orange
- **1 tbsp** *roughly chopped* basil
- **1 tsp** caster sugar

Meatloaf is quick to prepare: mix the meat and seasonings together and cook in a loaf tin as if it were one giant, sliceable meatball. Conveniently, you can bake small potatoes in the oven at the same time and make an easy roasted-tomato sauce. All in all, it's a satisfying meal with minimum fuss.

Different types of mince are good for this dish. Vary the spices, herbs or flavourings accordingly, such as five spice, dried oregano and grated orange rind with beef, or chopped, fresh marjoram and grated lemon rind with pork.

1. Preheat the oven to 190°C/Gas 5. Put the mince into a large mixing bowl and add the spices, garlic, basil, ½–¾ tsp fine sea salt and the egg. Mix well using your fingers to squish the flavourings properly through the meat. You'll be able to see when this has happened as the flecks of green herb will be dispersed throughout.

2. Use olive oil to lightly grease the base and sides of a 2 litre/25 x 14 x 7cm loaf tin. Put half the meat in the base of the loaf tin, pressing it down well. Crumble the feta on top (use more or less according to how cheesy you want to go). Put the rest of the seasoned meat over the cheese, pushing it down firmly.

A SATISFYING
MEAL WITH
MINIMUM FUSS

3. Put the small potatoes on a baking tray and drizzle over 1 tbsp oil. Season with salt and pepper and mix together.

4. If making the sauce, cut the tomatoes into quarters and put in a ceramic dish that can hold them in one layer, or near enough. Pour over the oil, sprinkle over the chopped chilli or chilli flakes and season with a little salt. Mix everything together.

5. Put the meatloaf into the oven and place the tray of potatoes and tomatoes on the shelf below.

6. After 1 hour, take everything out of the oven. Mush together the cooked tomatoes with a fork and stir in the orange juice and basil. Taste and season with a little caster sugar, if necessary.

7. Carefully turn the meatloaf out onto a chopping board or serving plate and cut into slices. A fair amount of liquid comes out of the meatloaf as it cooks. I pour this back over the meat once sliced to keep it juicy.

8. Serve the meatloaf hot with the baked potatoes and some sort of greenery, and the tomato sauce if you've made it.

CHORIZO &
MUSHROOM
SPELTOTTO

SERVES **4–5**

- **100g** dried mushrooms
- **1 litre** hot stock (instant is fine)
- **a knob of** butter
- **2 tbsp** olive or vegetable oil
- **1 stalk** celery, *finely chopped*
- **1 onion,** *finely chopped*
- **2 cloves** garlic, *finely chopped*
- **200g** chorizo, *cut into cubes*

- **300g** pearled spelt or barley
- **100ml** red or white wine
- **140g** cavolo nero or other well-flavoured cabbage

to serve:
- lemon juice
- *finely chopped* flat-leaf parsley
- *grated* parmesan

Filling and comforting, this is a great dish to get you through the winter shivers. It's a version of risotto made using the grain spelt rather than the traditional rice, hence the name.

1. Put the dried mushrooms in a bowl and cover with about 250ml of the stock. Leave to soak while you get on with the rest of the recipe.

2. Heat the butter and oil in a large saucepan and gently fry the celery, onion, garlic and chorizo over a medium-low heat for 10–15 minutes, until the onion is soft and infused with the lovely flavours and fat that come out of the chorizo.

3. Stir the pearled spelt or barley into the pan so that the grains are coated with the oil. Pour in the wine, remaining stock and the mushrooms with their soaking water. Give everything a good stir. Cover, turn up the heat and bring to the boil, then turn the heat down and simmer for 15 minutes. Add the cabbage, then continue to cook for another 15–25 minutes, stirring occasionally, until all the liquid is absorbed.

4. Serve in bowls with a squeeze of lemon juice, a scatter of parsley and a good helping of grated parmesan. This keeps well, covered in the fridge, for leftovers.

Spelt has a delicious flavour and some find it more digestible than other grains. Pearled barley can be used as an alternative.

MUSTARDY
CELERIAC GRATIN

SERVES **4** AS A MAIN COURSE;
6–8 AS A SIDE DISH

- **350g** celeriac, *peeled & very finely sliced*
- **1 large** baking potato (about 300g), *peeled or scrubbed & cut into 1cm slices*
- **2** banana shallots, *finely sliced*
- **3 tbsp** *finely chopped* flat-leaf parsley
- **1½ tbsp** capers
- **50–100g** air-cured ham, eg parma, serrano or a British one (optional)
- **300ml** full-fat crème fraîche
- **500ml** milk
- **1½ tbsp** Dijon or grainy mustard
- **1 clove** garlic, *finely chopped*

Celeriac is often served raw in a mustardy sauce as celeriac rémoulade. This gratin uses the same flavour combination to make a dish that can be served as a main course, along with a salad, or as a side dish with a Sunday roast.

Celeriac looks like an asteroid and has coarse, knobbly skin that needs to be cut off first. Then use a big knife to cut your big beast into quarters; it is then easier to cut these smaller pieces as thin as possible. Alternatively, use a mandolin, the side of a box grater or a food processor. However you do it, slice just before cooking as the flesh discolours once cut.

If your celeriac is small, substitute the rest of the weight with more potatoes.

The gratin is great on its own or alongside meat, fish or vegetables. Cook sausages in the oven at the same time as the gratin. To roast a chicken alongside, start the chicken off at a high temperature (220°C/Gas 7) for 15 minutes, then turn down the oven, slide in the gratin and continue to cook for about 1 hour, or until the chicken is cooked and the celeriac is tender. The gratin is also good with smoked mackerel, simply cooked fish or alongside a salad or steamed greens.

1. Preheat the oven to 180°C/Gas 4. In a large bowl, mix the thinly-sliced vegetables (apart from the garlic) with the chopped parsley, capers and ham, if using. Season with pepper and a flick of salt. Tumble the mixture into a medium-sized, not-too-deep dish – mine is 20cm square and 5cm deep.

2. Heat the crème fraîche and milk in a small pan. Stir in the Dijon mustard and garlic and season with salt and pepper. Bring to a gentle boil. Pour the liquid over the gratin. It won't cover the veg – that's fine.

3. Put the dish in the oven and bake for 1 hour 15 minutes, or more, until the vegetables are tender. Cover the top with foil if it is getting too brown. The timing depends on how finely you have cut your celeriac and what else you have in the oven at the same time.

Cumin **Paprika** **Cannell**

WINTER

WARMERS

MOST OF THESE

RECIPES ARE

STRAIGHTFORWARD

AND NEED ONLY

TIME

Turn on the oven, take a few well-chosen ingredients and add some fragrant spices or herbs; make a cup of tea or pour a glassful; then leave the One Pot to cook. This is your recipe for a winter warmer.

When it is cold, we turn inwards to domesticity: the hug of the sofa and a comforting plate of stew. We gather around a table to find warmth, nourishment and company.

The kitchen and hob turn into a dynamic form of radiator. It is the hearth of the home, as well as the heart. The oven is turned on much more often and I fill it up with One Pots to make the most of the heat.

Such cooking is reminiscent of the cooking of centuries past, when energy was more tangibly scarce and so had to be well used. This chapter reaches back to many classic recipes in the One Pot repertoire, be it hot pots, chicken pie or a comforting roast.

Most of these recipes are straightforward and need only time. Make the One Pots the night before or over the weekend: reheated, these recipes provide perfect midweek sustenance. Some recipes have relatively large quantities, as leftovers are always welcome.

Time brings about a miraculous transformation. As a dish cooks, the tough cut turns tender and spices impart their fragrance. Taste a One Pot as it simmers and you notice changes even within half an hour. Then reheat the next day and see how it has continued to evolve.

ORANGE & CORIANDER BEEF WITH HERB DUMPLINGS

SERVES **5–6**

- **1 tbsp** olive or vegetable oil
- **1.1kg** beef shin, *cut into large chunks*
- **½ tbsp** plain flour
- **250ml** red wine
- **500ml** beef or chicken stock (instant is fine)
- **2** onions, *sliced*
- **4 cloves** garlic, *finely chopped*
- **5 stalks** celery, *cut into large chunks*
- **6** carrots, *cut into large chunks*
- **6 strips of rind** from an orange
- **1 tbsp** coriander seeds, *roughly crushed*
- **2** bay leaves
- **1 tbsp** Japanese soy sauce (¾ tbsp if using stronger-flavoured Chinese soy sauce)

herb dumplings (optional but cosy):
- **150g** self-raising flour, plus extra to dust
- **75g** *ready-shredded* suet
- **1 tbsp** *finely chopped* coriander leaf
- **125ml** cold water (approx.)

Beef goes beautifully with orange, as does orange with coriander seeds. Put them together for a harmonious trio. The dumplings are optional, but adding them makes more of a substantial One Pot.

Shin of beef is very good value. With a bit of careful thought about flavourings, it makes as good a stew as any prime cut and is much better than the tasteless cubes of beef often sold as 'stewing beef' in supermarkets. Try to get the meat in big chunks, as these are easier to brown well and keep their succulence. They should fall apart with just a push of a spoon once cooked.

1. Preheat the oven to 170°C/Gas 3. Heat the oil in a large casserole over a medium-high heat. Put the meat into the pot and brown the pieces on both sides, letting it sit, undisturbed, for a few minutes in order to get a good colour. You'll know when the meat is ready to turn as it will come away easily rather than sticking to the bottom of the pan. Brown in two or three batches: it is best not to overcrowd the pan as this lowers its heat and stops the meat browning quickly and well.

2. Return all the meat to the pan. Scatter over the flour and cook for a minute or so, stirring. Pour in the wine and let it bubble away as you scrape up all the tasty remnants from the base of the pot. Add the stock along with the rest of the ingredients – the chopped vegetables, orange rind, coriander seeds, bay leaves and soy sauce. Season well with pepper. You may not need salt after adding the soy sauce, depending on how salty your stock is. Taste the liquid about halfway through the cooking time and add salt if necessary.

3. Put the casserole, covered, into the preheated oven for 2½ hours, or until the meat is spoonably tender. You can cook the dish in advance, leave it to cool and refrigerate, covered, for up to 3 days.

4. An hour or more before you want to eat, or while the stew is cooking, make the dumplings. Mix the flour, suet and coriander together in a bowl. Season with plenty of salt and pepper. Use a table knife to gradually stir in enough water to make a dough and knead, first in the bowl and then on a floured work surface, until the dough forms a cohesive whole. Roll into a ball, then cut this into four and each of these pieces into 4 again, so you have 16 small dumplings. Roll them into balls, each around the size of a walnut in its shell.

5. Turn the oven up to 200°C/Gas 6. Add the dumplings to the pot, cover and cook for 15 minutes. Take the lid off the pot, roll the dumplings over and continue to cook for another 15–30 minutes, uncovered, until the dumplings are cooked through and the stew has reduced slightly. Taste and add more salt if necessary.

CHEATY CHICKEN & MUSHROOM PIE

SERVES **6−8**

- **2 tbsp** olive or vegetable oil
- **3 shallots,** *finely chopped*
- **2 stalks** celery, *finely chopped*
- **4 rashers** smoked back bacon, *roughly chopped*
- **2 leeks,** *cleaned, trimmed & cut into 1cm slices*
- **1 clove** garlic, *finely chopped*
- **250g small** chestnut mushrooms, *halved*
- **a slosh** of whatever booze is about (if it's sherry, so much the better)
- **300ml** ready-made cheese sauce
- **300ml** crème fraîche
- **3−4 tbsp** *finely chopped* soft herbs: eg chives, parsley, chervil, tarragon (include 1 tbsp chopped tarragon, if possible)
- **6** chicken thighs, without skin or bone, *each cut into 6 chunks*
- **500g** ready-made butter shortcrust pastry
- **1** egg, *beaten*

A pie is, for some, the ultimate One Pot meal, with its crisp pastry crust broken to reveal a filling that's full of different flavours and plenty of tasty sauce. What a dish to put on the table for everyone to share! This chicken pie takes two shortcuts. Ready-made cheese sauces don't generally have enough oomph for my taste, but used here as part of the well-flavoured white sauce, they make life easier and the pie more possible mid-week. It's easy enough to make your own shortcrust pastry, but a bought version, made with butter, is another handy shortcut.

1. Preheat the oven to 190°C/Gas 5 and put a baking tray in the oven to heat up. Pour the oil into a large, ovenproof sauté pan, about 30cm diameter and 8−10cm deep. Add the chopped shallots, celery and bacon and cook over a medium-low heat for around 10 minutes, stirring occasionally. Add the leeks, garlic and mushrooms to the pot and continue to cook for 10 minutes, stirring occasionally.

2. Pour in the booze and scrape up any residue from the base of the pan. Stir in the cheese sauce, crème fraîche and chopped herbs, then add the chunks of chicken. Season with black pepper and stir well. Simmer for a couple of minutes, until the sauce is heated through, taking care it doesn't catch on the bottom. Take the pan off the heat and leave to one side to cool slightly.

3. Roll the pastry out into a circle large enough to cover the dish. Put a pie funnel (or egg cup) in the centre of the chicken mixture and lower the pastry over the pie, tucking it over the top of the meat. Trim off the excess pastry.

4. Roll out the pastry trimmings and cut them into shapes to decorate the pie (perhaps the first letter of each of the names of your guests; a chicken; love hearts...). Place these decorations on top of the pastry, sticking them on with a brush of beaten egg, then brush everything carefully with the remaining egg.

5. Put the pie on the hot tray in the preheated oven for around 1 hour, turning it around once or twice so it cooks evenly. The top should be golden, the centre bubbling and the chicken cooked. You can leave it in the oven, temperature turned down to 100°C/ Gas ½ to keep warm for 30 minutes or so until you're ready to eat.

6. Serve with green vegetables and some sort of potato, if you like.

Sorrel is a great addition to a chicken pie. This lemony-tasting leaf is the first green in the garden, or can be found in farmer's markets. For me, it is a harbinger of spring at a time when you are more than ready to move on from winter. Use about 25g, roughly chopped, and add it with the rest of the herbs.

Potatoes go with pies. Pie and mash is especially comforting. The stuffed cheesy baked potatoes with horseradish (see page 38) can be cooked in the oven at the same time.

A brilliant short-cut to a homemade white or cheese sauce is to simply put 300ml milk, 20g plain flour and 20g of butter, cut into small pieces, into a medium saucepan. Whisk together as the milk heats and the sauce miraculously comes together and thickens. No fussing around with a roux, and no lumps. Season with a grating of nutmeg, 2 tbsp grated parmesan, ¼ tsp flaky sea salt and a grind of pepper.

COTTAGE PIE
WITH A
TILED ROOF

SERVES **6–8**

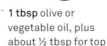

- **1 tbsp** olive or vegetable oil, plus about ½ tbsp for top
- **100g** chorizo, *finely chopped*
- **2 stalks** celery, *finely chopped*
- **2 onions**, *finely chopped*
- **2 carrots**, *finely chopped*
- **1 leek**, *finely chopped*
- **150g** mushrooms, *finely chopped*
- **500g** beef mince
- **2 x 400g** tins chopped tomatoes
- **1½ tbsp** tomato purée
- **2 tbsp** Japanese soy sauce (slightly less if using stronger Chinese soy sauce)
- **1 tsp** dried herbs (eg marjoram, oregano or thyme)
- **1kg** potatoes, *scrubbed & cut into 1cm thick slices*

Cottage pie is a great way to make mince go further. This one also adds a variety of vegetables to a dish that appeals even to veggie-phobes. There is a fair amount of chopping involved here, but it's followed by the short-cut of using sliced potatoes to top the pie – hence the 'tiles' – instead of going to the bother of making mash. Chorizo adds Spanish spice and a touch of heat to the mix.

The amount of mince can be increased by 100–200g to make the dish go further, or if you are feeding bigger meat-eaters.

1. Put the oil into a large sauté pan over a medium heat and gently sweat the chorizo with all the chopped vegetables, apart from the mushrooms. Stir occasionally until soft (about 15 minutes).

2. Add the mushrooms to the softened vegetables, increase the heat slightly and cook until they have given out their liquid and it has evaporated (about 5 minutes).

3. Add the mince, chopped tomatoes, tomato purée, soy sauce and herbs. Grind over some pepper. Mix everything together well. Cook over a medium heat for 15 minutes, stirring occasionally. Taste and adjust the seasoning as necessary. Meanwhile, preheat the oven to 200°C/Gas 6.

4. Place the sliced potatoes on top of the mince in concentric circles, overlapping to fit all the potatoes on top. Brush lightly with oil and season well with salt and pepper. Put a lid on the pot (or cover it with foil) and place in the oven for 30 minutes. Remove the lid and cook for another 30–40 minutes to brown the tiles of your cottage roof.

BUTTERNUT SQUASH & STILTON GRATIN

SERVES **4–6**

- **2** red onions, *finely chopped*
- **3 cloves** garlic, *finely chopped*
- **1 large** butternut squash (about 1.2kg), *peeled & finely sliced*
- **3 medium** potatoes, *peeled or just scrubbed & finely sliced*
- **1½ tbsp** *finely chopped* rosemary or sage, or 2 tbsp *finely chopped* chives
- **200g** stilton, *roughly chopped*
- **a knob of** butter, to grease the dish
- **300ml** whipping cream

Stilton adds a rich, tangy flavour to the cream in this tasty gratin. This is a meal in itself, served with a green salad, or can go alongside a piece of meat or fish.

Stilton is one of the treasures of British food. The best ones of all are those made with animal rennet – Colston Bassett and Cropwell Bishop, two of the best producers, both make traditional stiltons this way, as does Stichelton, a non-pasteurised cheese of the same family. For this dish you can use any kind of stilton; it's a great way to use up your Christmas truckle or slab. Perhaps because it's blue, people wrongly think it is an ageing cheese, but kept too long (or too warm) it can become too strong and fiery. Eat it up while still in its prime.

1. Preheat the oven to 180°C/Gas 4. Mix the vegetables, herbs and stilton together in a bowl. Grease a gratin dish with butter. Tip the bowlful into the dish and push it down slightly.

2. Heat the cream in a small pan until just below boiling. Season with a little salt and pepper. Pour the hot cream over the gratin so it oozes down between the layers. Top the gratin with a grind of black pepper.

3. Place in the preheated oven for 50–60 minutes, until the vegetables are tender and the top nicely browned.

DAUPHINOISE
POTATOES

SERVES **5** AS A MAIN COURSE;
7 AS A SIDE DISH

¨ **20g** butter
¨ **300ml** whipping
or double cream
¨ **100ml** milk
¨ **2 cloves** garlic,
finely grated

¨ **¼ tsp** *freshly grated*
nutmeg
¨ **1kg** floury potatoes
(eg King Edward),
peeled & cut into slices
about 5mm thick
¨ **15g** *grated* parmesan

The smell of a garlicky, creamy dauphinoise is one of the most warming welcomes to a home.
I used to laboriously layer up potatoes with slivers of garlic, butter and seasoning. Then I realised you can just infuse the liquid with these flavours and add it hot to the sliced potatoes, making the preparation quicker and easier, but the result just as delicious.

Potato varieties vary between waxy, firm types (such as Charlotte) and floury or fluffy varieties, (King Edward and Maris Piper). I've used both kinds in dauphionise potatoes and they give different results. Probably because cream and garlic are involved I love them all, but ultimately my favourite kinds of spud to use are the fluffys.

Whipping cream is less rich than double cream and good for a dauphinoise. It will rise up whilst cooking, so use a big enough dish and, if in doubt, rest assured any spillages will be caught by your baking tray. Double cream is also good and means you can make the dish go further by serving smaller portions.

Beetroot makes a beautiful, pink dauphinoise. Substitute about a third of the potatoes for finely sliced, peeled beets.

1. Preheat the oven to 170°C/Gas 3. Use half the butter to grease a gratin dish about 20cm in diameter and 8–10cm deep.

2. Put the cream and milk in a medium-sized pan. Add the garlic and nutmeg, then season well with black pepper and about 1 tsp flaky sea salt. Bring slowly to a gentle boil, watching the liquid doesn't boil over (the sort of thing that happens in my kitchen). As soon as it's boiling, remove from the heat and set to one side.

3. Layer up the potato slices in the greased dish. Pour over the hot liquid, making sure the garlic comes out of the pan and is dispersed fairly evenly over the gratin. Sprinkle over the parmesan and grind over a little more black pepper.

4. Put the gratin in the oven on a baking sheet and cook for 45 minutes to 1 hour, or until the potatoes are tender and the top nice and brown, covering with foil or a lid if the top is browning too much.

5. Leave to sit in the turned-off oven for another 10 minutes before serving, or up to 20 if this is convenient.

CHICKEN WITH BACON, GARLIC & HERBS

SERVES **4–6**

- **50g** butter
- **1 tbsp** olive or vegetable oil
- **1 chicken** (about 1.5kg)
- **170g** smoked streaky bacon, *roughly chopped*
- **10 cloves** garlic, *peeled*
- **100ml** white or red wine
- **500g** potatoes, *unpeeled, cut into large chunks*
- **leaves from 5 thyme sprigs** or leaves from 3 tarragon stalks, *roughly chopped*
- **300ml** chicken stock (instant fine; fresh better)
- **juice of ½–1** lemon

This classic dish combines chicken and potatoes with garlic, wine, smoked bacon and flecks of thyme or tarragon. It's the sort of comforting meal to eat in a bowl for supper with friends or family: One Pot cooking at its simple, tasty best.

1. Preheat the oven to 170°C/Gas 3. Melt the butter with the oil over a medium-high heat in a pan that ideally fits the chicken quite snugly. Season the chicken with salt and pepper and brown in the pan, first on its underside and then on each breast, turning it over carefully with two wooden spoons. Remove from the pan and put on a plate.

2. In the same pan, brown the bacon and the cloves of garlic. Pour in the wine and let it bubble up briefly. Add the potatoes, herbs and stock. Return the chicken to the pot. Put a lid on, bring the liquid to the boil and bake in the oven for 1–1½ hours, or until the juices run clear when you insert a knife into the thickest part of a thigh. Carefully stir the spuds around about halfway through.

3. Place the chicken on a large plate. Taste the juices and add lemon juice, salt and pepper, to taste.

4. Cut the bird into 4–6 portions as desired and spoon over the sauce. Serve with a green salad.

Cooking a whole bird is the most economical way to eat chicken and makes high-welfare birds much more affordable. After the meal, use the bones for stock.

THAI MUSSELS WITH NOODLES

SERVES **4**

- **200g** flat Thai rice noodles
- **1kg** mussels
- **1 tbsp** vegetable oil
- **4 small** shallots, *finely sliced*
- **1 thumb** root ginger, *peeled & finely chopped*
- **2 cloves** garlic, *finely chopped*
- **½** red chilli, *deseeded & finely chopped*
- **3** pak choi, *stems cut into 2–3 cm slices, leaves roughly chopped*
- **250g** shiitake mushrooms, *sliced*
- **1 stalk** lemongrass, *cut into three pieces*
- **1 x 400g** tin coconut milk
- **½ tbsp** fish sauce
- **1 tbsp** Japanese soy sauce (or slightly less of stronger Chinese)
- **1** kaffir lime leaf (optional but good)
- **juice of 1** lime
- **about 20** basil leaves (Thai basil best of all)
- **a large handful** of coriander leaf
- **about 20** mint leaves

Winter dishes can be light as well as warming. This fast and fragrant bowlful heats you up in the most cheering way, with its Thai flavours and heat, creamy coconut and beautiful rich nuggets of sweet, orange shellfish. As well as making the most of a bagful of mussels, it's the sort of midweek meal that usefully accepts chopped-up leftovers such as scraps of chicken, roast pork or potatoes. The ingredient list seems long but (apart from cleaning the mussels) the cooking can be done, start to finish, in 15 minutes or so: chop, chop; stir, stir; eat.

1. Put the noodles in a shallow dish and cover with just-boiled water. Leave to soak for 10 minutes.

2. Meanwhile, prepare the mussels by washing them in running cold water and pulling off the beard that attached the mussel to its rope or rock. Discard any that are cracked or remain open when tapped. Bash the three pieces of lemongrass with something heavy – the end of a large knife or the tin of coconut milk – to help release the flavour.

3. Heat the oil in a wok over a high heat. Add the chopped shallots, ginger, garlic and chilli and stir-fry for a couple of minutes. Add the pak choi and mushrooms and stir-fry for 2–3 minutes, until nearly cooked.

WINTER DISHES CAN BE LIGHT AS WELL AS WARMING

4. Add the lemongrass, coconut milk, fish sauce and soy sauce, and also the lime leaf, if using. Quickly drain the noodles and add to the pan, stirring well to incorporate.

5. Finally, add the mussels, give them a stir and put a lid on the wok. Cook for a couple of minutes, until the mussels have opened (discard any that don't).

6. Add the lime juice and herbs, taste and adjust the seasoning if necessary. Serve in large bowls.

When buying mussels, the best value are those that feel heavy in the hand.

The rise of the rope-grown mussel industry is a great success story. Produced on ropes suspended from rafts in clean sea water, the shellfish are safe and not gritty. In these days of concern about over-fishing and the environmental impact of fish farming, rope-grown mussels are squeaky-Green.

Store mussels in the fridge in a colander on top of a plate, and cover them with a damp cloth so they feel nice and moist and cool; as if still blissfully submerged in a Highlands sea loch. They are said to last for a week out of the water, if kept at a constant, cold temperature, but are best of all eaten as soon as possible.

LANCASHIRE
HOT POT

SERVES **6**

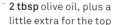

" **2 tbsp** olive oil, plus a little extra for the top
" **6** loin or chump lamb chops (or 12 smaller cutlets)
" **700ml** lamb or chicken stock (instant is fine or homemade instant, see note)
" **2 tsp** Worcestershire sauce
" **2 tbsp** redcurrant jelly
" **3** onions, *sliced*
" **3 large** carrots, *each cut into 4 chunks*
" **3 stalks** celery, *cut into chunks*
" **1 small** swede (about 350g), *peeled & cut into 3cm chunks*
" **1kg** potatoes, *thinly sliced*
" **50g** pearl barley or spelt (optional)
" **3** bay leaves (optional but good)

Lancashire hot pot is a lip-smacking dish that makes the most of the meat, fat and bones of lamb chops to flavour root vegetables and gravy. Mine is made in a wide sauté pan in order to get lots of crispy potatoes, but you can also make it in a deeper pan and layer up the spuds a bit more.

1. Preheat the oven to 220°C/Gas 7. Heat 1 tbsp of the oil in a wide, ovenproof pot over a high heat. Brown the lamb chops on both sides, cooking the meat in batches so as not to overcrowd the pan. Season the lamb on both sides as you go with salt and pepper.

2. While the meat is cooking, mix the stock with the Worcestershire sauce and the jelly. In a bowl, mix together the chopped onions, carrots, celery and swede.

3. Remove the last of the browned lamb from the pot. Pour the remaining 1 tbsp of oil into the pot and tip to ensure the base is oiled all over. Layer up the ingredients for your hot pot. Start with half the potatoes, half the mixed veg, the meat, the barley or spelt, if using, then the rest of the veg. Tuck in the bay leaves, if using, and season with pepper and a little salt as you go (but be careful with the latter as there will be salt in the stock and on the meat). Finish with the rest of the potatoes. Try to spread the ingredients evenly so that each serving spoonful will get a bit of everything.

4. Pour the stock over the dish. Depending on your pot, you may not need all of it; don't pour in so much that it covers the potatoes. Season the top of the potatoes with a couple more grinds of pepper, a sprinkle of sea salt and a drizzle of olive oil.

5. Put the pot in the hot oven for 20 minutes, then reduce the temperature to 170°C/Gas 3, cover with a lid or foil, and cook for another 2 hours, or until the lamb is tender. The top of the hot pot should have browned. If not, raise the temperature to 220°C/Gas 7 for 10 minutes or until the spuds turn an appetising glossy brown.

6. Leave the hot pot out of the oven for about 5 minutes to settle, then serve on its own or with some buttered cabbage.

Lamb chops are often expensive so I tend to go for what looks like best value for money on the day, ideally chump or loin chops, but sometimes best end or middle neck cutlets, which come from nearer the front of the animal. I use less meat and more root vegetables than some recipes because the beautiful savoury juices and fat from the lamb soak into the veg and make them extra tasty. If you are feeding meat lovers, simply add more chops.

Pearl barley is a good addition as it soaks up the gravy and adds bulk to the dish. Don't use too much or you won't have any gravy; these small grains are like little sponges.

A homemade version of instant stock for this dish is made by dissolving 1½ tbsp Marmite in 200ml cider and 500ml just-boiled water

BETTY'S VEGGIE HOT POT

SERVES **6**

" **50g** dried mushrooms
" **300ml** cider or stout
" **400ml** hot water
" **1½ tbsp** olive or vegetable oil
" **3** onions, *sliced*
" **1½ tbsp** plain flour
" **30g** butter
" **800g** potatoes, *peeled or unpeeled, cut into thin slices*
" **3 large** carrots, *peeled or unpeeled, cut into large chunks*
" **3 stalks** celery, *cut into large chunks*
" **200g** mushrooms (Portobello or chestnut best of all)
" **½ small** swede (300g), *peeled, cut into 3cm chunks (optional but good)*

As any *Coronation Street* fan will recognise, this recipe refers to the famous hot pot served in the Rovers Return pub in Britain's longest-running soap opera. Betty was the redoubtable barmaid who pulled pints right up until the actor was in her nineties; latterly sitting down for rests, but still making pithy remarks beside the bar. Betty-the-barmaid was famous for her hot pot, a classic Lancashire dish made with lamb, but Betty–the-actor was vegetarian, and so is my friend Debbie, who writes scripts for *Corrie*. I wanted to come up with a veggie version of this winter warmer. So here it is for you, Debbie, and in fond memory of Betty.

1. Preheat the oven to 220°C/Gas 7. Put the dried mushrooms into a bowl and pour over the cider or stout and hot water. Leave to soak for 20 minutes or so, whilst you prepare the rest of the dish.

2. Pour the oil into a casserole and add the sliced onions. Cook over a low heat, stirring occasionally, for 10–15 minutes, until softened.

3. Sprinkle the flour over the softened onions and stir for a couple of minutes to cook out the raw flavour. Remove the onions and put to one side. Drain the mushrooms, collecting the soaking liquid in a small saucepan.

4. Melt half the butter in the still hot pan and swirl it around to ensure it covers the base. Line the bottom of the dish with half the potatoes. Layer up the vegetables, chestnuts and barley, tucking in the bay leaves and seasoning with pepper and a little salt as you go. I tend to do: potatoes, carrots, chestnuts, barley, dried mushrooms, celery, fresh mushrooms, swede (if using). Finish with the rest of the potatoes. When you serve the dish, you will need a big spoon to dig into all the layers for each helping.

200g pre-cooked chestnuts, *roughly chopped*

a small handful (50–70g) pearl barley

3 bay leaves

2 tbsp redcurrant jelly

1½ tbsp Marmite

2 tsp soy sauce

5. In a small pan, combine the redcurrant jelly, Marmite, soy sauce and mushroom soaking water in the pan. Heat this for a minute or so, stirring, to melt it all into an instant stock, then pour over the vegetables.

6. Season the top of the potatoes with a couple more grinds of pepper and a sprinkle of sea salt. Top with the remaining 15g butter, in little dabs.

7. Cover the hot pot and put in the oven for 45 minutes. Uncover and cook for another 45 minutes, covering it again if the potato gets too brown. This is good served with buttery, well-peppered cabbage.

Peeling veg is not always necessary, especially for rustic food like this. For this dish, I tend to just scrub the spuds and carrots, but I peel the swede as the skin is tough. Plenty of flavour and micronutrients lie in the skin (though so do pesticides in non-organic veg).

Pickled walnuts are a great addition if you have them. Slip in about 3, each cut into 6 pieces, as an extra layer somewhere in the middle of the dish.

OX CHEEK
DAUBE

SERVES **6–8**

- **3** ox cheeks (about 1.3kg in total), *each cut into 3-4 pieces*
- **2 tbsp** olive oil
- **3** onions, *finely chopped*
- **6 cloves** garlic, *finely chopped*
- **3 stalks** celery, *cut into chunks*
- **2** leeks, *cleaned, trimmed & cut into chunks*
- **4 large** carrots, *peeled or scrubbed, cut into chunks*
- **3** turnips (about 300g), *peeled, cut into large chunks*
- **375ml** (½ bottle) red wine
- **300ml** beef or chicken stock (instant is okay; fresh better)
- **2** bay leaves
- **1 tbsp** Seville orange marmalade
- **½ tbsp** dried oregano, thyme or marjoram

In his book *Simple French Food*, Richard Olney makes the distinction between a daube and other kinds of stew. For the latter, the meat is first browned and the ingredients tend to keep their own character within a harmonious whole. In a daube, all the ingredients are put into the pot at the same time and are cooked long and slow so that the ingredients 'eventually melt with the aromatic, succulent, gelatinous strains into a single languid and caressing note'. Heaven.

1. Preheat the oven to 150°C/Gas 2. Put everything in a casserole dish, seasoning well with salt and pepper. Stir together, put a lid on and place in the oven for 3 hours, stirring the ingredients around after 2 hours.

2. The daube is ready when the beef is tender enough to push apart with a wooden spoon. Serve everyone with the rich, melting meat and a share of the vegetables.

3. This goes well with potatoes, be they mashed, boiled or baked.

Ox cheeks are cheap and have an intensely beefy flavour and melty texture when cooked long and slow. Or use another slow-cook cut such as shin, cut into big chunks.

Plenty of wine is key to a rich and delicious daube. Do not stint.

Olney advises adding a little sugar to the daube. I've added Seville orange marmalade to the pot instead, as beef is so good with orange. Works a treat.

RED THAI FISH CURRY

SERVES **4–6**

This quick curry perks you up in winter with its healthy fish, green leafy veg and warming Asian spices.

Use any kind of fish in this dish: whatever white fish looks good. The salty-sweetness of hot-smoked salmon isn't authentically Thai, but goes well with the flavours of this cuisine. This recipe is ideal for using up a good-value packet of hot-smoked salmon scraps and offcuts.

Thai flavours are about the balance of hot, sour, sweet and the fragrantly pungent. Taste the dish at the end and vary these elements according to your preferences.

- **1 tbsp** vegetable oil
- **2–3 tbsp** red Thai curry paste
- **1 x 400g** tin chopped tomatoes
- **1 x 400g** tin coconut milk
- **250g** firm squash (eg butternut; this is about ¼ medium one), *peeled, cut into 3cm pieces*
- **500g** green vegetables, (eg broccoli, cabbage, okra), *trimmed, cut into large bite-sized pieces*
- **3 tbsp** fish sauce
- **2 tbsp** lime juice, plus extra to serve
- **2 tbsp** dark or light brown sugar
- **300g** hot-smoked salmon, *in large flakes*, or 500g white fish, *cut into large chunks*
- **a large handful** of basil, *roughly torn*
- **a large handful** of coriander, *roughly chopped*
- chilli flakes or chilli sauce (optional)

1. Pour the oil into a large saucepan and add the curry paste: use more or less according to how hot you like your curry. Stir for a couple of minutes, then add the tomatoes. Fill the tomato tin up with water and pour this into the pan, swilling out any remaining juices at the same time. Stir in the coconut milk.

2. Add the squash to the pot, cover with a lid and bring to the boil. Turn down the heat and simmer for 10 minutes. Add the green veg and simmer for another 5–10 minutes, or until the vegetables are cooked. Stir through the fish sauce, lime juice and brown sugar. Taste and adjust the seasonings as you like.

3. Stir in the flaked salmon or white fish, along with half the basil and coriander. Cook for a couple of minutes, until the salmon is hot or the white fish is just done, then sprinkle over the rest of the herbs. Taste and adjust, if necessary, adding more lime, sugar, fish sauce or chilli heat with some chilli flakes or a dollop of chilli sauce.

4. Serve the curry on its own, or with rice or noodles, and squeeze over a little extra lime at the end.

LAMB WITH GARLIC, ANCHOVIES & ROSEMARY

SERVES **6**

- **1 tbsp** olive or vegetable oil
- **½ shoulder** of lamb (approx 1.3 kg, shank end is best)
- **2** onions, *roughly chopped*
- **3 stalks** celery, *roughly chopped*
- **4 cloves** garlic, *finely chopped*
- **3 wide strips** orange peel, plus juice of 1 orange
- **2 x 400g** tins chopped tomatoes
- **150ml** (a smallish glass) white wine
- **4 large sprigs** of rosemary
- **1 x 60g** tin anchovies, *drained*

A One Pot version of the classic dish of lamb roasted with garlic, anchovies and rosemary, this is super-easy and makes its own sauce as it cooks.

1. Preheat the oven to 220°C/Gas 7. Heat the oil in a large pot over a medium-high heat and brown the lamb on both sides. Remove the lamb and put to one side.

2. Turn the heat down and gently fry the onions, celery and garlic in the oil for 10 minutes, or until softened, stirring occasionally. Add the rest of the ingredients and stir well to combine. Bring to the boil and season with a little salt (not too much; the anchovies will break down and season the sauce) and a few grinds of black pepper.

3. Return the lamb to the dish and bake in the oven for 30 minutes, uncovered. Turn the heat down to 170°C/Gas 3 and cover. Cook for a further 2 hours, removing the lid for the final 30 minutes to allow the sauce to reduce a little. The meat should be soft enough to fall apart when scooped with a spoon. Check the seasoning and adjust if necessary.

4. Serve with greenery and some crusty bread, or potatoes baked in the oven along with the lamb (you could also cook small chunks of potato in the sauce to make more of a substantial One Pot).

PEPOSO

SERVES **6**

" **1.2kg** shin of beef,
cut into large chunks
" **10 cloves** garlic,
finely chopped
" **100g** tomato purée

" **¾ tbsp** freshly ground
black pepper
" **300ml** red wine
" **about 200ml** water

This Tuscan beef-and-pepper stew is said to date back to Renaissance Florence when it was made by the tile makers who would leave the dish to cook in their kilns as the tiles baked. I love the simplicity of putting five ingredients into a pot and letting them come together over time.

1. Put everything in a pot, adding enough water to just cover the meat. Season with 1½ tsp flaky sea salt.

2. Simmer, covered, for 2 hours then take the lid off and cook for another 1–1½ hours, stirring occasionally, until the meat falls apart.

3. Serve with mashed potato, or as a sauce for pasta.

Use more red wine if you like; some prefer to use a bottle of wine per kilo of meat and to cook the dish for longer. This is a slightly more economical version.

A neat way to measure pepper is grind it onto a piece of paper then fold this up to funnel the grains into a measuring spoon.

ROAST PORK BELLY WITH APPLES

SERVES 4–6

1.2kg–1.5kg pork belly, *skin scored at 1cm intervals with a sharp knife* (a butcher will do this for you)

¨ **1 tbsp** thyme leaves
¨ **4–6 medium** baking potatoes (or cut large ones in half)
¨ **4–6** red-skinned apples
¨ greenery of some sort

gravy:
¨ **1 tbsp** plain flour
¨ **a good splash** of apple juice or booze eg. cider or wine
¨ flavourings, as necessary (eg soy sauce, Marmite, apple jelly, apricot jam)

Pork belly is a reasonable value, lip-smacking cut of meat. A nicely roasted piece keeps you warm and happy in winter with its layers of fat, tenderly soft meat and crisp crackling. As the meat cooks, your whole home is scented with roast pork. Baking apples at the same time gives you instant apple sauce to cut through the fattiness of the meat. I got the idea from a Devon apple juice and cider maker, Tash, of Heron Valley Organic Drinks, who runs her family's company in an idyllic land of otters and apples, where pigs doubtless snuffle for windfall apples in the orchards.

The trick to getting the crackling nice and crisp is to dry out the fat as much as possible by keeping it in the fridge for a day and giving it a good whack of heat at the end of cooking.

To roast the potatoes instead of baking them, peel the spuds, boil them for 5 minutes, drain well and sprinkle with plain flour. Roll in the fat on the roasting tray and roast beside the pork.

1. When you come back from the shop, keep the meat in the fridge, uncovered, for at least a couple of hours and ideally overnight to help it dry out; this is one of the secrets of good crackling. Remove from the fridge 30 minutes before cooking, place on a sturdy roasting tin and cover the skin with about ½ tbsp flaky sea salt, rubbing it in well.

2. Preheat the oven to 180°C/Gas 4. Use kitchen paper to wipe off the excess salt and any moisture that has come off the skin. Not all the salt will come off, but this is part of the seasoning. Depending on how much is still on the meat, add a little more. Scatter over the thyme leaves and grind over plenty of black pepper. Rub this seasoning well into the cracks and all over the skin.

3. Roast the meat in the oven for 1 hour. Add the baking potatoes to the roasting tray and cook for a further 30 minutes. Run a knife around the equator of the apples, making just a shallow cut into the skin to prevent them from bursting in the heat and lay them on the tray beside the potatoes. Bake for another 30 minutes.

KEEPS YOU WARMLY HAPPY IN WINTER

4. After 2 hours total cooking time, take the roasting tray out of the oven and turn up the heat to 240°C/Gas 9. Check to see if the apples are soft and the potatoes cooked. Remove to a serving plate and keep warm. Pour off the fat into a saucepan and put the meat back in the oven, along with any apples and potatoes that need more cooking.

5. Roast the meat for another 10–15 minutes to crisp up the crackling. Turn the heat off and put the serving dish of potatoes and apples back in the oven to keep warm. Leave the door slightly open so the oven is warm, but not hot, while the meat rests.

6. Meanwhile, steam one or more green vegetable and keep the water.

7. Place the meat on a serving platter and keep warm. Sometimes the last blast of oven heat burns the fat in the tray, so I make the gravy in a saucepan instead, using some of the reserved fat. Either way, combine the plain flour with 1½ tbsp of the fat and stir over a low heat for a minute or so. Gradually add the hot water from the steamed greens and a good splash of apple juice or booze – cider is best, but anything you have to hand. Bring to the boil and cook until thickened. Taste and adjust seasoning as necessary, adding some Marmite or soy sauce and a spoonful of jelly or jam (apricot is good) to give it more flavour.

8. To carve, I cut the crackling off the meat, then cut the meat into thick slices along with bone. Serve the pork alongside some crackling, potatoes, greens and an apple. Sauce liberally with gravy.

DUCK SOUP WITH ORANGE & SOBA NOODLES

SERVES **4**

- **200g** soba or rice noodles
- **4** spring onions, *cut into long shreds, including the green part*
- **40g** cabbage, *very finely sliced*
- **100g** mangetout
- **½ thumb** root ginger, *peeled & cut into fine slivers*
- **½–1** red chilli, *cut into fine slices, with or without seeds, to taste*
- **2 tbsp** Japanese soy sauce (slightly less if using stronger Chinese soy sauce)
- **1 tbsp** fish sauce
- **1 tbsp** brown sugar
- **60ml** (¾ of a small glass) dry sherry (optional)
- **juice of ½–1** lime
- **1** orange
- **2 tbsp** *finely chopped* coriander
- **2 tbsp** *finely chopped* mint

duck stock:
- **2** duck legs
- **5** spring onions, *roughly chopped*
- **8cm** unpeeled root ginger, *sliced*
- **1** star anise
- **1 stalk** celery, *cut into chunks*
- dried orange peel (optional; see note)

Healthy, warming and refreshing, this meal-in-a-bowl is a good January to March dish to cheer up the end of winter (and is delicious at any other time of year, too). Uncomplicated in terms of technique, it showcases the Asian flavours that go so well with duck.

Orange or clementine peel can be put in a recently turned-off oven and left to dry out, then stored in an airtight container and used as a flavouring in stocks such as this.

Soba noodles are sold in health food shops and some supermarkets. Made with buckwheat, they have a good nutty flavour and smooth, firm texture.

1. First make the duck stock. Put the duck legs in a large pan with the rest of the stock ingredients. Cover with 2 litres of cold water and bring just to the boil. Skim off the scum that rises, turn the heat down and simmer, uncovered, for 2 hours.

2. Drain the stock into a large bowl, or another pan, through a colander. Remove the duck legs and allow to cool slightly. Discard the rest of the flavourings. Remove the skin from the duck. Take the meat off the legs and pull or cut into medium-sized pieces.

3. Cook the soba noodles in plenty of boiling, slightly salted water until tender (about 8 minutes). You can also use rice noodles which generally just need soaking in hot water for 10 minutes; follow the instructions on the packet.

4. Reheat the stock in a large pan and add all of the other ingredients, apart from the orange and herbs. Bring to the boil over a high heat and allow to bubble away for 2 minutes. Meanwhile, peel the orange and cut the flesh into thin semi-circles. As you do this, make sure you catch all the juice and add this to the pot.

5. Turn off the heat. Taste the stock and adjust the seasoning if necessary, remembering that you are going to add orange, herbs and meat to the mixture, which will all oomph up the flavour.

6. Put the noodles into large bowls. Divide the duck between the plates and spoon the hot stock on top, dividing the vegetables as evenly as possible. Place a couple of orange segments on the top of each bowl and scatter over the chopped herbs.

TRACKLEMENTS
BAKED BEANS

SERVES **10–14**

- **500g** dried pinto or haricot beans
- **1 tbsp** olive or vegetable oil
- **2 medium-large** onions, *finely chopped*
- **4 cloves** garlic, *finely chopped*
- **2 stalks** celery, *finely chopped*
- **1.5kg** smoked gammon, *on the bone*
- **300ml** posh tomato ketchup
- **2 tbsp** muscovado sugar
- **2 tbsp** wholegrain mustard
- **juice of 1** lemon

Here is one of the easiest, cheapest and most delicious recipes for feeding a crowd. The dish is so flavourful that just a large spoonful is enough for a portion alongside a fluffy baked potato and a salad or green vegetable. A top recipe for Bonfire Night parties, the leftover beans are then great to have on hand for further meals. The idea of using posh ketchup to spice up baked beans (and the basis of this recipe) comes from Guy Tullberg of the excellent Tracklements company. His delicious ketchup, naturally, is best of all.

Add spices, to taste, if your ketchup is mildly flavoured, such as 3 cloves, 1 cinnamon stick, 1 dried chilli.

Make this veggie by leaving out the ham, using well-flavoured instant vegetable stock and adding spices such as smoked paprika and chilli, to taste.

If too salty – some hams are saltier than others – add more lemon juice to the dish.

Other sauces to play around with in this recipe include Worcestershire, Tabasco, horseradish and onion marmalade.

You can cook this on the hob rather than in the oven, but take care it doesn't catch on the bottom.

1. Cover the beans with plenty of cold water and soak overnight.

2. Preheat the oven to 120°C/Gas ½. Heat the oil in a large, heavy-bottomed pan. Fry the chopped onions, garlic and celery in the oil over a medium-low heat, stirring occasionally, until soft (about 10–15 minutes).

3. Drain and rinse the beans in cold water, then return them to the pan. Nestle the gammon in amongst the beans and cover with water (you'll need about 1 litre). You won't cover the gammon but don't worry about this, just turn it over halfway through cooking.

4. Cover the pan with a lid and cook in the oven, for 1½ hours, adding more water if it looks too dry. Remove the pan from the heat and gently lift the gammon onto a carving or chopping board.

5. Cut away the outside skin and discard. Cut the meat into small chunks (about 3cm) and put these back into the pan. Add the ketchup, sugar and mustard and stir in well.

6. Put the pan back into the oven for 1 hour with the lid on, then remove the lid and cook for a further hour so that the sauce thickens. Serve with a baked potato or crusty bread and a salad.

BEEF IN
BEER

SERVES **4–6**

- **900g** brisket, *boned, in one piece, left unrolled*
- **2 stalks** celery, *cut in half*
- **a small bundle** of parsley & thyme, *tied up with string*
- **1** bay leaf
- **500ml** beer, (ideally a bitter or IPA)
- **3 large** or 6 medium carrots, *cut into large chunks*
- **2** leeks, *trimmed, cut into large chunks*
- **6 medium** potatoes, *scrubbed, cut in half*

This quietly delicious dish combines two traditional British ingredients: beef and beer. Brisket is a cheap cut, with fat that melts to produce a rich broth that is beaded with tasty little globes of flavour. The bitterness of the beer – a hoppy bitter works best – adds an extra element to the stew that mellows perfectly over the long cooking time.

1. Preheat the oven to 170°C/Gas 3. Put the beef in a large pot with the celery, herb bundle and bay leaf. Pour over the beer and add enough water (or beef stock) to nearly cover. Season with ½ tsp flaky sea salt.

2. Cover with a lid and bring to the boil, then put the pot in the oven to cook for 2 hours.

3. Add the vegetables into the pot and cook for another hour, or until the meat is tender. Remove the herb bundle. Taste the broth and add more salt if necessary.

4. Serve slices of the meat in large bowls with the vegetables and a few spoonfuls of broth. You could also float some whole flat-leaf parsley leaves on top to add some colour. A swipe of Dijon mustard is a good addition, both for colour and for taste.

If you want this to go further, add more potatoes, serve with hunks of bread, or cook dumplings on the top for the last 30 minutes of cooking.

Brisket is one of the best cuts for making leftover dishes. I like to serve this stew for 3–4 people for a weekend lunch or supper, reserving the leftover meat and vegetables for another dish, such as hash (fry a chopped onion; stir in leftover potato and any other leftover cooked veg; stir in the chopped up brisket; season well and cook until piping hot). You can also use the remaining stock as the base of a good soup.

Carrots keep their sweetness much better if left in larger chunks, or even whole.

TUSCAN
MEATLOAF

SERVES 4–6

" **30g** dried porcini mushrooms
" **1 slice** crustless white bread
" **3 tbsp** milk
" **500g** lean beef mince
" **1 small** onion, *finely chopped*
" **1 clove** garlic, *finely chopped*
" **30g** air-dried ham eg parma, serrano or a British version, *finely chopped*
" **20g** *grated* parmesan
" **1 egg**, *lightly beaten*
" **3 tbsp** dry breadcrumbs (optional)
" **1 tbsp** butter
" **1 tbsp** olive oil
" **100ml** white wine
" **1 x 400g** tin chopped tomatoes
" **a pinch** of sugar

I love how this posh version of meatloaf is packed with Italian 'umami' (ultra-savoury) flavours: parmesan, air-cured ham, mushrooms and tomatoes. Resist the temptation to add herbs or more tomatoes to the sauce: it sounds simple but tastes just right.

This is the pimped-up version of the meatloaf in the Simple Suppers chapter (see page 68) and suitable for entertaining. The one disadvantage of this recipe, adapted from Marcella Hazan's Tuscan Meat Roll in her classic book *The Essentials of Classic Italian Cooking*, is that it is so delicious people tend to come back for more and your hoped-for leftovers soon disappear.

1. Put the dried mushrooms in 500ml warm water. Leave to soak for 30 minutes.

2. Meanwhile, tear the bread into pieces and place in a small pan with the milk over a low heat. When the bread has soaked up the milk – just a minute or so – turn off the heat and allow to cool. Mush up the mixture, using a fork or the back of a wooden spoon.

3. Drain the mushrooms, reserving the liquid to use as a tasty stock in another dish, and chop into small pieces.

4. Put the mince in a mixing bowl and add the bread, onion, garlic, ham, parmesan and egg. Season with plenty of freshly ground black pepper and ½ tsp sea salt. Mix together carefully with your hands until everything is well combined. Form into a large ball and put on a chopping board or work surface.

HOPED-FOR LEFTOVERS SOON DISAPPEAR

5. Carefully roll the meat into a large cylinder about the shape of a small loaf (7cm in diameter and about 20cm long). Flatten a little with the palms of your hands. If you like, you can roll it in dry breadcrumbs. This thickens the sauce slightly and improves the look a bit. I tend to have Japanese panko breadcrumbs in the cupboard so it is easy to do; otherwise I might not bother.

6. Heat the butter and olive oil together in a saucepan that is just long enough to take the length of the meatloaf. Brown the meat on all sides over a medium-high heat, carefully turning it over – two wooden spoons, or a spatula and a wooden spoon, are good tools for this task.

7. Pour in the wine and let it bubble up, stirring in the residue from the bottom of the pan. When it has reduced by half, add the tomatoes and a pinch of sugar. Bring to the boil then turn down the heat and cook over a gentle heat for 30 minutes, covered, and a further 30 minutes with the lid slightly askew so the sauce reduces down. Turn the meatloaf carefully 2 or 3 times during cooking.

8. Leave to cool slightly, then serve in thick slices with the sauce spooned on top. This is great with baked potatoes or a potato salad plus a lightly dressed rocket salad.

TWO-HEAT
CHILE CON CARNE

SERVES **10**

¨ **2–4** chipotle chillies (depending on heat levels & the number of people who want a hot chile)
¨ **2** ancho chillies
¨ **2 tbsp** dripping or good lard or 3 tbsp olive or vegetable oil
¨ **3 large** red onions, *sliced*
¨ **3 cloves** garlic, *finely chopped*
¨ **1.8kg** shin of beef, *cut into large chunks*

¨ **a large bunch** coriander, *stalks & leaves separated & chopped*
¨ **2 tsp** dried oregano
¨ **2** bay leaves
¨ **2 tsp** ground cumin
¨ **1 x 6cm** cinnamon stick
¨ **700g** passata
¨ **500ml** beef stock (instant is fine)
¨ **1 tbsp** cider vinegar
¨ **1 tbsp** dark muscovado sugar
¨ **20g** dark chocolate

Some-like-it-hot, some not. This version of chile con carne has proper chunks of meat and Mexican flavours, including their dried chillies, or *chiles*, as they call them in Mexico. Just before the meat goes in the oven, you can divide it into two pots, one hot with chillies and the other with the great fiesta of Mexican flavours, but without the heat, or with less, to suit all palates. If possible, make the dish a day in advance of eating, as the flavours improve with time.

1. Put the chipotle and ancho chillies into hot water (leave them whole and with the seeds in) and leave to soak whilst you get on with the rest of the dish.

2. Preheat the oven to 150°C/Gas 2. Heat the dripping, lard or oil in a large pan and cook the onions over a medium-low heat for 10 minutes, or until soft, stirring occasionally. Add the garlic, beef, coriander stalks, herbs and spices to the softened onions and give it all a good stir. Add the passata, stock and cider vinegar. Season with ¼ tsp flaky sea salt, the muscovado sugar and chocolate, broken into pieces.

3. At this point you can decide how many of your guests like hot food. If some are unlikely to want chillies, then put their portions into another pot. Cut open the soaked dried chillies and discard three-quarters of their seeds. Finely chop the flesh add to the 'hot' pot, along with the soaking water and seeds. I tend to add some of the soaking liquid to the 'cool' pot to give it a bit of flavour and buzz.

to serve:
- **1 medium** red onion
- **3–4 tbsp** cider vinegar
- **2** ripe avocados
- plus: boiled white rice, sour cream, refried black beans (tinned or see page 176), nachos, lime wedges

4. Put a lid on the pots, bring to the boil and put in the preheated oven for 3 hours. Check occasionally and stir, adding a little more water if necessary.

5. While the chilli is cooking, prepare your bits and pieces for serving. Cut the red onion into very thin slices and put in a small bowl with a pinch of salt and the cider vinegar. Leave for at least 1 hour to make a quick, pink pickle.

6. Serve the chilli with rice and a swirl of sour cream, a spoonful of pink pickle, the sliced avocados, a dollop of refried beans, a scatter of chopped coriander leaf, nachos and lime wedges.

The extras that you serve with this dish make it beautifully colourful, with whites, pinks and greens against the dark meat. The bits and pieces don't take long to do and make the meat go much further. At its simplest you could just serve the chile with rice, sour cream, coriander leaf and a wedge of lime, though I would be loathe to miss out the quick pickle, which takes just a minute to make and looks and tastes great.

Mexican dried chillies can be bought from a specialist (www.coolchile.co.uk) and some supermarkets and delis. Chipotles are smoked jalapeños and have some heat. Anchos are milder, dried poblano peppers.

LOWER EAST SIDE PORK & PEAR STEW

SERVES 6–8

" **75g** butter
" **2 onions,** *sliced*
" **1½ tbsp** plain flour
" **25g bunch** of flat-leaf parsley stalks, *finely chopped*
" **¼ tsp** ground mace
" **3 cloves**
" **1 litre** beef stock (instant is fine)

" **200g** dried pear halves (see note below), *cut into 3 or 4 pieces*
" **1.4g** pork shoulder, *cut into 7cm chunks*
" **700g** celeriac
" **juice of ½–1** lemon
" **1–2 tbsp** *finely chopped* flat-leaf parsley leaves

I got the idea for this recipe in a fascinating book about the life of immigrant New Yorkers, *97 Orchard Road*. Tenement cooking in the nineteenth century meant going up and down flights of stairs as there was no running water in the apartments. One Pot cooking was almost a necessity in such circumstances and this must have encouraged many classic old-world dishes to continue, such as this German stew.

Dried pears are available at some supermarkets, health food stores and online. If unavailable, substitute dried apple.

Mace is the outer casing of a nutmeg and is a spice that is now much less used than its other half. I like its milder flavour and use it as a seasoning in stews, milk pudding and also in curries, spice cakes and biscuits.

Lemon slices are added to the original recipe but they look too much like the celeriac and have slightly too strong a flavour, so I just add lemon juice instead.

1. Melt the butter in a sauté pan that has a lid. Add the onions and soften them over a low heat, stirring occasionally (10–15 minutes). Sprinkle over the flour and leave to cook for a minute or two, stirring occasionally. Add the parsley stalks, mace and cloves, stir in the beef stock, then add the pears and pork. Season with salt and pepper, bearing in mind the saltiness of the stock.

2. Stir the ingredients together. Bring to boil, then turn down the heat and simmer for 15 minutes.

3. Meanwhile, peel the celeriac and cut into thin half-moon slices – don't do this too far in advance as it will discolour. Add the sliced celeriac to the pot and continue to cook the dish for 45 minutes, or until the meat is tender. Add the lemon juice at the end, to taste, and scatter over the parsley leaves. Serve with jacket potatoes and green veg, or just with a salad.

MY VERSION OF RICE & PEAS

SERVES **6−8** AS A MAIN COURSE;
MORE AS A SIDE DISH

- " **250g** mixed dried beans
- " **300g** long-grain rice
- " **1 x 400g** tin coconut milk
- " **6** spring onions, *roughly chopped, including the green part*
- " **2 bushy sprigs** thyme
- " **1** scotch bonnet chilli, *left whole, or cut in half for more heat*
- " **about 6** allspice berries, *lightly crushed* (optional but good)
- " lime wedges, to serve

This Jamaican classic works as a dish on its own, or as an accompaniment for a piece of roasted meat or fish, or a stew such as pepperpot (see page 161). If served as a main dish, I think it essential to cook the beans rather than opening a tin as the cooking water provides a tasty stock. 'Peas' in Jamaica are what we call kidney beans in the UK. I like to use the mixed bags of beans available in some supermarkets and health food shops instead – not at all authentic, but it adds different colours and shapes to the dish.

Scotch bonnet is the authentic and most delicious chilli to use here, with a fruity and distinctive flavour that adds much to the dish. You increasingly find them in supermarkets and always in shops near Caribbean communities. Watch out: they are hot. First-timers should leave the chilli whole and fish it out at the end, or just use a piece of the flesh, without the hot seeds, finely chopped.

Add more flavours to the cooking beans, such as 5 cracked allspice berries, 2 cloves of garlic and a big sprig of thyme, to get even more flavour from the bean water.

1. If you remember, soak the beans in plenty of cold water overnight. You don't need to do this, but it does cut down the cooking time. (I tend to soak and cook the beans the day before cooking the dish). Put the beans in a pot, covered with water. Bring to the boil and boil hard for 10 minutes, then turn down the heat and simmer, covered, until the beans are soft. How long this takes depends on the age of the beans and whether or not you've managed to soak them: generally 1–1½ hours.

2. When the beans are cooked, drain, reserving the cooking water, which is now full of flavour.

3. Off the heat, put the rice in the pot and stir in the coconut milk, spring onions, thyme, chilli and ¾–1 tsp flaky sea salt. I like to add the allspice berries, an authentic taste in Jamaican food. Pour 600ml of the bean water into the pot.

4. Bring the mixture to the boil over a high heat, turn down the heat and simmer, covered, for 20–25 minutes, or until the rice is tender and the liquid absorbed, adding a touch more just-boiled water from the kettle if needed, or more of the bean water.

5. Remove the scotch bonnet pepper (or mash it up and stir in, seeds as well, if your guests like really hot food – though beware, this is very hot). Serve with cooling lime wedges.

RICH MUTTON & CAPER STEW

8 SERVINGS

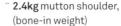

- **2.4kg** mutton shoulder, (bone-in weight)
- **3 tbsp** olive or vegetable oil
- **75g** plain flour
- **1.5 litres** lamb stock (or a mixture of lamb & beef or beef pho stock, see page 186)
- **2 large** onions, *roughly chopped*
- **3 large** carrots, *sliced*
- **2 stalks** celery, *sliced*
- **½ tbsp** juniper berries, *lightly crushed*
- **250ml** double cream
- **5 tbsp** capers, *drained & rinsed* (the small ones are best)

Mutton truly deserves its high status amongst those in-the-know. A number of chefs, as well as hill farmers, prefer mutton to lamb during the winter and spring, saying it is like well-aged beef compared to milder veal. The meat comes from sheep that are at least 2 years old, beyond the stage of both young lamb and year-old hogget. It used to be more popular than beef on the British table, yet has fallen away due to changes in supply and demand for meat, wool, milk and fat for tallow candles, all of which mean older sheep are now less economically viable. This sumptuous stew is slightly adapted from a recipe by the talented chef Robert Owen Brown. I first ate it at a Christmas lunch hosted by Booths, the excellent supermarket group which sells mutton from the grey-and-white Herdwick sheep that graze the natural pastures of the Lake District. The dish was so outstandingly good that a number of guests asked for the recipe.

1. Get your butcher to take the meat off the bone, or do it yourself. Cut the meat into large chunks – about 10 or so pieces – trimming off the excess fat.

2. Preheat the oven to 150°C/Gas 2. Pour 2 tbsp of the oil into a large casserole dish over a high heat. Brown the meat in batches on both sides, adding the last 1 tbsp of oil halfway through.

3. When you've removed the last batch of meat from the pan, add the flour and stir it around in the fat, letting it cook for a minute or so. Tip the browned meat back into the casserole. Pour the stock into the pan and, as it bubbles up, stir vigorously with a wooden spoon to scrape up any tasty gubbins stuck to the bottom.

4. Add the chopped onions, carrots and celery, then the juniper berries. Season with salt and plenty of black pepper. Stir everything together, then bring to the boil and put in the oven to cook for 3½ hours, or until the meat is so tender it can be pushed apart with a spoon.

5. Use tongs or spoons to remove the meat from the dish. Strain off the liquid and discard the veg.

6. Pour the liquid back into the pan, bring to the boil over a high heat and let it bubble away until reduced by about a third. Add the cream and boil away until the sauce has a nice thickness, about the same as pouring double cream, or slightly looser, as you like. Turn the heat down slightly, add the capers, then return the mutton to the sauce to heat through. Taste and adjust the seasoning if necessary.

7. Serve with boiled potatoes and simple greens, such as cabbage, or perhaps a tangy helping of watercress.

Mutton should be bought from a good butcher or farm to ensure it is well produced. The excellent book, *Much Ado About Mutton*, by advocate Bob Kennard, has a long list of suppliers and his website has plenty of information: www.muchadoaboutmutton.co.uk. Ideally, it should be hung for at least 10 days to 2 weeks or more to ensure it is tender and tasty. Meat from mountain and downland breeds, fed on a mixed and natural diet, is particularly special.

Advance cooking suits mutton. This is a classic example of how a One Pot dish can be made at your leisure and quickly reheated to serve to guests at your convenience. A couple of days in the fridge even improves the flavour.

Buy the mutton on the bone and you can make your own stock for the dish, following the instructions for beef stock (see page 30) or pho stock (see page 186).

CARIBBEAN
FISH PIE

SERVES **6**
(COULD BE MORE, BUT FISH PIE
IS ALMOST TOO EASY TO EAT...
AND PEOPLE TUCK IN)

- **700g** fish fillet, *cut into 4–5cm cubes*
- **500ml** whole milk
- **250ml** coconut cream
- **50g** butter
- **2 tbsp** plain flour
- **juice of 2** limes
- **large bunch** of coriander leaf, *roughly chopped*
- **1 large sprig** of thyme, leaves removed
- **8** spring onions, *roughly chopped, including the green part*
- **200g** large, peeled, raw prawns
- **300g** spinach
- **4** hard-boiled eggs, *quartered*

Sweet potato mash:
- **750g** sweet potatoes, *peeled & cut into large chunks*
- **500g** regular potatoes, *peeled & cut into smaller chunks*
- **75g** butter, plus extra for topping
- **½ tsp** *freshly grated* nutmeg
- **a large pinch** of ground allspice

A big fish pie is a mighty fine dish to put on the table. This version is full of the bright tastes of the Caribbean and has sunny orange sweet potato mash on top.

Fish pie mixes can be found in fishmongers. Otherwise, its good to have a mix of fish fillets, including about a third of the mixture as smoked fish if possible.

Typical Caribbean spices include allspice (called pimento in Jamaica) and nutmeg. Caribbean herbs include thyme and coriander. All these combine with tangy lime to make a lively flavour. You don't need to add chilli to spice up this dish.

1. First make the mash. Put all the potatoes in a pan, cover with water and add ½ tsp flaky sea salt. Bring to the boil, then turn down the heat and simmer until tender (about 10 minutes). Drain well and mash thoroughly with the butter, nutmeg and allspice. Season with more salt and a good grind of pepper, to taste.

2. Now for the filling. Put the chunks of fish in a wide, shallow pan and add the milk and coconut cream. Bring to the boil slowly, over a medium-high heat, then turn off the heat, cover with a lid and leave for a few minutes. Remove the fish from the pan and leave to cool. Meanwhile, preheat the oven to 180°C/ Gas 4.

FULL OF THE BRIGHT TASTES OF THE CARIBBEAN

3. Melt the butter in a large saucepan. Add the flour and stir for a couple of minutes so it cooks a little. Gradually add the hot coconut milk mixture that was used for poaching the fish. If the liquid is hot, it helps to stop lumps forming. Stir well as you add the liquid, use a whisk and beat hard if lumps form.

4. Add the lime juice, coriander and thyme leaves. Season with salt and pepper. Stir in the chopped spring onions, then gently mix the fish and prawns into the mixture.

5. Cook the spinach leaves over a high heat in a lidded pan, so they collapse. Drain well in a colander, pushing out any excess liquid.

6. Spoon the fish mixture into a large baking dish (about 30cm diameter and 10cm deep, or thereabouts). Spread the spinach over the top and carefully nestle the boiled egg quarters in the mixture.

7. Place large spoonfuls of the mash all over the top and use the back of the spoon to spread them out. Dot with a little more butter. I like to use a fork to make a criss-cross pattern of ridges in the top of the pie that crisp up as the pie cooks.

8. Put in the oven for about 30–40 minutes, until piping hot and slightly brown on top.

DESPERATE DAN
LAMBSHANK PIE

SERVES **6−8**

- **3−4** lamb shanks
- **2 tbsp** olive or vegetable oil
- **4** banana shallots or small onions, *finely chopped*
- **2 large** carrots, *finely chopped*
- **2 stalks** celery, *finely chopped*
- **300g** button mushrooms, 150g *finely chopped, the rest halved*
- **400ml** red wine
- **500ml** water or lamb or chicken stock (homemade is best)
- **4 sprigs** thyme
- **1 tbsp** plain flour

suet pastry:
- **250g** ready-shredded beef suet
- **500g** plain flour, plus extra if needed
- **300ml** water
- beaten egg or milk, to glaze (optional)

This was our wedding pie, served with bones sticking out of the pastry, rather like Desperate Dan's 'cow pie' in the *Beano* cartoon. I admit it uses two pots, but it comes together in one and lots of guests asked for the recipe. I remember the chef, Sylvain Jamois, saying that you need plenty of wine and that's true. The scent of the lamb cooking in a rich, winey sauce is enough to create domestic bliss long after the 'I do'.

Advance cooking can be done by making the stew up to 3 days in advance and cooking it under the pastry on the day.

Suet pastry is not only delicious, but extra-easy to make and almost like play clay as it is so malleable and easy to roll.

1. Preheat the oven to 170°C/Gas 3. Season the lamb shanks with salt and pepper. Heat 1 tbsp of oil in a casserole dish over a high heat and brown the meat. Add half the chopped shallots or onions, carrots, celery and the finely chopped mushrooms.

2. Pour in the wine and let it bubble up, then add the stock and 2 thyme sprigs. Cover, then place in the oven for 3 hours, or until the meat is tender.

3. Meanwhile, heat another 1 tbsp of oil in an ovenproof sauté pan and soften the rest of the chopped onions, carrots and celery for 10 minutes over a medium-low heat, stirring occasionally. Add the halved mushrooms and continue to cook for another 5 minutes, stirring occasionally.

4. When the meat is cooked, strain off the veg and discard. Take the meat off the bone, cut into medium pieces and leave to one side.

5. Add the leaves from the 2 remaining thyme sprigs to the vegetables in the sauté pan and sprinkle over the flour. Stir in the strained, winey liquor. Bring to the boil and bubble away for a few minutes to thicken slightly. Return the meat to the pan and taste, adjusting the seasoning if necessary. Remove from the heat and leave to cool.

6. To make the pastry, mix the suet and flour in a bowl. Add a touch of salt and plenty of pepper. Use a table knife to roughly stir the water into the dry ingredients, then use your hands to finish it off, kneading the dough into a rough ball. If the mixture is too wet to handle, knead in a little more flour. Place the dough on a lightly floured work surface and continue to knead for a minute or so, until the dough holds together in a ball.

7. Roll the pastry out to just under 1cm thick. Put the lamb shank bones in the middle of the pie filling. Drape the pastry over half the dish, then use one hand to lift the bones and poke them through the pastry as you lower it down over the rest of the pie. This isn't a neat procedure for me, though Sylvain did it beautifully. It doesn't matter if you have holes in the pastry; the gravy soaking through is a most appetising look. Tuck the pastry over the meat. If you like, glaze with beaten egg or milk.

8. Preheat to 200°C/Gas 6. Put the pie into the hot oven for 45–50 minutes, until the pastry has browned and the gravy is bubbling up. Serve, if you wish, with mashed potato and steamed greenery.

GAMMON & BEANS

SERVES 6–8

- **2 cloves** (optional)
- **2kg** gammon (smoked is best)
- **250g** split dried fava beans
- **3** carrots, *cut into 3 large chunks*
- **2 stalks** celery, *cut into 4–5 large chunks*
- **3 cloves** garlic, *finely chopped*
- **2 bay leaves**
- **500ml** cider
- **1 litre** water
- **a squeeze** of lemon juice, if needed
- **2 tbsp** *roughly chopped* flat-leaf parsley
- olive oil, to serve

Gammon provides its own stock that mixes with beans to make a sauce for the meat. I like the luxurious, velvety texture of beans in this dish and the way they are at least as important as the meat, if not more. It is always useful to have some gammon in the house and I cook a larger piece than needed in order to have meat for sandwiches and other meals.

Ham hocks are a good-value alternative to a gammon in this recipe and the sort of budget cut you spot in farmer's markets. You just need one to flavour the dish, or two if you want more meat.

Dried fava beans are much appreciated in Egypt and the Middle East. We used to export all the beans grown in the UK, or use them for animal feed. An enterprising and eco-aware East Anglian company, Hodmedods (www.hodmedods.co.uk), now package and sell British beans in the UK. Unlike many dried beans, there's no need to soak these split beans before cooking.

1. If using, stick the cloves into the gammon, then put everything but the lemon juice, parsley leaves and oil in a pot. You want the liquid to just cover the meat so add more or less, as necessary (if it's a big or awkward sized gammon that is hard to cover, try to nearly cover and turn it over halfway through cooking). Put on a lid and bring to the boil, then turn down the heat and simmer for 2 hours.

2. Remove the meat from the pot and discard the cloves. Leave to cool for 10 minutes on a plate and then tip the juices released from the meat back into the pot. Use a stick blender to whizz up the beans to get a nice soupy texture that's still slightly chunky. Check the sauce for seasoning. A few grinds of black pepper are a good idea and a squeeze of lemon if the mixture is too salty.

3. Serve the bean mixture in bowls with slices of gammon on top, a sprinkling of parsley and a swirl of oil.

OVEN-DRIED
TOMATOES

MAKES A BOWLFUL, FEEDS PLENTY

¨ **16–20** tomatoes,
   cut in half
¨ **2 tbsp** caster sugar
¨ **½–1 tsp** chilli flakes

¨ **1 tsp** dried oregano
   (optional)
¨ **2–3 tbsp** olive oil,
   or more if needed

One Pot cooks often have the oven on and it is handy to have recipes for dishes you can cook alongside your stew or whatever else is on the go. In the late autumn and winter, tomatoes lack flavour and sweetness. This method imparts plenty of both. The semi-dried tomatoes can then sit in the fridge in a bowl, ready to transform many a One Pot or other dish, be it pasta sauce, stew, sandwich or pizza.

1. Put the tomato halves on to a baking tray large enough for them to sit in a single layer.

2. Mix together the sugar, chilli flakes and oregano, if using, with ½–1 tbsp flaky sea salt. Sprinkle evenly over the tomatoes. Put in a medium-low oven (about 160°C/Gas 3) for 2–3 hours, or for as long as your other food is cooking. You can dry them for as long as you want; they become more chewy and intense in flavour the longer you leave them.

3. Put the tomatoes into a small bowl and pour over enough olive oil to just cover. Keep in the fridge, covered.

You can cook this at various temperatures as long as the oven temperature is below 180°C/Gas 4 or so, adjusting the time accordingly.

Leave the tomatoes to cook in the oven with the door closed after you've turned it off, so they continue to dry out in the residual heat.

ANDREA'S LIGHT CZECH DUMPLINGS

MAKES **40** (GOOD FOR FREEZING)

- **2 tsp** dried yeast or 1½ tsp instant yeast
- **270ml** warm water, at blood temperature
- **1 tsp** caster sugar
- **500g** fine semolina, plus extra for dusting
- **1 large** egg, *lightly beaten*

A good addition to the One Pot cook's repertoire is the dumpling. These ones are so special you can even eat them as a main dish, rather than with a stew or soup. I was given a masterclass in this yeasted style of dumpling by a family friend, Andrea, who grew up in the Czech Republic where making them is a household skill, done with love and attention. The result is very much worth the effort; light yet filling. Add herbs or other seasonings to the dough as you like.

1. If using dried yeast, put in a small bowl with the warm liquid and sugar, stir and leave for 10 minutes, until it froths up. Pour into a large bowl or a food mixer fitted with a dough hook and add the semolina, and 1 tsp fine sea salt. If using easy-blend yeast just put all these ingredients into the bowl together. Add the egg.

2. Mix everything together with a wooden spoon for 10 minutes, or for 5 minutes in a food mixer, until the dough is smooth and less sticky.

3. Dust the top of the dough with semolina and cover the bowl with a clean tea towel. Leave the dough to rise in a warmish place for 1 hour, or longer. It should roughly double in size.

4. When the dough has risen, liberally dust the work surface with semolina. Knock the air out of the dough by pushing down onto it. Cut into eight pieces. Roll each piece into a cylinder about 5cm thick. Roll each piece into a long cylinder. Dust a chopping board with more semolina and place the cylinders on it to prove for 10 minutes or so, covered lightly with a clean tea towel.

5. Meanwhile, get a large pan of water on to boil, or a large steamer. Boil or steam the dumpling rolls for 20 minutes, turning them over after 10 minutes if boiling. Do not open the lid of the steamer, if using. You will need to cook the dumpling rolls in batches or one at a time as the dough expands slightly as it cooks.

6. Take the dumpling rolls out of the pan and immediately prick each one about 10 times on each side to let out the steam and help keep them soft.

7. Andrea likes to cut the dumplings with a thread to help them keep their bounce. Put a long piece of cotton thread under each roll and cross over the ends to slice off a dumpling about 2-3cm thick. Repeat for the rest. (I must admit I just use a knife.)

8. The dumplings keep in the fridge for a few days or freeze well, wrapped as a whole roll in clingfilm and cut up once defrosted, or wrapped in smaller parcels of ready-cut dumplings. Steam to reheat.

Serve these dumplings as the starchy component of a stew, or in a soup. They can also be served as a starter or main course, with chopped onions sizzled in plenty of fat until crispy brown, as is the Czech way.

Andrea did a stirring form of kneading, which is hard work by hand: she said her 7-year-old daughter, Georgie, was quick to hand the bowl and spoon back to mum. So did I. Andrea was brought up in a place where dumplings are part of the household and has the special muscles for it, holding the bowl in the crook of one arm and using the spoon to transform the sticky dough into something more malleable. A mixer with a dough hook is much easier, if less character-and-muscle building.

Yeast takes longer to rise in cold weather. Andrea's mother used to put her dough in the bed under the duvet to keep it warm in their snowy mountain village. In London, she tends to put the bowl in the kitchen sink, partly surrounded by warm – not hot – water.

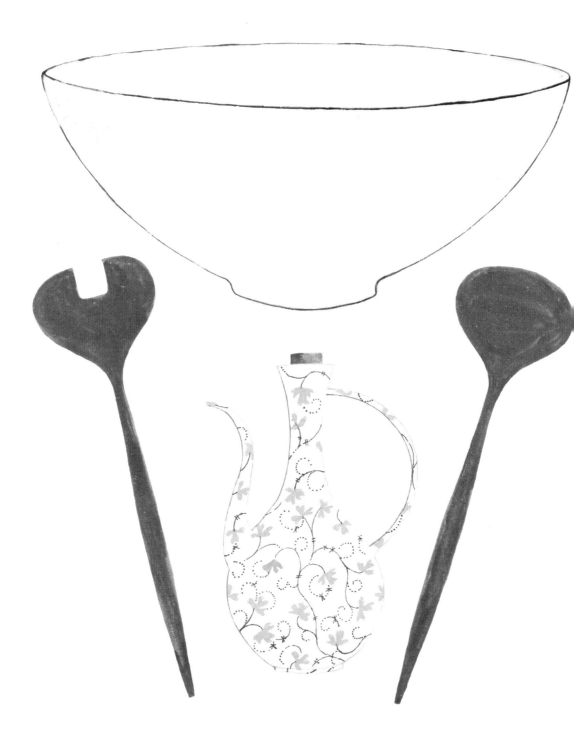

SUMMER
SPREADS

ONE POTS

FOR WHEN THE SUN

MAKES YOU WANT TO

FLOP RATHER THAN

RUSH AROUND THE

KITCHEN

One Pots shift in the summer. The emphasis is now on fresh vegetables, fish and bright, light flavours. We want to spend less time in the kitchen and more time outside. The oven goes on less often and One Pot cooking moves to the hob.

Summer is the time when people float in and out of the home, and so it is helpful to have a few adaptable One Pots in the fridge, ready to feed ever-changing numbers.

Feeding friends and family in these months is often about putting a selection of dishes on the table for people to help themselves. Make a One Pot, then lay out cheese, fruit, salad and bread to complete the meal. The recipes in this chapter can be eaten alone, or enjoyed as part of a summer spread.

In the summer and early autumn, shops and gardens have an abundance of seasonal vegetables, so meals are orientated towards making the most of this glut. There are recipes in this chapter for some of the more substantial summer veg, such as turnips and kohlrabi, that make light meals more satisfying.

For inspiration, I've looked at the recipes of One Pot cooks in hot countries, who have evolved many ways to make food that suits the summer. This chapter travels to Provence, Italy, Greece, Morocco, the Middle East and Jamaica to find One Pots for when the sun makes you want to flop rather than rush around the kitchen.

GREEK LAMB WITH DILL & CHICKPEAS

SERVES **6**

- ¨ **1 tbsp** olive or vegetable oil
- ¨ **½ shoulder** of lamb (approx. 1.3kg, shank end is best)
- ¨ **2** onions, *sliced*
- ¨ **1 stalk** celery, *sliced*
- ¨ **2 cloves** garlic, *finely chopped*
- ¨ **2 x 400g** tins chickpeas, *drained & rinsed*
- ¨ **juice of 1** lemon
- ¨ **3 tbsp** *chopped* dill
- ¨ **250ml** white wine
- ¨ **1 tsp** ground allspice

Pots can make you dream of cooks near and far. This recipe is inspired by a green-glazed earthenware pot that was given to us as a wedding present by my friend Deborah Colman. She brought it back from the Cycladic island of Sifnos, where the potter sells his wares beside one of the beaches. Debs says that families use the same faithful dish each week to cook their Sunday chickpea soup. One ingredient that makes Greek food taste authentic is dill. Instead of using red wine with lamb, this dish is bright with white wine, lemon juice, dill and just a touch of allspice to mellow the flavour.

1. Preheat the oven to 170°C/Gas 3. Heat the oil in a casserole dish with a lid and brown the whole piece of meat on both sides over a high heat. Remove from the pan and put to one side.

2. Turn down the heat to medium-low and add the onions, celery and garlic to the pan. Stir them into the fat then cook for 5 minutes to soften slightly, stirring occasionally.

3. Add the chickpeas, lemon juice, dill, wine, allspice and 1 tsp flaky sea salt. Mix, then nestle the lamb back in the pan.

4. Put the casserole dish in the oven and cook for 3 hours, or until the lamb is tender enough to fall off the bone.

5. Serve the meat and chickpeas with spoonfuls of sauce, greenery or a green salad and some kind of starch – crusty bread is fine.

Butter beans can be used instead of chickpeas. Whichever you use, the pulses soak up the juices, adding another texture to the dish as well as making the meat go further.

GIGANTES PLAKI

SERVES **6** AS A MAIN COURSE; **10** AS A SIDE DISH

- **400g** dried butter beans or 4 x 400g tins, *drained & rinsed*
- **4 tbsp** olive oil, plus 1 tbsp to serve (ideally Greek),
- **2 large** onions, *finely sliced*
- **2–4 cloves** garlic, *finely chopped*
- **2 tbsp** tomato purée
- **2** bay leaves
- **2 x 400g** tins chopped tomatoes
- **1** lemon, *finely grated zest*
- **1 tsp** dried, or 1 tbsp fresh, oregano, *roughly chopped*
- **4 tbsp** *chopped* dill

You could call these 'Greek baked beans'. As it happens, they do go beautifully on toast, especially on open-textured Mediterranean style bread such as sourdough. I can imagine dishes of these being brought back home from the village oven on a Greek island to feed a large tableful. It's a useful supper dish and makes good leftovers for quick lunches or a lunch box. The flavours improve with time so even if you are going to serve the dish in one go for a party, try to bake your beans a day or two in advance.

The large gigantes beans from Greece are the authentic bean for this dish. I've substituted butter beans, but do use gigantes if you can find them online or in a Mediterranean food shop. They look good and absorb flavours well.

Different herbs work well in this dish. Substitute the dill with the same quantity of chopped basil or flat-leaf parsley or 3 tbsp in total of chopped mint. I've also used thyme and hyssop from my garden instead of oregano.

Barbecues need ballast and a dish of gigantes plaki, made in advance, goes well with sausages, lamb, fish and vegetable kebabs.

1. If using dried beans, soak them overnight in plenty of cold water. Drain and put into a large pan. Cover with fresh water, bring to the boil, then turn down the heat and simmer for around 1 hour, until tender but not too soft. Drain, reserving the liquid.

2. Preheat the oven to 180°C/Gas 4. Heat the oil in a large, ovenproof pot and add the onions and garlic. Cook over a medium-high heat for 5 minutes, stirring occasionally. Turn the heat down to medium-low and cook gently for 15–20 minutes, stirring occasionally, until soft and sweet.

3. Add the rest of the ingredients to the softened vegetables, apart from 1 tbsp of the chopped dill. Add 300ml of the cooking liquid if cooking your own beans, or otherwise 300ml of just-boiled water, and season well with salt and pepper. Bring to the boil.

4. Put the dish in the preheated oven, covered, and cook for 1–1½ hours, or until the beans are completely soft. Add a dash of hot water or bean stock if they are starting to look dry. Cook for a final 30 minutes with the lid off.

5. Top with a final scattering of fresh chopped dill and drizzle over the last tbsp of olive oil. Serve on toast rubbed with garlic and drizzled with olive oil, perhaps with some feta or goats cheese crumbled on top.

COUSCOUS WITH ROASTED VEGETABLES & LEMON-HERB DRESSING

SERVES **6–8**

- **200g** couscous (barley, wholewheat or large wheat couscous are best)
- **double the volume of couscous** in hot vegetable stock (about 500ml, instant is fine; I use mushroom)
- **1 medium** butternut squash (about 1kg), *peeled, deseeded & cut into 4cm chunks*
- **3** peppers, *deseeded, each cut into 8 long strips* (ideally use different colours)
- **3** red onions, *cut into quarters through the root & peeled*
- **2 tbsp** olive oil
- **1 x 400g** tin chickpeas, *drained & rinsed*
- **100g** pistachio nuts, *roughly chopped* and/or 100g feta, *roughly crumbled*
- **50g** dried apricots, *chopped*

This colourful and healthy summery dish is easy to make in advance. Roasting deepens and sweetens the flavours of the vegetables, then a sprinkling of chopped dried apricots enhances this sweetness and is balanced by the tart lemon juice and sumac.

1. Preheat the oven to 200°C/Gas 6. Put the couscous in a small bowl and add the hot stock. Stir and leave to soak while you roast the vegetables.

2. Spread the butternut squash, peppers and onions on a large baking tray in a single layer. Season lightly with salt and pepper – not too much as there is more seasoning in the dressing. Drizzle over the oil and toss well to coat.

3. Roast the vegetables for 20 minutes. Add the drained chickpeas and stir in. Roast for another 20–30 minutes, turning the vegetables once, until they are slightly caramelized at the edges.

lemon-herb dressing:
- **juice of 1** lemon
- **3 tbsp** good olive oil
- **1 small clove** garlic, *crushed*
- **7 tbsp** *chopped* flat-leaf parsley or chives
- **2 tbsp** *chopped* mint
- **1 tsp** sumac, plus 1 tsp to finish (optional but good)

4. While the vegetables are cooking, make the lemon-herb dressing by whisking together all the ingredients. Season with salt and pepper, but go steady on the salt if you are adding feta.

5. In a serving bowl, combine the couscous and dressing, taking time over this to ensure the grains are well coated and the herbs evenly dispersed. Mix in the roasted vegetables, chopped pistachio nuts and chopped apricots. If you are serving this with feta, alongside or instead of the nuts, mix this in carefully right at the end.

6. Sprinkle the top of the dish with sumac (about 1 tsp) and serve warm or at room temperature.

Couscous comes in various forms. I particularly like barley couscous for its slightly different flavour. Wholewheat couscous is also tasty, or make the dish with large wheat couscous, cooked in advance, according to packet instructions (generally simmered in salted water for 10 minutes).

Herbs can vary according to preference and what you have to hand. Use around 9 tbsp (or more) of chopped, mixed herbs in total, or 4 tbsp if using just mint. Mint is a distinctive and delicious herb in Middle Eastern food but one of the strongest in flavour. It is best kept in balance with other kinds, especially flat-leaf parsley.

Advance cooking is fine with this dish (though it's best eaten on the day) and leftovers are excellent. If making in advance, keep in the fridge, covered, and crumble the feta over just before serving.

HONEY JERK PORK WITH MANGO SALSA & PLANTAINS

SERVES **6**

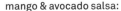

- **3½ tsp** jerk seasoning
- **juice of 2½** limes
- **4 tbsp** honey
- **2** pork tenderloins (about 500–550g each)
- **2** ripe plantains
- **1 tbsp** olive or vegetable oil

mango & avocado salsa:
- **1** mango, *pitted & cut into 2cm dice*
- **1** avocado, *peeled & cut into 2cm dice*
- **3** spring onions, *finely chopped*
- **2 tbsp** *finely chopped* coriander leaf
- **1 tbsp** *finely chopped* mint
- **¼ tsp** salt
- **juice of ½** lime
- **1 tbsp** olive oil

Spicy food from a hot country is great for summer dining. Pork tenderloin from high welfare animals can be bought surprisingly cheaply considering it is a tender, quick-cook cut and I love it done Jamaican jerk-style and served with a salsa.

1. Mix together the jerk seasoning with the juice of 2 limes and 2 tbsp of the honey in a shallow ceramic or plastic bowl. Cover the pork loins in the marinade and ideally leave in the fridge, covered, for at least 30 minutes or overnight, turning it over from time to time.

2. Preheat the oven to 180°C/Gas 4. Peel the plantains and cut on an angle into slices 1.5–2cm thick. Line a baking tray with foil and lay the slices on one side.

3. Put the tenderloins on the other side of the baking tray. Pour the rest of the marinade over the meat and roast for 20 minutes in the preheated oven. Baste the meat with the marinade and drizzle over another 2 tbsp honey, then cook for a further 10 minutes. Leave to rest for 5 minutes then cut on the diagonal into 2cm thick slices.

4. While the meat is cooking and resting, make the salsa. Mix everything in a serving bowl and leave to one side for the flavours to mingle. Its best not to make this too far in advance or it loses some freshness.

5. Squeeze half a lime over the plantains and sprinkle over plenty of salt. Use a fish slice or spatula to loosen the plantains from the tray and toss so they are seasoned all over. Serve the plantains and salsa alongside the pork, perhaps with a green salad as well.

For a more chargrilled look and taste, heat a frying pan or griddle over a high heat. Take the pork out of the marinade, pat dry and sear it on each side (5–6 minutes in total). Then cook in the preheated oven for 20 minutes, or until cooked through, adding the extra honey for the last 10 minutes of cooking.

You can cook the pork and plantains in advance (ideally so they are ready just before your guests arrive) and serve the dish warm or cold.

Plantains can be found in some supermarkets and greengrocers near Caribbean communities. For this recipe get the black-skinned ripe fruits, as their sweetness goes well with the spicy jerk meat.

CHILLED SOBA NOODLES WITH SMOKED MACKEREL

SERVES **6**

- ¨ **300g** soba noodles
- ¨ **100g** mangetouts
- ¨ **3** smoked mackerel fillets, *skinned*
- ¨ **1 tbsp** sesame oil, plus extra to serve
- ¨ **½ tbsp** rice vinegar
- ¨ **3** spring onions, *finely chopped, including the green part*
- ¨ lime juice, to serve

miso aubergines (optional):
- ¨ **3** medium aubergines
- ¨ vegetable oil for greasing
- ¨ **5 tbsp** white miso
- ¨ **½ thumb** root ginger, *peeled & finely grated* or ½ ball crystallized ginger, *finely chopped*

Soba noodles are eaten chilled in Japan as a refreshing summer dish. In this version, I've added smoked mackerel to make a One Pot meal.

I've also given the option of it turning into a vegetarian Two Pot dish using the dark intensity of soft aubergine, topped with a strong miso paste. Both versions offer a good contrast to the gentle soba noodles with their firm texture and nutty, buckwheat flavour. Fresh, crisp mangetouts and spring onions then make this a satisfying lunch or light supper dish.

1. Bring a large pan of salted water to the boil. Add the noodles and cook for 6 minutes. Add the mangetouts to the pan and continue to cook until the noodles are just tender (about 2 minutes or so). Drain and put in a large bowl. Break the mackerel into large flakes. Add to the bowl.

2. Stir the sesame oil and rice vinegar into the noodles, combining so the noodles are well coated in oil and the mangetouts and mackerel are evenly dispersed among the noodles. Leave to cool completely, then cover and put in the fridge to chill for at least 1 hour – up to 24 hours is fine.

3. For the miso aubergines, cut the aubergines in half and score them in a criss-cross at 3cm intervals, right down into the flesh, but not so you pierce the skin. Put them skin-side up on a lightly oiled baking tray and place under a hot grill for around 10 minutes, or until the skin has hardened almost to a shell and the flesh inside is soft.

" **3 tsp** honey
" **1 tbsp** Japanese
   soy sauce
" **3 tbsp** mirin
" **1½ tbsp** lime juice
" **2 tbsp** sesame
   seeds, *toasted*

4. Whilst the aubergines are cooking, make the miso mixture by whisking together the rest of the ingredients (apart from the sesame seeds) in a small bowl. This is an intense, salty mixture, which goes well with the relatively bland noodles and silky aubergine flesh. If you want to make it less salty, replace the soy sauce with water.

5. Turn the aubergines over and spoon the miso mixture onto the flesh, gently pushing it down into the grooves. Grill for around 5 minutes, checking after 3 minutes and turning the aubergines around so the miso topping grills evenly: it should be patched with brown, but be careful not to burn it.

6. Scatter the sesame seeds over the aubergines and leave to cool. These are best eaten at room temperature, but will keep happily in the fridge for a day or so.

7. When ready to eat, spread the chilled noodle mixture on a big platter. If using, place the aubergines on top. Scatter the chopped spring onions over the whole dish. Just before serving, you can squeeze over a little more lime juice and perhaps an extra quick slick of sesame oil.

The mangetouts are cooked with the noodles to save on washing up. You could also very lightly steam these on the day – just to the point where they are post-crunch – and stir them into the noodles just before serving.

Use any kind of miso, if making the aubergines. I prefer white miso as it's sweeter and less salty. If you use a darker, stronger kind, then taste your mixture before adding the soy sauce and use water instead to loosen the mixture if it is already salty and intense. The taste should be strong, but not overpowering

SUMMER ROAST
CHICKEN

Serves 4-6

- **1.2kg** small potatoes, *larger ones cut in half*
- **3** peppers, *deseeded & each cut into 4 long strips (a mix of colours is good)*
- **2** red onions, *quartered*
- **4–6** cloves garlic, *finely chopped*
- **6** tomatoes, *quartered*
- **1** aubergine, *cut into 2cm cubes*
- **3 tbsp** olive oil
- **1 x 1.5kg** chicken
- **1 tbsp** balsamic vinegar
- **about 20** basil leaves, *roughly torn*

Roasts can be summery and this one is as much about the season's bountiful vegetables as the meat. A garlicky roasted ratatouille, made in the same baking tray as the chicken, acts as both accompanying vegetable and sauce and makes this a One Pot roast. This is a good choice for relaxed summer entertaining as there is no last-minute fussing over gravy.

Use the biggest baking tray you have to spread out the ingredients and help get the chicken skin as crispy as possible amongst all the steamy veg.

This dish is good warm as well as piping hot and can be made slightly in advance of eating. I might finish it off just before guests arrive and leave it in a low (100°/Gas ½) oven until ready to eat.

1. Preheat the oven to 220°C/Gas 7. Mix all the vegetables together on the largest baking tray you have; ideally they should be in more-or-less one layer. Drizzle over 2 tbsp of oil. Season everything generously with salt and pepper.

2. Place the chicken on top of the vegetables, in the centre of the tray. Drizzle the remaining 1 tbsp of oil over the chicken and season well with salt and pepper.

3. Roast the chicken and vegetables for 15 minutes. Turn the heat down to 200°C/Gas 6 and continue to cook for 15 minutes, then stir around the vegetables and potatoes that surround the chicken so they brown evenly. Continue to cook for another 30 minutes.

4. Check that the chicken is cooked by piercing the thickest part of the thigh with a sharp knife; the juices should run clear.

5. Place the chicken on a carving board. Stir the vegetables together with the chicken juices, balsamic vinegar and basil leaves. Season if necessary with more salt and pepper. Serve the chicken hot or warm with the vegetables alongside.

HERB
OMELETTES

SERVES **4**

"" **6 medium** eggs
"" **50ml** milk
"" **20g** *finely chopped* herbs (mix of any 2 or more of basil, dill, flat-leaf parsley, chives & tarragon)
"" **a small knob** of butter, plus more for the tray

filling:
"" **300–400g** cooked vegetables, *chopped into smallish pieces* (see note), or use a mix of tasty salad leaves
"" **4 tbsp** crème fraîche
"" **1 tsp** creamed horseradish

Omelette aux fines herbes is a classic of the French kitchen and an easy supper dish to rustle up from a box of eggs. This recipe makes the dish more substantial by using whatever leftover vegetables you have to hand to make a filling. The idea for the recipe came from Yottam Ottolenghi's *Plenty*, a book that has greatly fostered the trend to put vegetables back in the centre of the plate. He makes the omelettes thinner than usual, so they can act as a wrap, and also makes your box of eggs go even further.

You can make the omelettes in advance, keep them in a warm oven (100°C/Gas ¼) then fill just before serving. If making the day before, keep in the fridge, layered with pieces of greaseproof paper. Reheat in a 180°C/Gas 4 oven for around 5 minutes, or until hot, then fill.

Fillings I like: cooked and well-drained spinach with finely chopped spring onions; cubes of beetroot and cooked chard; chickpeas in a lemon-herb dressing roasted carrots dusted with ground toasted cumin seeds.

Add cooked potatoes, cut into cubes, to any of these fillings to make them more substantial.

1. Crack the eggs into a bowl and whisk with the milk and a good seasoning of salt and pepper. Stir in the herbs.

2. Melt the butter in a small frying pan (around 20cm diameter) over a high heat.

3. Pour a quarter of the egg mixture into the pan. Swirl the mixture around so it covers the base of the pan.

4. Cook until the omelette is starting to set on the bottom (a minute or so), then gently lift up one side, ideally using a palette knife or spatula, and tip the pan so the runny egg runs into the gap. Leave to cook briefly, until the omelette is completely set on the base and the top has no pools of liquid.

5. Lift or tip the omelette carefully out of the pan and place on a lightly buttered baking tray. Add a little more butter to the pan, if necessary, and cook the other 3 omelettes, placing them each time on top of the last with a piece of greaseproof paper between.

6. Heat up the vegetables for the filling, either in the omelette pan or in a microwave. Mix the crème fraîche with the creamed horseradish and spread thinly over the omelettes followed by a spoonful of the filling. Roll up the omelettes. Serve with a salad and bread.

TORTILLA

SERVES **4–6**

¨ **3 tbsp** olive oil,
plus 1 tsp (Spanish or
Portuguese olive oil
best of all)
¨ **4 banana shallots**
or 2 medium onions,
finely sliced

¨ **2 cloves** garlic,
finely chopped
¨ **500g** waxy potatoes,
peeled
¨ **8 medium** eggs
¨ **50g** parmesan, *grated*

The basis of this tortilla is a box of eggs and some potatoes cooked in plenty of tasty olive oil. It's as simple as that – and as complex. An omelette is fast and takes minutes; a tortilla is slow and takes an hour. The thicker tortilla also takes practice. You must get to know how it works in your particular pan and how to turn it over without a mess. (If you do make a mess at first, no matter. You can't make an omelette without cracking eggs and a few slightly duff ones can be renamed as chopped omelette.) Once mastered, you have an excellent dish that is portable enough to be taken on a picnic or in a lunchbox to provide the basis for a lunch, supper or outdoor summer brunch. A tortilla is also adaptable as you can add herbs and all sorts of other bits and pieces – bacon, chopped black olives, roasted peppers, spring onions and so on.

1. Heat the oil in a small frying pan over a medium-low heat and gently fry the shallots or onions and the garlic, stirring occasionally, until softened (about 15 minutes). Season with a little salt to help stop the onions from burning.

2. While the shallots are cooking, cut the potatoes into slices that are as thin as possible. You can do this in a food processor or on a mandolin, or on the slicing side of a box grater – watching your fingers as these sharp slits are treacherous to fingertips. I tend to use a box grater for about two-thirds of each spud and cut the last bit with a knife.

3. Add the potatoes to the pan with the onions, season well – 1 tsp flaky sea salt and lots of black pepper – and mix together. Leave to cook over a low heat for 30 minutes, stirring every 4 minutes or so to get the potatoes to cook evenly.

4. Meanwhile, crack the eggs into a large bowl, add the grated cheese and whisk together. Tip the potatoes and shallot mixture into the eggs. Use a spatula to remove any bits stuck to the base of the pan and add 1 tsp of oil. Tip the egg and potato mixture back into the pan.

5. Leave the tortilla to cook for 15 minutes over a medium-low heat, moving the pan around occasionally. After 10 minutes, gently ease a spatula around the edge of the tortilla and tilt the pan so any loose egg fills the gap.

6. When the tortilla looks almost set on top, use a spatula to gently ease under the tortilla. Get a big plate – or, if you have one, another frying pan – and place it over the pan. Turn it over so the tortilla tips out. Then slide the tortilla back into the pan, or continue to cook in the new pan, for another 15 minutes. Eat hot, or warm, or cold from the fridge.

You can also finish off the tortilla in an oven. Cook the tortilla in a pan with an ovenproof handle. Preheat the oven to 180°C/Gas 4 and, instead of flipping the tortilla, cook it in its pan in the oven for a final 10 minutes.

Additions can be made to a tortilla, but on the whole I'm against using leftover cold potatoes as these have a certain stale flavour that is much less delicious than potatoes freshly cooked in olive oil.

SLOW-COOKED
TURKISH BEANS

**SERVES 4 AS A LIGHT LUNCH;
8 AS PART OF A SPREAD**

- **100ml** olive oil
- **2** onions, *finely sliced*
- **3–4 cloves** garlic, *finely sliced*
- **200g** green beans or sugarsnap peas
- **2** leeks, *trimmed, cut into 2cm slices*
- **10** cherry tomatoes, or 3 larger ones, *roughly chopped*
- **2 tbsp** *roughly chopped* soft herbs such as basil, chervil or dill
- **juice of ½** lemon
- **1 tsp** honey or 1½ tsp caster sugar
- **a small pinch** of chilli flakes
- **100ml** water
- **3–4 tbsp** Greek yoghurt or goat's curd, to serve

Beans often come in a glut and here's a great way to use them up. Vegetables are usually cooked briefly, but low-and-slow is another route, as championed by food writer Paula Wolfert in her book *Mediterranean Clay Pot Cooking*. This method turns plain beans into a central dish that can be served either on its own or as part of a summer meal.

1. Heat the oil in a large pan with a lid and soften the onions slightly for a few minutes, stirring occasionally.

2. Add the rest of the ingredients to the pan, apart from the yoghurt, and season with ½ tsp flaky sea salt. Scrunch up a circle of greaseproof paper that's slightly larger then the pan's diameter, briefly wet it under a running tap, then tuck over the veg so they cook in their own juices.

3. Cover with a lid and cook the dish very slowly on a low heat for at least 1 hour, or until the beans are ultra-tender and the rest of the ingredients have collapsed into a sauce, adding a splash more water if necessary.

4. Eat warm or at room temperature. Just before eating, taste and adjust the seasoning if necessary, and spoon over the yoghurt or goat's curd.

Olive oil is crucial to give a rich density to the dish. Don't be tempted to reduce the quantity.

The Turks might sprinkle the top of this with their characteristic pepper, *kirmizi biber*, which is why I've put some chilli flakes into the mixture.

LENTILS WITH BASIL & GOAT'S CHEESE

SERVES **4–8,** AS A MAIN COURSE
OR PART OF A SPREAD

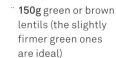

- **150g** green or brown lentils (the slightly firmer green ones are ideal)
- **2–3 cloves** garlic, *crushed*
- **juice of ½** lemon
- **5 tbsp** good olive oil
- **a large handful** of basil, *finely chopped*
- **100g** goat's cheese, *crumbled*

This recipe is adapted from *The Pauper's Cookbook* by Jocasta Innes, first published in 1971 and still in print. Innes wrote her classic after she had left London affluence for love and an impoverished, bohemian life in Dorset, where she lived on £20 a week. Hedgerow foraging and making-do with big bags of storecupboard staples were a necessity and a number of One Pot recipes feature. Not every cookbook feels rooted in a home kitchen, but this one could have its words splattered with sauces, such is the sense that the recipes are tried-and-trusted. In the 1970s, lentils were a byword for a type of knit-your-own stodge. But this recipe feels a long way from worthy seventies food and is a noble dish for rich and poor alike.

Salmon or trout work especially well with these lentils, both in looks and taste.

Sorrel is excellent addition or replacement for the basil. This lemony herb is easy to grow in a garden or tub, flourishing from early spring onwards, and is sometimes sold in farmer's markets and farm shops.

1. Put the lentils in a medium pan, cover with cold water by about 5cm and add the garlic. Bring to the boil, then turn down the heat and simmer for 20–25 minutes, or until the lentils are tender.

2. Put the lemon juice and olive oil in a serving bowl. Drain the lentils and put in the dish. Season with salt and pepper, to taste; plenty of pepper is a good idea with lentils. Add three-quarters of the basil.

3. Turn the lentils over in the dressing to mix well. You can make the dish up to this point a day in advance and leave in the fridge, covered. Bring out of the fridge an hour or so before serving.

4. Scatter over the rest of the basil and the crumbled goat's cheese and serve at room temperature, with plenty of crusty bread.

COOK-AHEAD FENNEL & SAFFRON RISOTTO

SERVES **4**

- **1 tbsp** olive oil
- **2 banana shallots** or 3–4 ordinary ones, *finely chopped*
- **1 clove** garlic, *finely chopped*
- **1 bulb** of fennel, *trimmed & chopped into small pieces* (reserve any feathery fronds to scatter over the top)
- **200g** short-grain risotto rice
- **75ml** white wine
- **750ml** well-flavoured vegetable stock (fresh is best, or good instant)
- **about ½ tsp** saffron threads, *soaked in 2 tbsp warm water for 20 minutes*
- **30g** unsalted butter
- **50g** *finely grated* parmesan
- **3 tbsp** *roughly torn* basil or *finely chopped* chives
- **a squeeze** of lemon juice, to taste

There are friends who can sit easily beside you chatting while you stir a risotto; but it's not always straightforward to have people in the kitchen when trying to concentrate. And, alas, there are other times when the cook is alone in the kitchen, stirring the risotto, listening to laughter in the room next door. This cook-ahead dish makes an evening more relaxed and happy for all concerned, especially for a cook who is also the host. I got the idea for this risotto from Shaun Hill's cookbook *How to Cook Better*, which 'does wot it says on the tin' and shares much kitchen wisdom. His trick of partially cooking risotto in advance is just one of the useful tips in the book that I've adopted. I imagine many restaurants cook risotto this way to make the service a bit quicker.

1. Heat the oil in a large saucepan, add the chopped shallots, garlic and fennel and cook over a medium-low heat until soft (about 10 minutes).

2. Add the rice and stir around so it is coated in the oil, then cook for 4 minutes on a low heat, stirring every 30 seconds or so to stop it sticking to the bottom of the pan. Season with about ½ tsp flaky sea salt and a good amount of black pepper.

3. Pour in the wine and boil, briefly, to reduce slightly. Add 250ml of the stock along with the saffron and its soaking water. Bring to the boil. Cover and leave off the heat until the stock has been absorbed. At this point you can halt the cooking. Leave to cool, then cover and keep in the fridge if you are more than an hour in advance of finishing the cooking.

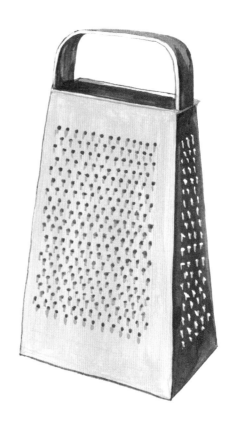

4. Around 10–15 minutes before you want to eat, add the rest of the stock to the rice, straight from the fridge. You can either do this all in one go, bring the liquid to the boil and then simmer, stirring occasionally, until the liquid has been absorbed by the rice. Or – if you want to chat to a friend by the stove – heat the liquid and add it to the rice gradually, as you do with an authentic risotto.

5. Stir in the butter, parmesan, herbs and lemon juice. Taste and adjust the seasoning if necessary. I serve a green salad afterwards, or you could have it alongside the risotto.

Saffron is a luxurious ingredient and its colour and flavour combine with the freshness of the basil and fennel to make this dish a summer treat. Saffron varies enormously in price and quality. Look out in Spanish specialist stores for good-value saffron, or get hold of some excellent British saffron (www.norfolksaffron.co.uk). Don't touch large 'bargain' bagfuls of saffron, which are likely to be adulterated. Good-quality saffron is more powerful and you will need to use less; too much can taste medicinal. Try a smaller amount first then add more, if necessary, next time you make the dish.

Use this method to cook any vegetable risotto up to a day in advance of eating – just keep it in the fridge, covered, once cooled. This is especially useful if you are coming back from work shortly before guests arrive.

HONEYED

TURNIPS

SERVES **4** AS A LIGHT MAIN COURSE;
8 AS PART OF A SPREAD

¨ **1 tbsp** basic olive oil
¨ **800g** turnips,
   *trimmed, peeled,
   left whole if small
   or cut into 4–5cm
   chunks if larger*

¨ **2 tbsp** honey
   (ideally a light one
   such as orange
   blossom or wildflower)
¨ **juice of 2** oranges
¨ **4 tbsp** *finely chopped
   chives*

Root vegetables are useful to One Pot cooking, providing carbohydrate substance to a dish. This is as true in summer as it is in winter. Turnips are a much under-rated root that are especially good when young, tender and juicy in early summer. The citrus honey glaze coats the turnips, giving a counterbalance to the vegetable's brassica tang, and their white flesh has a beautiful pearly gleam that echoes the shine of the honey.

1. Heat the oil in a large pan over a medium-low heat and add the turnips, ideally so they are more-or-less in a single layer. Add the honey and three-quarters of the orange juice. Season well with sea salt and black pepper.

2. Wet a piece of greaseproof paper, slightly larger than the diameter of the pan, and scrunch it up. Place over the turnips, tucking it down slightly over the sides. Bring the liquid to the boil, then cover with a lid, turn down the heat and cook slowly for 45 minutes, or until the turnips are nearly tender.

3. Remove the paper and turn the turnips over. Bring the liquid to the boil and reduce until it becomes thick and sticky, turning the turnips over again as they brown slightly.

4. Remove from the heat. Stir in the chopped chives and remaining orange juice, to taste. Serve warm or at room temperature.

To make this dish more substantial in a way that is meaty, cheesy or vegan, scatter over 10–12 roughly chopped slices of salami, 100g crumbled feta, or 100g toasted almonds – or two or more of these.

KOHLRABI WITH LEMON & POPPY SEEDS

SERVES 4 AS A LIGHT MAIN DISH;
8 AS PART OF A SPREAD

- **500–600g** kohlrabi
- **10** dried apricots
- **2 tbsp** olive oil
- **½** lemon, *finely grated zest & juice*
- **1 tbsp** poppy seeds
- **3 tbsp** *finely chopped dill*
- **100g** feta, *roughly crumbled* or 100g pistachio nuts, *roughly chopped*

Kohlrabi is an asteroid of a vegetable that catches the eye, but does not often drop into the shopping basket. This crunchy brassica is well worth cooking as I discovered when one arrived in my veg box and I needed to find a way to use it up. Now I seek out its strange pale-green form in markets and greengrocers.

Kohlrabi's best qualities are captured in this refreshing summer salad. What might look like a root is actually a swollen stem with a mild yet satisfying flavour that is reminiscent of a broccoli stalk, but with much more snap and sap. The juicy texture, in particular, is what makes this oddity a star.

Poppy seeds, like kohlrabi, are a popular ingredient in Germany and other northern European countries. You only need a tablespoonful for this salad and, since they contain oil, it is best to keep the packet sealed in the fridge or in a cool cupboard, using them up withing a few months. Bread, cakes and biscuits are the classic ways to do this, but they are also good sprinkled over salads, curries and homemade granola.

Dried cherries are a good alternative to dried apricots. Use 50–75g.

1. Trim the stems and base off the kohlrabi. If you are using a large one, peel it as well. Cut into 1cm slices, then cut the slices into thick matchsticks (1–2cm thick). Cut the apricots into slivers.

2. In a serving bowl, mix the olive oil, lemon zest and juice, poppy seeds and dill. Season with ¼ tsp flaky sea salt. Add the kohlrabi and toss well in the dressing so every matchstick gets a coating. Scatter over the feta or pistachios.

3. Chill in the fridge, covered, for at least 30 minutes. Taste before serving, adjusting the seasoning if necessary.

KEDGEREE

SERVES **6**

" **40g** butter
" **2 large** onions,
finely sliced
" **1** lemon, *finely grated
zest & juice*
" **2** bay leaves
" **600g** smoked haddock
" **200ml** milk
" **500ml** water
" **250g** basmati or other
long-grain white rice,
*soaked for 30 minutes
& drained*
" **100g** frozen peas
(optional)
" **150g** cold-water
prawns, *cooked &
peeled*
" **3 medium** eggs
" **6 tbsp** *finely chopped*
herbs (I like flat-leaf
parsley, perhaps mixed
with dill & chives)

spice mix:
" **4** cardamom pods
" **1 tsp** cumin seeds
" **1 tsp** coriander seeds
" **½ tsp** turmeric

Eaten hot or warm, kedgeree is great
for supper, lunch or the classiest
kind of brunch. Instead of the usual
curry powder, this recipe uses a light
and fragrant mix of freshly ground
spices. For a short-cut, use 1 tsp or
so of a good-quality garam masala.

1. Melt the butter in a large pan over a
medium-high and sweat the sliced onions,
seasoned with a pinch of salt. After about
5 minutes, turn the heat down to medium-
low and continue to cook for another
15 minutes, stirring occasionally, until the
onions are soft and sweet.

2. To make the spice mix, remove the seeds
from the cardamom pods and roughly grind
with the cumin and coriander seeds. Stir the
ground spices and turmeric into the cooked
onions. Add the lemon zest along with the
bay leaves. Grind over a decent amount of
black pepper.

Hot-smoked salmon is a neat and simple
replacement for the smoked haddock.
No need to cook it; just flake and stir it in
at the end. However, it means there is
slightly less flavour in the cooking milk.

GREAT FOR SUPPER, LUNCH OR A CLASSY BRUNCH

3. Place the haddock on top of the cooked onions, skin-side up. Pour over the milk and water and cover with a lid. Bring to the boil, then turn the heat down and simmer for 5–7 minutes, until just cooked. Turn off the heat. Carefully remove the haddock from the pan and leave to one side until it becomes cool enough to handle.

4. Meanwhile, stir the rice into the pan, making sure it is well mixed into the onions. If using, also add the peas at this point. Bring the liquid back to the boil, then turn down the heat and simmer, covered, for about 12 minutes, until the rice is cooked. Stir the rice every so often and, if the liquid is absorbed before the rice is cooked, add a big splosh of hot water. Add the prawns to the pot right at the end so they warm through.

5. While the rice is cooking, boil the eggs to your liking. Some (like me) prefer them firmer than others. Do them for 6 minutes for soft-in-the-centre-of-the-yolk; 7–8 minutes for set. Once cooked, put the eggs into cold water until cool enough peel, then cut into quarters.

6. Take the skin off the haddock and remove any stray bones. Break the fish up into medium-sized pieces.

7. Stir the chopped herbs and lemon juice, to taste, into the cooked rice. Very carefully add the fish to the rice so you keep the pieces whole. Check the seasoning. Lay the eggs on top. If this is for lunch or supper, serve with a green salad.

EASY THREE-PEPPER SALAD

SERVES PLENTY AS A SIDE DISH,
SANDWICH FILLER OR PIZZA TOPPING

" **150ml** olive oil
" **6** peppers, *deseeded & finely sliced* (ideally different colours depending on what's cheap & good)
" **2 large** onions, *finely sliced*
" **4 cloves** garlic, *finely chopped*
" **a large pinch** of caster sugar

Big bags of colourful peppers are often good value in greengrocers and supermarkets. I used to always grill them and keep a bowlful, stored in oil, in the fridge to be added to salads, sandwiches or served alongside a main course. Then I discovered that you don't necessarily have to go to the trouble of all that roasting and peeling to get the soft flesh and luscious pepper-flavoured oil. This is the easy route to one of the most useful and colourful of summer standbys. Bring up to room temperature before serving, as befits Mediterranean food.

Cubes of root ginger (about 5cm square) and a couple of dried chilli peppers can be added to the mix at the start and removed once cool.

Basil is another excellent addition to the end dish, after cooking, and adds its fragrance to the oil.

You can cook this in a covered pot in a medium oven (150°C–170°C/Gas 2–3), when cooking something else to make the most use of the oven's heat.

1. Put all the ingredients into a medium-sized pan, reserving two of the chopped cloves of garlic for later. Cook over a low heat for 1½ hours, covered, stirring occasionally.

2. Stir in the other 2 cloves of chopped garlic. Season with salt, pepper and a large pinch of caster sugar.

3. Serve at room temperature.

POTATO & SMOKED SALMON SALAD

SERVES **4**

- **600g** Charlotte or other firm salad potato, *cut in half if large*
- **a little** olive oil
- **1–2 tsp** white wine (optional)
- **150g** smoked salmon, *cut into strips*

honey dressing:
- **2 tsp** honey (ideally truffle honey)
- **½ clove** garlic, *crushed*
- **juice of 1** lemon, *finely grated* zest of ½
- **¼ tsp** truffle salt (optional)
- **3 tbsp** good olive oil
- **3 tbsp** *finely chopped* flat-leaf parsley

A good potato salad is far more than a side dish. The salad moves from delicious to wonderful if you happen to have any truffle products in your kitchen. Rather than using truffle oil, I find truffle salt and truffle-infused honey are great ways to add this sexy feral flavour to all manner of foods, without breaking the bank completely.

Truffle salt and truffle honey are expensive, but much better value than truffle oil and clearly far less pricey than truffles themselves. Truffle salt is wonderful in scrambled eggs and to season mushroom pasta sauces. Truffle honey sexes up any kind of salad dressing or can be drizzled over cheese.

Dressing hot potatoes with white wine is a useful trick I've picked up from French cookery and can be used for any type of potato salad. Sometimes I simply add the wine to the spuds, then toss them in good olive oil and chopped herbs and season well with sea salt and pepper.

1. Put the potatoes in a small pan and cover with water. Add 1 tsp ordinary salt, bring to the boil then turn down the heat and simmer for 10–15 minutes, or until tender.

2. In a small bowl, put the honey, garlic and lemon juice. Season with the truffle salt (or substitute regular fine salt) and black pepper. Stir together so the honey starts to dissolve. Whisk in the olive oil and lemon zest. Leave while you get on with the rest of the dish.

3. Drain the potatoes and cut into large chunks (3–4cm). Put in a serving bowl. Sprinkle over the white wine, if you have it open. You can do this up to 2 hours or so in advance of serving.

4. At least 30 minutes and up to 1 hour before serving, put the smoked salmon into the salad bowl with the potatoes. Whisk up the dressing and stir in the parsley. Pour the dressing into the bowl and carefully turn the potatoes and salmon in the garlicky honey dressing. Season with a little more salt and pepper if necessary. Serve at room temperature.

BUTTERNUT SQUASH & GOAT'S CHEESE TART

SERVES **4–6**

¨ **2 medium** eggs,
plus 4 yolks
¨ **100ml** double cream
¨ **100ml** milk
¨ **2 tbsp** *finely
chopped* chives
¨ **3** spring onions,
finely chopped
**the bulbous half of
a medium** butternut
squash (about 450g),
*peeled & cut into
1cm semi-circles*
¨ **150g** log of goat's
cheese, *cut into
1cm circles*

pastry:
¨ **100g** plain flour,
plus extra to dust
¨ **50g** cold unsalted
butter, *cut into
small cubes*
¨ **1 medium** egg,
beaten

Colourful and attractive, this
summery tart is substantial enough
to be a main course or lunch. You
could serve it just with a salad, but
I also add potatoes, simply boiled
with mint leaves, which makes
the dish go further.

1. First make the pastry. Put the flour, ½ tsp
fine salt and the butter in a bowl and use the
tips of your fingers to rub the butter into the
flour. When it resembles breadcrumbs, add
the egg to the bowl and, using first the blade
of a table knife, then your fingertips, stir it
in, gradually gathering the crumbs until they
form one mass. Roll this together into a ball
and knead lightly to make it cohesive. Wrap
in greaseproof paper or clingfilm and leave
in the fridge for at least 30 minutes – it'll
keep here for up to 2 days.

2. Dust the work surface with flour and roll
the pastry out to a circle approximately
30cm in diameter. Pick the pastry up by
rolling it round your rolling pin and lower
it into a tart tin with a detachable base
that's about 25cm in diameter. Push lightly
but firmly into the tin. Rest in the fridge
for 15 minutes to 1 day (if doing this well in
advance, cover the pastry with cling film).

A SUMMERY TART FOR LUNCH

3. Preheat the oven to 190°C/Gas 5 and place a baking sheet on the shelf to heat through – this will help cook the base of the tart properly. Put a piece of baking parchment bigger than the base of the tart on top of the pastry, then cover with a layer of baking beans (dedicated clay ones or dried beans you can reuse for this purpose). Put the pastry case on the hot tray in the oven for 10 minutes. Remove the parchment and beans and cook the pastry for another 5 minutes to colour slightly.

4. Meanwhile, in a mixing bowl, whisk together the 2 whole eggs and 4 yolks with the cream and milk. Stir in the chopped chives and spring onions. Season with a pinch of fine sea salt and a good grind of pepper.

5. Remove the pastry case from the oven. Lay the pieces of squash in a circle around the edge of the case. Lay the slices of goat's cheese in a smaller circle inside the circle of squash. Put the final pieces of cheese and squash in the middle of the tart. Carefully pour the herby custard mixture over the squash and cheese. Grind some more pepper over the top.

6. Cook the tart in the centre of the oven for 35–40 minutes, until the squash is tender and the top is browning nicely. If the pastry is getting too brown, cover this outside rim with a piece of foil.

7. Serve hot, warm or at room temperature, with potatoes and a salad.

PROVENCAL TOMATO TART

SERVES **4–6**

- **1 x 250g** sheet of butter puff pastry
- plain flour, to dust (optional)
- **150g** pesto or 190g thick, ready-made tomato-based pasta sauce
- **250g** tomatoes, ordinary or cherry (the ripest you can find)
- **30g** anchovies, *drained & cut into 2cm pieces*
- **about 15** good-quality black olives, *pitted & roughly chopped*
- **8** basil leaves, *roughly torn* (optional)

Best made with ripe tomatoes and good-quality pesto, this intense tart nonetheless works fine with more standard fare. I sometimes even make it with the jar of pasta sauce on special offer in a shop and some just-about-okay tomatoes (though not the *most* wan). What you must use, however, is good puff pastry made with butter.

1. Preheat the oven to 220°C/Gas 7. If it isn't ready-rolled, roll out the puff pastry to A4 size on a floured work surface. Place on a baking sheet. With the tip of a sharp knife, score a line around the outside of the pastry about 2cm from the edge. Spread the pesto or other sauce in a thick layer over the pastry, up to the line.

2. Cut the tomatoes into slices around 2cm thick, or cut cherry tomatoes in half. Place on top of the pastry within the scored line, skin-side up if using cherry tomatoes and slightly overlapping if using standard. Scatter the anchovies and olives over the top of the tart and grind over some black pepper.

3. Bake in the preheated oven for 25 minutes, or until the pastry is browned and the tomatoes are giving out their juices. If you like, scatter over some torn-up basil.

4. Cut into 4 or 6 pieces, depending on appetites and whatever else you are serving. This is an intensely flavoured, rich tart and you can get away with a small piece alongside a good potato salad or crusty bread and lots of greenery.

SPANAKOPITA

SERVES **8–12**

" **1kg** spinach, or a mix of greens
" **3 medium** eggs
" **200g** feta cheese
" **25g bunch** dill, *fronds chopped*
" **25g bunch** chives, *finely chopped* (or use 15g mint)
" **¼ tsp** *freshly grated* nutmeg or ground mace
" **75g** melted butter or 3–4 tbsp olive oil
" **270g** filo pastry

This Greek greens pie is a handy way to provide vegetables as part of a summer spread and a good dish for vegetarians. Vary the cheese, herbs and greens as you like.

1. Preheat the oven to 160°C/Gas 3. Wash the spinach, removing any large stalks, and roughly chop. Put in a large pan, cover with a lid and cook over a medium heat for a few minutes, until wilted, stirring so it cooks evenly. Drain well in a colander, pressing out the water thoroughly with the back of a spoon, then place in a large bowl.

2. Crack the eggs into the greens, crumble in the feta, add the herbs and season with salt, pepper and nutmeg. Mix everything well (I find this is best done using my hands once the leaves are cool enough).

3. Brush a baking tray (about 30 x 20cm) with butter or olive oil and lay a sheet of filo pastry on it. Brush this with butter or oil and lay another one on top, brushing the top of this with the fat. Spread the greens mixture on top. Cover with the rest of the pastry sheets, buttering or oiling them as you go.

4. Put the pie in the oven to bake for 45–50 minutes, or until the top is nice and brown. Cut into 9 large pieces, or 12 smaller ones and serve alongside other dishes or as a main course with salads.

Chopped spring onions are another good addition to the pie, added along with the cheese.

Sesame seeds or nigella seeds are good to scatter on top. Use 3 tbsp sesame seeds or ½ tbsp nigella seeds.

Other greens can also be used. When making this in the winter, I use half spinach, half kale, with the stalks cut out and the leaves roughly chopped before cooking.

SUMMER
FISH TAGINE

SERVES **6**

- **1.5kg** firm fish, skinned, eg huss or monkfish, *cut into big chunks (about 6cm)*
- **3** peppers, ideally different colours, *deseeded & cut into 2cm strips*
- **6 large** vine tomatoes, *roughly chopped*
- **3** carrots, *cut into thick batons*
- **2 stalks** celery, *cut into batons*
- **18** green olives
- **2** preserved lemons, *pithy centres removed, skin finely chopped* or 2½ tbsp lemon juice
- **2** bay leaves
- **3 cloves** garlic, *finely chopped*
- **3 tbsp** *finely chopped* flat-leaf parsley
- **1½ tbsp** *finely chopped* coriander leaf
- **1 tbsp** honey
- **½–1 tbsp** harissa (optional but good)
- **1 tbsp** *chopped* mixed coriander & parsley leaves, to garnish

spice blend:
- **2 tsp** paprika
- **2½ tsp** turmeric
- **1 tsp** ground ginger
- **2 tsp** ground cumin
- **3 tbsp** olive oil
- **4 tbsp** (60ml) water

Here's a celebration of Moroccan-spiced fish and the sweet flavour and colours of summer vegetables, based on a dish that I ate in the coastal town of Essaouira. The tagine can be made the night before eating and reheated. The fish cooks for longer than normal and is almost a seasoning for the vegetables, as well as an ingredient.

1. Mix together everything for the spice blend in an ovenproof sauté pan with a lid. If you have time, marinate the chunks of fish in this spice mixture for an hour, or at least while you prepare the vegetables.

2. Preheat the oven to 180°C/Gas 4. As you chop the vegetables, add them to the pot with the fish and its spice marinade. Add the olives, preserved lemon or lemon juice, the bay leaves, garlic, chopped parsley and coriander, honey and 1 tsp flaky salt. Mix everything around gently with your hands.

A CELEBRATION OF MOROCCAN-SPICED FISH

3. Put the pot in the oven, with the lid on, for 45 minutes. Gently stir everything around and cook, lid on still, for another 15 minutes. Take the lid off and cook for a final 15 minutes, after giving the mixture another stir. The dish is ready when the vegetables are tender.

4. If you like, stir in the harissa (if some guests don't like hot food, serve them first, then stir in proportionately less) and scatter with a final flourish of chopped herbs. Serve with couscous or bread.

To make this an all-in-one-pot for four people, cut down the ingredients by a third and include 4 medium waxy potatoes, peeled and cut into 4cm chunks, added along with the other veg.

Adapt the vegetables to whatever you have to hand. This is also good made in the winter with pumpkin or squash.

A teaspoonful of ras al hanout, the classic Moroccan spice blend with rose petals, is a good addition to the spice mix.

Huss is a useful (and cheap) fish to use as it keeps firm. Instead of fiddly bones, the flesh falls away from a simple cartilage spine. A single fish is about right for six. To get big chunks, cut straight through the spine with a heavy knife. You can use any other fish instead, but if it is soft and flaky then add it just in the final 15 minutes of cooking.

FATTOUSH

**SERVES 4 AS A MAIN COURSE;
8 AS A SIDE DISH**

- **200g** sliced bread (dry is fine), *cut into 2cm strips*
- **1** red onion, *finely sliced*
- **juice of 1** lemon
- **½ small clove** garlic, *crushed*
- **50ml** good olive oil
- **1** cucumber, *chopped into chunks*
- **1** cos or 2 baby gem lettuce, *cut into thick slices*
- **12** radishes, *trimmed & finely sliced*
- **2 tbsp** *finely chopped* mint
- **6 tbsp** *chopped* flat-leaf parsley
- **4 tbsp** coriander leaf, *chopped* (optional)
- **8** ripe tomatoes, *cut into chunks* (quality matters in this dish; get the best you can)
- **1½–2 tbsp** sumac

This refreshing and substantial Middle Eastern salad is a great lunch or light supper dish and a great way to use up stale bread. It also works well as part of a summer spread or as an accompaniment to a piece of meat, or fish or a vegetarian main.

1. Preheat the oven to 150°C/Gas 2 and put the strips of bread on a baking tray in the oven for 10 minutes. This will dry out the bread, making it crisp enough to hold its own in the salad without going soggy.

2. Put the sliced onion in a serving bowl with the lemon juice, crushed garlic and olive oil and leave for at least 10 minutes to soften.

3. Chop up the rest of the ingredients as directed, and add them to the bowl, but don't mix into the dressing just yet and leave the bread to one side.

4. Shortly before eating, toss everything together, including the bread, sprinkle the sumac on top and serve.

The bread must be crunchy in a good fattoush, writes Anissa Helou in *Lebanese Food*. Instead of lemon in the dressing, she uses 3 tbsp of sumac, mixed with the oil, for a salad that feeds four.

Pitta bread, grilled or toasted, is good in the salad, which is useful as it goes stale quickly and needs eating up.

POTTED
SHRIMPS

SERVES **6**

" **200g** unsalted butter
" **1** lemon, *finely grated zest* plus a squeeze of juice

" **¼ tsp** mace
" **¼ tsp** cayenne pepper, to taste
" **200g** peeled shrimps

In the days of larders, all manner of meat and fish were potted as a traditional way of preserving food under a layer of fat. Nowadays, we mostly eat refrigerated potted shrimp, but I still like to make my own as it is super-easy and fun to play around with the seasoning. Once or twice I have laboriously peeled shrimps myself, but must admit this is a kitchen task too far for me and now buy them ready-peeled from a fishmonger.

Put all the shrimps in one dish or more, as you like. The ramekins look more elegant and you can freeze one or two to have on hand for quick suppers.

Melt potted shrimps onto pasta with a squeeze of lemon juice and some finely chopped herbs. This excellent 'almost-ready' meal is quickly sorted if you have potted shrimps in the freezer or fridge.

Potting is a form of preservation but I'm always a touch careful with shellfish and eat these within 3 days if refrigerated, or otherwise freeze them.

1. Melt the butter and pour into a bowl. Add the lemon zest, a squeeze of juice and the other seasonings, making it more or less spicy as you like. If your butter is unsalted, add ¼ tsp flaky sea salt. Stir in the shrimps and coat well with the butter and spices. Warm through gently for 1 minute to help release their flavour into the butter.

2. Pour the mixture into a small serving dish or divide between 6 ramekins. Cover with clingfilm and refrigerate when cool.

3. Take the pots out of the fridge shortly before serving to soften slightly and serve with toast or good bread.

TERRINE

SERVES **8**

" **600g** pork shoulder
" **6 chicken thighs,**
without skin or bone
" **8 rashers** smoked,
streaky bacon,
finely sliced
" **250g** chicken livers
" **5 cloves** garlic,
finely chopped
" **2 tbsp** brandy
" **50ml** white wine
" **1** lemon,
finely grated zest

seasoning mix
(to be played around
with endlessly):
" **1 tsp** coriander seeds
" **1 tsp** juniper berries
" **½ tsp** chilli flakes
" **½ tsp** *coarsely ground*
black pepper
" **½ tsp** *finely grated*
nutmeg
" **2 tsp** *finely chopped*
sage
" **1 tsp** thyme leaves

A terrine is one of those cook-ahead dishes that positively improves with a day or two in the fridge, making it a convenient One Pot for summer entertaining. Fancy, layered ones in restaurants look good, but can lack oomph in the taste department. This homemade terrine isn't designed to win a Michelin star, but sure delivers on flavour.

Cheaper cuts, full of flavour and with enough succulent fat, are part of the essence of a terrine. I put together this combination (two good-value parts of pig and chicken) through a bargain 'three for £10' offer on higher welfare meat in a supermarket, and you'll also find them well-priced in a butcher's.

Seasoning is key to a terrine. This is a matter of the cook's taste and can be played around with endlessly. The combination of some strong green herbs, such as sage and thyme, and an interesting mixture of spices, plus a few slugs of tasty booze are what give the dish its character, with some citrus zest for freshness. I think you need a fair amount of salt, though some will want to use less.

Streaky bacon can be used to line the loaf tin and wrap over the top of the terrine to give a smarter appearance and extra flavour.

1. First make the seasoning mix. Put any whole spices – in my mixture, the coriander and juniper – in a mortar and crush with a pestle so they are roughly ground (they don't have to be pulverized). Mix in the chilli flakes, black pepper, nutmeg, sage, thyme and 2 tsp fine sea salt. You can also just grind everything together in a spice grinder, though its best to coarsely grind the peppercorns separately through a pepper grinder and cut up the sage.

2. Chop the pork shoulder and chicken thighs to ½cm dice. Though laborious, this is best done by hand to get the right texture, but you could put them through the large holes of a mincer (a butcher will do this for you), or whizz the meat up in a food processor if feeling pushed for time. I tend to cut the chicken by hand and whizz up the pork.

3. Tip the meat into a large bowl and add the finely chopped bacon. Trim the chicken livers of any white sinew and blood, chop into ½cm pieces and add to the bowl.

4. Add the seasoning mix, garlic, brandy, wine and lemon zest to the meat. Use both hands to mix everything together. Take a few minutes over this, using your splayed fingers to thoroughly combine the ingredients and massage the flavourings into the meats. Cover the bowl with clingfilm and leave in the fridge overnight, or at least for a few hours, to allow the flavours to develop.

5. Preheat the oven to 190°C/Gas 5. Put the meat into a large loaf pan or oblong terrine dish and cover tightly with foil, or with a lid on the terrine dish. Place on a baking tray in the oven for 45 minutes. Remove the foil or lid and cook for another 15 minutes or so, until brown on top.

6. Remove from the oven and leave to cool as quickly as possible by putting the base of the dish in a shallow dish of cold water.

7. Leave the terrine, covered, in the fridge for at least a day if you can; the flavours really do develop. You can make the terrine up to 3 or 4 days in advance.

8. Serve the terrine in thick slices with toast or good bread, some pickles and a salad, or with a gratin and a salad for a more substantial meal. I tend to have it with boiled and buttered new potatoes. Something about cold meat and hot potatoes is especially good.

EXPLORE
THE
WORLD

FAR AWAY CAN BE

CLOSE TO HOME

IN THE KITCHEN,

THE WORLD IS

YOUR ONE POT

The far away can be close to home in the kitchen. From East Asia to South India, from New Orleans to Hanoi, from Switzerland to Brazil, from Mexico to the Philippines: the world is your One Pot.

Happily, you don't necessarily need exotic ingredients to set out on these journeys. Many of the recipes in this chapter require nothing more unusual than root ginger and storecupboard spices. What makes them special is a different take on the familiar, or interesting One Pot techniques.

Other recipes in this chapter cater for cooks curious to try different flavours, and include ingredients that may need to be found further afield. As well as shopping online, it is well worth visiting a good Italian deli, Asian supermarket or Middle-Eastern greengrocer – whatever you have nearby or want to seek out. Such places are Aladdin's caves for the tastebuds and good to explore for an inspiring stock-up of stores.

This chapter contains most of the more complex dishes in the book. I make these longer dishes at the weekend or on holiday, when I have time to enjoy the ride and can fill my kitchen with the ingredients, scents, sounds and tastes of journeys near and far.

One Pots enable you to understand and enjoy the recipes from other home kitchens around the world. This is real food, not fancy restaurant fare; taste travel rather than tourism.

SRI LANKAN
BREAKFAST
EGG HOPPER

MAKES **6** HOPPERS
(**1–2** PER PERSON)

" **200ml** coconut cream
" **½ tsp** dried yeast
(slightly less if
easy-blend)
" **1 tsp** caster sugar
" **150g** rice flour

" **250ml–275ml** water
" **6** eggs, plus 2 egg
whites
" vegetable oil
" *chopped* coriander
leaf, to finish

Hoppers are Sri Lankan fermented rice pancakes that provide a bouncy-textured starch for a meal. Add an egg to each one and you have a complete one-pan dish. They are traditionally eaten for breakfast, though I more often serve them for brunch or lunch. They're also excellent with a dollop of leftover curry.

This sweet and savoury combination is typical of East Asia. The hoppers are also delicious eaten as a sweet pudding or brunch dish, with just a squeeze of lime juice and a sprinkle of brown sugar instead of the fried egg.

1. Put the coconut cream, dried yeast and sugar in a bowl and leave in a warm place to ferment for 45 minutes (you will start to see the odd bubble appear).

2. Mix the rice flour into the yeast mixture and whisk, adding enough of the water to get the mixture to the thickness of double cream. Cover and leave for 2 hours in a warm place, so it continues to bubble up slightly (this is a gentle fermentation so it won't rise). If you are making this the night before, leave it in the fridge overnight, covered, and bring it up to room temperature before cooking.

EXCELLENT WITH A DOLLOP OF LEFTOVER CURRY

3. Just before cooking, whisk the two egg whites until foamy, but not stiff. Fold these into the batter with ¼ tsp fine sea salt.

4. Heat a small, non-stick frying pan on a high heat. Wipe the pan with vegetable oil and pour in a small ladleful (about 60ml) of batter. Swirl around quickly to cover the base of the pan, place a lid on top and steam the pancake for a minute or so, until the centre has set.

5. Crack an egg into the centre of the hopper and cover with the lid again. Let it cook for about 2 minutes, or until the egg is done to your liking. (If, like me, you don't like runny yolks, flip the hopper over to let it cook for a minute on the other side.)

6. Sprinkle over some coriander and a grinding of pepper. Either serve immediately, or keep warm in a low oven until you have cooked all the hoppers.

BEEF
RENDANG

SERVES **6–8**

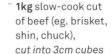

" **1kg** slow-cook cut
of beef (eg. brisket,
shin, chuck),
cut into 3cm cubes
" **4** cardamom pods,
*seeds removed &
roughly crushed*
" **1 tbsp** coriander seeds
" **½ tbsp** cumin seeds
" **1** cinnamon stick,
broken in half

" **1 x 400ml** tin coconut
milk (a good Asian
brand is best)
" **2** kaffir lime leaves
" **2 tbsp** palm sugar (or
light muscovado sugar)
" **2 tbsp** tamarind purée
" **100g** dessicated
coconut (fresh, or
frozen, grated even
better)
" **a squeeze** of lime
juice, if needed

This Indonesian dish comes together
in classic One Pot style, the flavours
combining and complementing
each other to make a satisfying
whole. Beef rendang is one of my
all-time favourite curries: coconut-
rich and deeply savoury. The recipe
originated as a means of preserving
meat and this is why the curry is
served as a dryish dollop, more as a
tasty seasoning to rice than a sauce.

I learnt this particular short-cut
method – it normally takes 8 hours
– at a course run by Fran, a French
woman who picked up cooking tips
from her East Asian in-laws and
now teaches them in East London
(www.lapancooking.com).

1. Put the beef in a medium-large pot and
cover with water. Cover with a lid, bring
to the boil, then turn down the heat and
simmer, still covered, for 2 hours.

2. Meanwhile, make the curry paste. Put all the
ingredients into a small blender and whizz
to get a smooth, aromatic paste.

3. Drain the beef, reserving the stock. (You may
or may not need this for the dish. If not, it is
deliciously savoury and worth saving for a
soup or sauce.) Wash the pan and put it back
on a low heat. Add the spice paste and cook
for 7 minutes or so, stirring to stop it burning.

4. Add the meat and the whole spices – the
cardamom, coriander seeds, cumin seeds
and cinnamon. Season with 1 tbsp flaky sea
salt (it takes about 1½ tbsp in total, but add
the salt in two stages as the curry reduces
down considerably.) Fry for 5 minutes,
stirring often, until the spices smell toasty.

curry paste:
- ¨ **2** onions, *roughly chopped*
- ¨ **10cm** root ginger, *peeled & roughly chopped*
- ¨ **8 cloves** garlic, *roughly chopped*
- ¨ **2 stalks** lemongrass, *finely chopped*
- ¨ **1–3 tsp** chilli flakes, to taste (2 is right for me but 3 makes it more intense)
- ¨ **1½ tbsp** turmeric
- ¨ **120ml** vegetable oil

5. Add the coconut milk, lime leaves, sugar and tamarind. The meat should be just covered with liquid – if not, add some of your beefy stock. Simmer, uncovered, until the chunks of meat are breaking apart and the sauce has reduced down – about 45 minutes. Stir from time to time to stop it catching on the bottom of the pot.

6. Meanwhile, toast the coconut in a dry frying pan over a low heat. Stir occasionally for the first couple of minutes, and then stir more-or-less constantly once the coconut begins to brown. Once it is all a nutty colour – but not so dark it is bitter-burnt – take off the heat and leave to one side.

7. When the beef is soft, stir in the toasted coconut. Simmer for another 10 minutes, stirring often, until it has reduced down slightly. It'll look like a mush rather than having chunks of meat. Taste and add more salt if necessary. I sometimes add a squeeze of lime juice at the end to get a bit more of a tart-sweet balance.

8. Serve with rice and salads. This is an intense curry and you need just a small dollop on each plate.

Toasting the coconut gives the rendang its characteristic colour and taste. Do this carefully as the coconut burns quickly, but do it thoroughly as you want the curry to have a nice dark colour and depth of flavour.

The traditional method of making beef rendang is to cook the meat with the spices and coconut milk for 8 hours, keeping a constant eye that it doesn't burn. This method, cooking the meat first, is relatively quick and easy. I tend to cook the meat, make the spice paste and toast the coconut the day before, to spread out the cooking process.

Palm sugar is the Asian version of maple syrup: boiled-down, concentrated sap. You can buy it in hard lumps or easy-to-use granules. Coconut palm sugar is especially delicious, but all varieties are special and worth seeking out to use in East Asian cooking. Jaggery, often made from cane sugar, is an Indian substitute.

If you want to make more of a saucy curry, stir in some of the beef stock at the end of cooking, bring to the boil for a couple of minutes, then simmer until it has the consistency you want.

JANSSON'S
TEMPTATION

SERVES **6–8**

˝ **1 kg** potatoes
(a firmer red-skinned
variety such as
Desirée is best)
˝ **2** red onions,
finely sliced
˝ **2 cloves** garlic,
finely chopped

˝ **2 x 50g** tins of
anchovies, *drained
& chopped*
˝ **25g** dill, *finely chopped*
˝ **1** lemon,
finely grated zest
˝ **75g** butter
˝ **400ml** whipping cream

This Swedish classic, traditionally made with plump, pickled Swedish anchovies, is also great with the tinned or bottled type that are such a handy storecupboard standby. This is a special accompaniment to a slice of meat or fish but it is most delicious on its own with a salad or some oven-dried tomatoes (see page 113). This recipe has become a favourite of my book group, who report that it is gobbled up by teens who don't normally touch anchovies.

1. Preheat the oven to 190°C/Gas 5. Peel the potatoes if you wish; I don't for this dish and just give them a scrub. Thinly slice the potatoes and cut them into matchsticks. Place in a large bowl.

2. Add the onions, garlic, anchovies, dill and lemon zest to the potatoes. Season generously with 1 tsp flaky sea salt and plenty of freshly ground black pepper.

3. Smear half the butter on the bottom of a sauté pan or 23cm square baking dish. Tip the potato mixture into the dish. Pour over the whipping cream and dot the top with the rest of the butter.

4. Put on a baking tray, in case the cream bubbles over the top, and bake for 1 hour 15 minutes, until the potatoes are cooked and the top is browned and crisp in parts, covering with foil at the end if necessary.

PEPPERPOT

SERVES **6**

- **700g** lean stewing beef, *cut into 3cm pieces*
- **750ml** beef stock (instant is fine)
- **3 sprigs** thyme
- **5cm piece** root ginger, *peeled & finely chopped*
- **2** onions, *finely chopped*
- **2 cloves** garlic, *finely chopped*
- **½–1** red chilli, *de-seeded & finely chopped* (ideally Scotch Bonnet)
- **2** bay leaves
- **6** allspice berries
- **1 x 400g** tin butter beans, *drained*
- **1 x 400ml** tin coconut milk
- **500g** sweet potato, *peeled & cut into 4cm cubes*
- **½ medium** butternut squash (about 500g), *peeled & cut into medium chunks*
- **6** spring onions, *roughly chopped*
- **200g** baby spinach, *washed*
- **1 handful** coriander leaf, *roughly chopped*

Like many One Pot dishes, this Jamaican classic is even better eaten the day after making. It's great to have in your repertoire as an alternative beef stew for cold nights.

Yam and pumpkin are authentic Jamaican additions to the root vegetables and a good substitute for either the squash or potato.

Dumplings are often added to the pepperpot. A Jamaican friend told me how the neighbouring households of his grandmother and aunt would share a pot for the stew, but add their own 'house-style' dumplings, one an indented disc, the other with twisted ends.

1. Put all the ingredients apart from the sweet potato, squash, spring onions, spinach and coriander into a large pot with a lid. Season with ½ tsp flaky sea salt. Bring to the boil over a high heat and skim off any scum that rises. Turn the heat down, cover and simmer for 15 minutes.

2. Add the sweet potato, squash, spring onions and spinach to the pot. You may need to add the spinach in 2 or 3 batches, stirring each one into the stew as it collapses.

3. Continue to cook over a low heat for another 45 minutes, uncovered, stirring occasionally, until the beef is tender. Check the seasoning and add more salt if necessary. Serve in big bowls with the coriander scattered on top.

BROWN DOWN
CHICKEN

SERVES **6**

- **12** skinless chicken thighs on the bone
- **3 tbsp** vegetable or olive oil
- **4 tbsp** granulated sugar
- **juice of 2** limes, plus 1 lime to serve
- **300g** long-grain rice
- **750ml** just-boiled water
- **200g** baby spinach leaves
- **2 tbsp** Japanese soy sauce (1½ if stronger Chinese soy sauce)
- **80g bunch** of coriander
- if you like it hot-hot-HOT, the rest of the ½ red chilli left over from the marinade, *finely chopped*

marinade:
- **3 cloves** garlic, *crushed*
- **6** spring onions, *cut into 2cm lengths, including the green part*
- stalks from the bunch of coriander, *finely chopped*
- **2 tsp** thyme leaves
- **1 tbsp** Japanese soy sauce
- **½** red chilli, *deseeded & finely chopped* (ideally Scotch Bonnet)
- **8** allspice berries, *lightly crushed*, or 2 star anise

'Brown down' is a traditional Jamaican technique that uses a little caramelised sugar and plenty of nice spice to make a dish that is full of Caribbean sass: sweet and hot is a party for the tastebuds. I've added rice to give the dish more substance but you can also just simmer the chicken in its brown down sauce (include the marinade) and serve any accompaniments separately.

1. Mix together the marinade ingredients in a shallow dish with ½ tsp sea salt. Add the chicken and coat well. If you have time, cover and leave in the fridge for at least 30 minutes or overnight.

2. Put a large pot with a lid on a medium-low heat. Add the oil, then sprinkle over the sugar. Let the sugar dissolve and cook until it starts to brown (about 6 minutes; but it depends on your pot and heat source so keep a close eye on it). Gently draw a wooden spoon through the sugar occasionally to help it dissolve.

A DISH FULL OF CARIBBEAN SASS

3. Scrape the marinade off the chicken and reserve. Place the chicken in the pan, turn the heat down to low and cover. Leave to cook for 10 minutes, then turn the chicken over, add the lime juice and cook for another 10 minutes, lid on.

4. Add the rice, just-boiled water and reserved marinade. Stir well. Put the lid back on and turn up the heat. Bring to the boil, then lower the heat and cook for about 15 minutes, or until the water has been absorbed and the rice is nearly cooked.

5. Turn off the heat and stir in the spinach. Cover and leave for another 10 minutes. Stir in the soy sauce and the final flourish of chopped coriander leaf, along with the rest of the chilli, finely chopped, if you want a bit more heat.

6. Serve the brown down chicken with a slice of lime for squeezing over the whole dish.

GOULASH

SERVES **5–6**

" **2 tbsp** good-quality
    lard, goose fat or
    olive oil
" **1kg** chuck, or other
    braising beef,
    cut into 5cm chunks
" **2** onions, *sliced*
" **1 clove** garlic,
    finely chopped
" **1 tsp** caraway seeds

" **2 tbsp** paprika
" **1 tbsp** tomato purée
" **250g** tomatoes,
    chopped
" **200g** roasted peppers
    (either from a jar
    or homemade),
    cut into thick strips
" **150ml** sour cream

Goulash is the sort of dish debased by school dinner hell, but it's time to reclaim its qualities and banish thoughts of watery slop and mean gristle. Proper Hungarian food has a sophisticated flamboyance that is achieved by getting the details right. In particular, it is important to use good fat and a decent amount of paprika.

Paprika is made from ground-up, dried red peppers and varies in heat and flavour. The Hungarians have 8 grades of paprika, such is their devotion to the spice. For this dish you can either use one of the milder forms, such as the *édesnemes* or 'noble sweet', or the generic paprika sold in supermarkets. For a hotter goulash, use hot paprika, or standard paprika with a pinch of chilli powder added.

1. Preheat the oven to 170°C/Gas 3. Melt the lard or goose fat in a heavy-based pot with a lid over a medium-high heat. Brown the beef on both sides in the fat. Do this in batches to keep the pan hot so the meat browns well, removing the pieces to a bowl once done.

2. Add the onions to the cooking fat in the pan, scraping up the tasty goo in the bottom of the pan. Turn down the heat and cook over a medium-low heat for 10 minutes, or until softened, stirring occasionally.

3. Add the garlic, caraway seeds, paprika and ½ tsp flaky sea salt to the pot and cook, stirring often, for 2 minutes. Add 200ml water, the tomato purée and the chopped tomatoes. Return the beef to the pot and mix it in well.

4. Bring the goulash to the boil, covered, then put in the oven and cook for 1½ hours. Add the peppers and continue to cook the mixture for another 30 minutes, or until the meat is completely tender.

5. Leave to cool for 5 minutes. Stir in the cream. Serve with salad or green vegetables and either dumplings or potatoes.

CHICKEN TAGINE WITH GREEN OLIVES & PRESERVED LEMONS

SERVES **4–5**

- **8** chicken thighs, ideally with skin & bone
- **½ tbsp** olive oil
- **1 large** onion, *grated*
- **3 cloves** garlic, *finely chopped*
- **2** preserved lemons, *pithy centres removed, skin finely chopped*
- **150g** green olives, *pitted & roughly chopped*
- **600g** potatoes, *cut into wedges* (I scrub but don't peel)
- **400ml** water
- **1** chicken liver, *trimmed & roughly chopped* (optional)
- **1–2 tbsp** *roughly chopped* coriander leaf

spice marinade:
- **½ tsp** ground ginger
- **1½ tsp** turmeric
- **1½ tsp** ras al hanout
- **2 tbsp** coriander stalks, *chopped*
- **juice of 1** lemon

Real Moroccan food is not to be found in restaurants but in homes, as I learnt on holidays staying at Orchard of the Shooting Star, a villa near Marrakech, with my friends Alice and Ed, and later when in the dusty countryside between Marrakech and Essaouira, on a work trip with Belazu, a company that imports Mediterranean ingredients. We ate a version of this classic tagine in the home of one of their suppliers, Omar Lamaidi. My version is simpler – in Morocco, a team of women simmered whole birds, then skilfully fried them in plenty of hot oil to crisp up the skin – but adopts tips from Moroccan kitchens, such as using just a small amount of liquid, grating rather than chopping the onion to make a sauce, and the particular blend of herb and spices.

1. Mix together the spice marinade in a non-metallic dish. Add the chicken and massage it thoroughly into the meat. If you have time, cover and leave in the fridge for at least 30 minutes and, if possible, overnight.

2. Wipe the marinade off the chicken (reserve it). Heat the oil in a casserole dish and fry the chicken on both sides until brown.

3. Add the onion, garlic, preserved lemons, green olives, potatoes and water. Stir in the marinade. Bring to the boil, turn down the heat, cover with a lid and cook for 35–40 minutes, until the meat is tender. If using the liver, stir it in and continue to cook for 5 minutes.

4. Serve the chicken with its sauce on its own, garnished with a scattering of coriander leaf. I might also serve a salad, and couscous for extra carbohydrate to satisfy big appetites.

MUJADDARA (LENTILS WITH BULGUR)

SERVES **8** AS A LIGHT LUNCH;
MORE AS A SIDE DISH

- **250g** coarse bulgur wheat
- **250g** brown or green lentils
- **1.2 litres** water
- **1 tbsp** baharat or other Middle Eastern spice mix, or ground cumin
- **2 cloves** garlic, *finely chopped*

basic toppings (to be varied or added to according to storecupboard):
- **3 tbsp** olive oil
- **3 large** onions, *sliced*
- **3 tbsp** *chopped* mint or 5 tbsp *chopped* flat-leaf parsley
- **a squeeze** of lemon juice per person
- **1 dollop** chilli sauce, per person

Grains and pulses can be totally transformed from plain fare to good nosh by simply putting two or more kinds together. My first visit to Koshari Street, in St Martin's Lane, London, came as a revelation. They specialise in the Egyptian street food staple, koshari, made from a mixture of lentils, rice and vermicelli, plus chickpeas as part of the topping, which sounds like carb-overload, but is so entirely satisfying and delicious that I immediately looked into other such recipes and came across mujaddara. The dish epitomises how cheap One Pot food, well spiced, can be a winner. Crucially, you jazz up the dish at the last minute with various additions, such as crispy fried onions, chilli sauce, herbs, sumac or dukkah (a crunchy combo of spices and seeds): the savoury adult equivalent of the sprinkles kids put on ice cream.

1. Soak the bulgur in plenty of water for around 15 minutes.

2. Meanwhile, put the lentils in a medium-sized pan with the water, spice, garlic and 1 tsp flaky sea salt. Stir, bring to the boil, then turn down the heat and simmer, uncovered, for 15 minutes.

3. Drain the bulgur and stir into the lentils. Bring to the boil again, then simmer, covered, for another 15 minutes, or until all (or nearly all) of the water has been absorbed by the grains. Stir occasionally.

4. While the grains are cooking, heat the oil in a frying pan over a medium heat and cook the onions until crispy and brown, taking care they do not burn by stirring occasionally, more towards the end. Turn the heat off before they go too dark as they will continue to cook in the residual heat.

5. Serve the mujaddara with a sprinkle of chopped herbs, the crispy onions, a squeeze of lemon juice and a dollop of chilli sauce.

This is a large amount so the dish can
stretch over several meals – mujaddara
is great with sausages, cold meat, a
piece of fish or as part of a mixed meze.
If halving the quantity of lentils and
bulgur, add a little less than half the
spice mix or cumin (1 tsp should do it)
or it may be too strong.

Baharat or other Middle Eastern spice
mixtures tend to be a combination of
cinnamon, cloves, cardamom, nutmeg,
ginger, cumin, coriander, peppercorns
and perhaps paprika, or a touch of cayenne
pepper. If you want to keep it simple, just
add ground cumin, either ready ground
or toasted in a pan and ground. I also
follow what they do in Koshari Street and
add a good sprinkle of dukkah, a Middle
Eastern seed, nut and spice mix.

Bulgur is a nutty and nutritious grain
with plenty of protein and minerals.
Use the coarse kind for this recipe. You
can also use long-grain white rice
as a substitute.

Lentils are cheap but need not feel
worthy, as this dish shows. Green lentils
hold their shape best and cost a little bit
more. But I've used whatever came to hand
– brown and also a mixture of red and
green in the dish – and they all work fine
(don't use all red though, too mushy).

PASTILLA FOR BEGINNERS

MAKES **1** x **23**CM PASTILLA
(SERVES **8**)

¨ **4** chicken thighs, *without skin or bone*
¨ **1 tbsp** olive or vegetable oil
¨ **150g** whole blanched almonds

¨ **2 tbsp** icing sugar, plus 2–3 tsp icing sugar, to finish
¨ **4 medium** eggs, *beaten*
¨ **2 tbsp** lemon juice

One of the classics of Moroccan cooking, Pastilla is a pie with thin pastry enclosing a sweet and spicy meat filling. The prepararation takes a bit of time, but you can space this out over two days, and all in all it is an interesting dish to make and rewarding to set upon the table. We're lucky to have the cookbooks by American foodwriter Paula Wolfert, who has collected recipes from decades spent in Moroccan homes and this recipe is loosely adapted from one of hers. Wolfert writes that in the city of Fes, a centre of culinary excellence, the pie is never less than a mighty 50cm in diameter. Mine is smaller than this: a pastilla for beginners, if you like.

Pastilla is classically made with pigeon. This recipe uses confit duck as well as chicken to get some of the darkness and flavour of the original meat.

Vary the meat as you want. Use 2 more chicken thighs if you don't have a confit duck leg. If available, you could also use pigeon meat. You want about 500g of meat-off-the-bone in total.

Advance preparation spreads the work out. Make the filling up to 24 hours before you cook the pie. Cool the mixture as quickly as possible and store it in the fridge, covered.

1. Mix together the ingredients for the spice paste in a medium saucepan with a lid, including the saffron water. Nestle the chicken thighs in the spiced liquid, bring to the boil, then turn the heat down and simmer, lid on, for 25–30 minutes, or until the meat is cooked through to the bone. Turn the chicken over once or twice to prevent it drying out and add a little more water if necessary.

2. While the chicken is cooking, heat 1 tbsp of oil in a frying pan and brown the almonds over a medium-low heat, shaking them around regularly after a couple of minutes and taking care they do not burn. Set aside 32 of the almonds and coarsely chop the rest. Mix the chopped almonds with the 2 tbsp icing sugar and set aside.

3. Remove the cooked meat from the saucepan and, when cool enough to handle, shred or chop into smallish pieces (about 3cm).

4. Turn the heat down under the pan containing the chicken juices, so that the liquid just simmers, and add the beaten eggs. Cook gently for a few minutes over a low heat, stirring often as if making scrambled eggs. You want the eggs to set lightly to give the mixture a curdy texture that's looser than scrambled eggs; it will set more in the pie.

- **2** preserved lemons, *pithy centres removed, skin finely chopped*
- **4 tbsp** *finely chopped* parsley
- **1½ tbsp** *finely chopped* coriander leaf

- **1** confit duck leg (about 175g), *roasted, skinned & shredded*
- **100g** unsalted butter
- **1 x 270g** packet of filo pastry

spice paste:
- **1 tbsp** olive oil
- **1 large** onion, *coarsely grated*
- **½** cinnamon stick
- **½ tsp** ground ginger
- **¼ tsp** *freshly ground* black pepper

- **¼ tsp** turmeric
- **½–1 tsp** saffron, (quantity depending on strength), *crushed & soaked in 150ml water for 20 minutes*

5. Stir in the lemon juice, chopped preserved lemon peel, herbs and a big pinch of sea salt. Return the chopped chicken and add the duck, taste and add more salt if necessary. Remove the cinnamon stick.

6. Preheat the oven to 220°C/Gas 7, with a large baking tray inside to help to make the pie's base crisp. Melt the butter in a small pan. Take a shallow pie dish that's around 23cm diameter, or use a cake tin with a removable base. Butter the bottom and sides of the pie dish well – be lavish with the butter.

7. Assuming your packet of filo consists of 6 large sheets, cut them in half to make 12 smaller sheets. Double up 10 of these to create 5 squares of pastry, sticking each together with melted butter. Lay these double sheets of filo around the pie dish, at an angle, overlapping them by around 2cm and so that half the pastry overhangs the rim in a triangle shape. Butter the filo pastry that is on the base of the pie dish and lay one of the remaining two pieces on top, so the base of the pie dish is now covered in pastry. Butter all the pastry on the base and sides once more – again, be lavish.

8. Spread the almond and icing sugar mixture on the bottom of the pie. Cover with the meat and spicy egg mixture. Place the last piece of pastry in the centre of the pie, and brush with butter. Gently lift the overhanging pastry and fold it into the centre. Brush everything with butter again. You should have about 1 tbsp or so of melted butter left.

9. Bake the pie on the hot baking tray in the preheated oven for 20 minutes, turning it around if necessary to ensure it browns evenly. Take the pie dish off the baking sheet and loosen it carefully by running a knife around the edge of the dish. Wearing oven gloves and taking care you do not burn yourself, place the baking sheet on top of the pie and flip it so that the pie turns out onto the baking tray. Brush with the remaining butter and put back in the oven for 10 minutes.

10. This is best eaten hot or at least warm. To decorate, lay 8 lines of 4 almonds radiating out from the centre of the pie, like bicycle spokes (you will cut 8 slices of pie between these) and dust the top with icing sugar, more or less according to taste. Serve on its own, in a slice, as a starter, or with Moroccan salads for a main course.

PORK
ALENTEJO

SERVES **4–6**

Portuguese cooking is full of wonderful pork recipes. This classic, from the central Alentejo region, is one of the most delicious combinations of surf 'n' turf that you could possibly imagine.

- **450g** lean pork (leg or loin), *cut into 3cm cubes*
- **1 tbsp** olive oil or ¾ tbsp good lard
- **1 large** onion, *sliced*
- **150ml** water (or white wine or dry sherry)
- **700g** medium waxy potatoes, *peeled & cut into 3cm cubes*
- **250g** whole clams (see note on how to de-grit)
- **100g** ready-cooked clams (not stored in vinegar)
- **a good squeeze** of lemon juice
- **80g bunch** of coriander, *leaves roughly chopped*

marinade:
- **3 cloves** garlic, *finely chopped*
- **1½ tsp** paprika
- **2 tbsp** olive oil
- **100ml** white wine or dry sherry
- **2 bay leaves**
- stalks from the bunch of coriander, *finely chopped*

1. Put the marinade ingredients in a shallow, non-metallic container, ideally large enough to contain the pork more or less in a single layer. Turn the pork cubes in the marinade so they are well coated. Cover and leave to marinate in the fridge, turning occasionally, for as long as you can (up to 24 hours, though 15 minutes is better than nothing).

2. Heat the oil or lard in a sauté pan over a medium-low heat, and soften the sliced onion with a pinch of salt for about 10 minutes, stirring occasionally. Add the pork and marinade plus the water, potatoes and ½ tsp flaky sea salt. Increase the heat and bring to the boil. Turn the heat down, cover with a lid and simmer for 15–20 minutes, or until the pork is tender and the potatoes nearly cooked.

A DELICIOIUS COMBO OF SURF 'N' TURF

3. Add the clams in their shells and cook for a few minutes, covered, stirring around once or twice, until the shells open; discard any that don't. Add the ready-cooked clams and leave to heat through.

4. Squeeze over lemon juice, to taste. Scatter the whole dish with the coriander leaf. Serve in large shallow bowls, with bread to mop up the most delicious juices.

Lard is a good cooking medium for this dish because pork is so central to Portuguese cooking, though it can be hard to get hold of good-quality stuff. The cheap packs taste iffy to me, quite apart from the ethics of industrial pig farming. Better lard can be found in some butchers and farmer's markets.

Clams can be extra-expensive. To economise, use a combination of clams-in-the-shell and ready-cooked bottled or frozen shelled ones. Cockles are an excellent alternative.

To de-grit clams the Japanese (and most effective) way: put the shellfish in a sieve and suspend them in a saline solution – 1 tbsp salt dissolved in 500ml water – so the water just covers the mouths of the clams. Cover with foil, so the clams think they are in a nice underwater environment (and not the fridge of someone who is about to eat them). Leave for 3 hours and the clams will expel their grit. You can also rinse the clams thoroughly in running cold water. What you mustn't do is leave shellfish in a bowl of ordinary water, as they die.

RED BRAISED
PORK

SERVES **6**

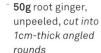

- **50g** root ginger, unpeeled, *cut into 1cm-thick angled rounds*
- **6** spring onions, *cut into 4 long strips on the diagonal, including the green part*
- **3 cloves** garlic, *finely chopped*
- **12** shiitake mushrooms, *quartered*
- **1** butternut squash, *peeled if you like, deseeded & cut into 4cm chunks*
- **1.2kg** pork shoulder, *cut into 3cm slices*
- **2 tbsp** vegetable oil
- **500ml** stock (instant is ok; homemade better here)
- **3 tbsp** light or Japanese soy sauce
- **100ml** sherry
- **4 tbsp** soft brown sugar
- **2** star anise
- noodles or rice, to serve

Chinese red-braised dishes are made from meat cooked in a stock that reduces down to a sticky sauce. On the Chinese table, the dish would be served with a number of other dishes. I've added butternut squash and mushrooms and left a little more liquid to make it more of a One Pot.

I love the simplicity of this dish: a bit of chopping, then everything goes into the pot to work its magic.

Pork shoulder is one of the One Pot cook's most useful ingredients. Not only is the cut delicious and excellent value for money, but you don't have to fuss too much about timing as it doesn't dry out quickly like more expensive cuts such as leg and tenderloin.

Don't bother to peel the ginger, but do cut it into angled round pieces so it is easily distinguished from the pieces of meat. You can eat the ginger, which becomes mild and soft through cooking, though it won't be to everyone's taste.

1. Preheat the oven to 170°C/Gas 3. Put all the ingredients in an ovenproof sauté pan. Bring the liquid to the boil then put in the oven with the lid half-off for 1 hour.

2. Remove the lid and continue to cook for another 1½ hours, or until the meat is tender and the liquid much reduced. Stir and turn the meat about every 20 minutes. You can continue to cook the dish for longer if you want a more reduced sauce.

3. Serve with rice or noodles, or just with a salad or stir-fried greens.

PORK
ADOBO

SERVES **4**

¨ **700g** pork cheeks, *cut into 5cm chunks* (or belly pork)
¨ **2 tbsp** *finely chopped* garlic (about 6 cloves)
¨ **2 tbsp** *finely chopped* peeled root ginger
¨ **2 tsp** dark brown muscovado sugar
¨ **½ tsp** chilli flakes
¨ **4 tbsp** cider vinegar
¨ **80ml** Japanese soy sauce
¨ **200ml** water
¨ **500g** waxy potatoes (eg Charlotte), *cut into 4cm chunks*

Those with a taste for the strongly savoury – my fellow salt 'n' vinegar crisp addicts – will love this tangy pork dish from the Philippines, a delicious combination of vinegar and soy sauce, with a little chilli heat and plenty of garlic and ginger. I particularly like to use pork cheeks in this dish. If you can't find them, use belly pork instead.

1. Preheat the oven to 160°C/Gas 3. Put everything apart from the potatoes in a medium-sized pot.

2. Cover the pot with a lid and cook in the oven for 1 hour. Add the potatoes and stir. Cook, uncovered, for another hour, or until the meat is tender and the potatoes cooked.

3. Serve with spicy salad leaves, such as mizuna or rocket.

VINDALOO

SERVES **6**

- **600g** pork shoulder, *cut into 6cm chunks*
- **2 tbsp** olive oil
- **4** onions, *sliced*
- **80g bunch** coriander, *stalks finely chopped, leaves roughly chopped*
- **6** tomatoes, *roughly chopped*
- **450g** waxy potatoes, *cut into 5cm chunks (no need to peel)*
- **1 tbsp** brown sugar

spice paste:
- **2 tbsp** cider vinegar
- **6 cloves** garlic, *roughly chopped*
- **a thumb** of root ginger, *peeled & chopped*
- **1–3** green chillis *(deseeded for less heat, if desired)* or ½–2 tsp chilli powder, to taste
- **1 tbsp** coriander seeds
- **½ tbsp** cumin seeds
- **1 tsp** turmeric
- **1 tsp** black peppercorns
- seeds of **6** cardamom pods
- **6cm** cinnamon stick

Vindaloo has become a stereotype of curry-house laddery, but its original version is far more sophisticated and delicious. This tartly refreshing curry hails from Goa in South India, formerly a Portuguese colony. It is flavoured with a marinade of wine and garlic, as well as the famed chilli, which is why the name comes from the Portuguese dish *carne de vinha d'alhos* (meat with wine and chilli).

1. Put all the ingredients for the spice paste, apart from the cinnamon, into a small grinder along with 1 tbsp water and whizz until you have a paste. If you don't have a grinder, finely grate the ginger and garlic and finely chop the chilli. Crush the coriander, cumin and cardamom in a mortar and pestle. Grind the peppercorns in a pepper grinder onto a sheet of paper you can fold to tip the spice into a measuring spoon. Mix everything together apart from the cinnamon.

2. Rub the spice paste into the pork, add the cinnamon stick to the dish and leave to marinate in a shallow, non-metallic dish. If you are in rush this can just be left while you cook the onions, but ideally marinate the meat, covered in the fridge, for a couple of hours or overnight.

3. Pour the oil into a large pan and slowly cook the onions over a medium-high heat for 5 minutes, stirring occasionally to make sure they don't burn on the bottom. Turn the heat down and continue to cook slowly for 30 minutes, stirring occasionally.

4. Add the coriander stalks, chopped tomatoes, potatoes and sugar to the pan along with the meat and its marinade. Season with 1 tsp flaky sea salt. Pour in 200–300ml water, but no more; this should be a thick curry and the vegetables will release water as they cook. Cover with a lid and bring to the boil, then turn the heat down and simmer for around 1¼ hours, or until the meat is tender enough to push apart with a wooden spoon.

5. Stir in the coriander leaf just before serving the curry with rice.

Chillies are variable in taste and heat. You can nibble a little of a fresh one to check its heat first and use more or less accordingly. If in doubt, take out the seeds and the white veins as these are the hottest part. I've given the option for a relatively mild amount of chilli, but this is traditionally a hot dish and many will want more.

REFRIED
BEANS

SERVES **6–8**

- **3 tbsp** good-quality lard or olive oil
- **2** red or white onions, *finely chopped*
- **4 cloves** garlic, *finely chopped*
- **2** bay leaves
- **1 tsp** dried oregano or epazote (a Mexican herb that is used with beans)
- **1 tsp** cumin seeds
- **4 tbsp** *finely chopped* coriander stalks
- **large pinch** of chilli flakes
- **500g** home-cooked black or pinto beans (see notes) or 2 x 400g tins of black or pinto beans, drained
- **250–300ml** vegetable stock or bean cooking water

to serve
- **100g** *crumbled* white cheese, eg Lancashire
- **1** lime, *cut into wedges*
- **about 2 tbsp** *finely chopped* coriander leaf
- warm tortillas or rice & salad

Refried beans, a staple of Mexican cooking, suffers from being regarded as a side dish rather than a more central part of a meal. Give those beans some love and they are transformed. The beans are best served as a well-flavoured dollop alongside white rice or warmed tortillas and salad or vegetables.

I often make this in double quantities, especially if going to the trouble of cooking the beans from scratch. Leftovers are a useful standby to have in the fridge for quick bursts of protein and flavour for mid-week lunches.

1. Heat the fat in a heavy-based pan over a medium-low heat and soften the onions and garlic for about 10 minutes, stirring occasionally. Add the bay leaves, oregano, cumin, coriander stalks and chilli flakes and stir around for a few minutes.

2. Add the beans and 250ml of the stock or bean cooking water and cook for 10 minutes, stirring occasionally, adding more liquid if necessary to prevent the mixture getting too dry; you are after a creamy texture. Mash the beans with a potato masher once they are soft and season with flaky sea salt. The amount you use will depend slightly on whatever else you might put on the plate, but they do take a fair amount of salt. Start with ¼ tsp and increase as needed.

3. Remove the bay leaves and serve with cheese crumbled on top, a wedge of lime and a scattering of coriander leaf, with warm tortillas or rice and salad.

GIVE THOSE BEANS SOME LOVE

Cooking the beans yourself is a good idea because the texture and taste are better than tinned and you get a tasty stock alongside. Soak 250g dried beans in plenty of cold water overnight, drain, put in a pan with more water and, if you like, some extra flavours such as bay leaves and a couple of cloves of garlic. Bring to the boil, cover, and leave to simmer until reasonably soft (about 1 hour, but check as the cooking time for beans varies according to their age and quality).

Two key elements turn beans (yawn) into refried beans (yum). The first is seasoning. Coriander stalks and leaves, cumin, chilli flakes and oregano or, if you have it, the Mexican herb epazote (available from www.coolchile.co.uk), make a great deal of difference, as does plenty of garlic. Then give the beans some juicy fat. Lard is authentic and if I don't have any then I chop off some slightly fatty bacon rinds (from 6 rashers will do) and cook them slowly in a frying pan to render out the fat. Olive oil also works fine and makes it into a vegetarian dish.

A quick red onion pickle is also delicious with refried beans and adds a bright pink to the dark dish. In a small bowl, mix ½ tbsp honey with 1½ tbsp cider vinegar and a pinch of sea salt. Finely slice 2 large red onions and soak them in the dressing for at least 1 hour, or overnight.

MOLE POBLANO

SERVES **8**

" **1.5kg** chicken
" aromatics for the cooking water:
1 onion, *halved*,
1 carrot, *chopped*,
1 stalk celery, *chopped*
" **2 tbsp** good lard or olive oil
" **1** onion, *finely chopped*
" **2 cloves** garlic, *finely chopped*

" **1** red pepper, *deseeded & finely chopped*
" **1 x 400g** tin chopped tomatoes
" **1 small** banana, *finely chopped*
" **10g** dark chocolate (at least 70% cocoa solids)
" **1 tbsp** *finely chopped* coriander leaf

Mexico's national dish traditionally has more than 30 ingredients and is made with turkey in order to provide a feast for a large tableful. My version is simpler, but still has a rich mix of dried Mexican chillies, nuts and spices to make a smooth, dark brown sauce with many taste sensations. The dish takes time but is a feast both at the table and for the cook, who is surrounded by all the scents of the Mexican kitchen. I've added the secret ingredient of Tia Nena, a woman in her 80s, who made the best mole I've ever eaten in her home-restaurant in the hills above Veracruz on the Caribbean coast. As she stirred her big pot (her arm was almost shorter than her stirring spoon), she told me to add a small amount of banana to give the dish a fruity boost.

1. Place the chicken in a pot that's just the right size for it and not too big. Add the aromatics and 1 tsp flaky sea salt. Just cover the bird with water. Bring to the boil, then turn down the heat immediately. Skim off any froth, cover and cook gently for 1 hour 20 minutes, or until a knife pushed into the thickest part of the thigh shows no red juices. Remove the chicken from the pot and leave to cool slightly, reserving the stock to make the sauce.

2. While the chicken is cooking, start making the spice paste. Open up the chillies and remove the seeds. Briefly toast them, skin-side down, in a dry frying pan over a medium heat, just until they start to smell fragrant (about 1½ minutes). Soak the toasted chillies in warm water for 15 minutes.

3. Use the same dry frying pan to toast, in turn, the sesame seeds, then the pine kernels and then the blanched almonds over a medium-low heat, stirring each one after a minute or so to ensure they don't burn. They are ready when they smell toasty. Put the seeds, nuts and the spices (apart from the cinnamon) in a small grinder or liquidizer with 2 tbsp of the chilli-soaking water and grind to get a paste. Add the soaked chillies with 2 tbsp more of the soaking juice and the raisins and whizz it all up again.

spice paste:
- **2** mulatto chillies
- **1** ancho chilli
- **1** pasilla chilli
- **20g** sesame seeds, plus 2 tbsp to garnish
- **20g** pine kernels
- **20g** blanched almonds
- **½ tsp** coriander seeds
- **2** allspice berries
- **¼ tsp** anise or ¼ star anise
- **2 cloves** (optional)
- **30g** raisins
- **½** cinnamon stick

4. Put the lard or oil into a pan over a medium-low heat and gently cook the onion, garlic and chopped red pepper until soft. Add the tomatoes, banana and the spice paste along with the cinnamon stick. Cook for another 10 minutes to develop the flavours, stirring often so the mix doesn't burn.

5. Add 600ml of the stock from the chicken pot and the chocolate. Bring to the boil, then turn down the heat and simmer, uncovered, for 40 minutes, or until the mixture has thickened slightly. Remove the cinnamon and whizz the sauce up in a liquidizer. You can then sieve it, but I don't bother. Pour the sauce back into a pan and reheat. Taste and season with more salt, if necessary.

6. While the sauce is cooking, cut the legs off the chicken and divide into drumstick and thigh. Take the rest of the meat off the bones and chop into large 2-bite pieces.

7. Mix the meat into the sauce to reheat. Sprinkle sesame seeds and coriander leaf over the top and serve with refried beans (see page 176), rice and an avocado and red onion salad. The green, brown, black and white plateful looks dramatic and tastes wonderful.

Dried Mexican chillies have fascinating flavours, spanning from a tart fruitiness to tarry tobacco. As you remove the seeds, this recipe is about how they taste rather than their heat. A mix is authentic, but you could also use 2 rather than 3 kinds. Ancho chillies are now available in some supermarkets but all can be bought online from Mexican specialists.

Advance cooking is a good idea as the sauce develops and mellows in flavour over a day or two, and is best of all on days 3, 4 and 5. Reheat thoroughly before serving.

CLAYPOT
VEGETABLES

SERVES **4–6**

" **2 tbsp** vegetable oil
" **2 banana shallots,** *finely sliced*
" **2 cloves** of garlic, *finely chopped*
" **1 thumb** root ginger, *peeled & finely chopped*
" **1 red pepper,** *deseeded & sliced*
" **1 green pepper,** *deseeded & sliced*
" **1 carrot,** *peeled & cut into batons*
" **2 courgettes,** *cut into thick batons*
" **100g** green beans or mangetout, *trimmed*
" **2 pak choi,** *stems roughly chopped, leaves left whole*

" **150g** shiitake mushrooms, *halved if large*
" **300g** firm squash (eg. butternut), *deseeded, peeled & cut into small chunks*
" **400g** firm tofu, *cut into 4cm chunks* (optional but good)
" **4 tbsp** Japanese soy sauce
" **½ tsp** chilli flakes, or to taste
" **1 tbsp** sesame oil, plus more to drizzle
" **1 large handful** coriander leaf, *roughly chopped*

Claypot cooking brings together many different ingredients to make a satisfying whole. The claypot itself gains a patina of flavour over time, but any saucepan or flameproof casserole dish with a lid will do. As with a stir-fry, there are a large number of ingredients in the dish, but not much work is required other than initial chopping. It's a great way of using lots of vegetables and can be adapted to whatever you have in your kitchen. What seems like a large amount of vegetables cooks down as they release their juices. There's very little liquid added to the dish; it all comes from the veg.

1. Heat the oil in a large pan or wok with a lid over a high heat. Stir-fry the shallots, garlic and ginger in the hot oil for a couple of minutes. Add the rest of the vegetables and tofu, if using, and stir together.

2. Add the soy sauce, chilli flakes, sesame oil and 2 tbsp water. Stir well to mix these flavourings with the vegetables. Put a lid on, turn the heat down to medium low and cook for around 30 minutes, stirring a couple of times.

3. When the vegetables are tender the dish is ready. Taste and adjust the seasonings if necessary and serve on top of plain boiled rice with coriander leaf and a final drizzle of sesame oil.

To add a flavoursome fish element, substitute 2 tbsp of the soy sauce with oyster sauce and stir in 150g cooked and peeled north Atlantic or cold water prawns towards the end.

To add meat, cut 6–7 skinned and boned chicken thighs (about 450g meat) into large pieces and add at the beginning along with the vegetables. Check the meat is cooked through before serving.

Dry or medium sherry is a good substitute for the water.

JAPANESE CHICKEN HOT POT

SERVES **6**

6 chicken thighs, *boned & skinned, each cut into 4–5 pieces*

125g shiitake mushrooms, *shallow cross cut into top*

10cm piece of kombu

a thick thumb of unpeeled root ginger, *cut into about 6 long slices*

3 sweet potatoes, *peeled & cut into 5cm cubes* or 100–250g udon noodles (optional)

200g cabbage, *finely sliced*

6 medium carrots, *cut into 2cm thick slices on the diagonal*

100g watercress or other spicy green such as mizuna

3 spring onions, *finely chopped, including the green part*

cheaty ponzu dipping sauce:

4 tbsp Japanese soy sauce

2 tbsp mirin

2 tbsp citrus juice (ideally 1 tbsp of lemon & 1 tbsp of lime)

Japanese One Pot dishes, less well known than sushi and sashimi, are well worth discovering. Their secret isn't so much about long cooking, but the effective layering of flavours and textures. This easy dish transports your kitchen table somewhere else, especially if you make it with the umami-rich kombu. In Michael Pollan's exploration of braises and other slow One Pots in *Cooked*, he describes the deeply savoury taste of umami as a secret of good stock. Using such ingredients as kombu is a trick worth adopting for One Pots in general.

1. To make the cheaty ponzu, mix all the ingredients together.

2. Put the chicken, shiitake mushrooms, kombu and ginger slices in a medium-sized pot and cover with water. If you are using sweet potatoes, add them now. Bring to the boil, then turn down the heat and simmer for 20 minutes, or until the chicken is cooked all the way through.

3. Add to the pot the sliced cabbage, sliced carrots and noodles, if using, and continue to simmer for 5 minutes, or until the carrots are tender and the noodles cooked.

4. Divide the watercress between 6 bowls. Place the chicken, carrots, cabbage and noodles on top. Ladle over enough of the cooking broth to just cover the ingredients. Scatter with the spring onions.

5. Serve little bowls of the ponzu dipping sauce alongside, or stir it into the pot, to taste, just before serving.

Kombu is a crucial ingredient in this dish and available online, in Japanese stores and healthfood shops. The magic of this dish lies in its 'umami' quality, a Japanese term describing an intensely savoury taste. Certain ingredients, here the mushrooms and kombu, have this natural glutamate quality in spades and are better than the artificial monosodium glutamate.

Ponzu is a sauce that is traditionally served alongside Japanese One Pot dishes, as well as grilled food, and literally means 'vinegar punch'. It is a tart sauce that can also be umami-rich when the ingredients are simmered with kombu and katsuobushi flakes from dried tuna. In an utterly inauthentic way, I add such seasonings to the One Pot and make a very basic version of the sauce. If you want to make your own more authentically, simmer the soy sauce and mirin with a 5cm piece of kombu and 1 tbsp katsuobushi for 5 minutes, then strain off the flakes and kombu and stir in the citrus juice. It's also a great seasoning sauce for steamed vegetables.

PRAWN, PINEAPPLE & TAMARIND LAKSA

SERVES **4**

- **250g** cooked, shell-on, north Atlantic or cold water prawns
- **a little** vegetable oil
- **700ml** water or chicken stock
- **2 sticks** of lemongrass, *bashed a bit to release flavour*
- **2 tbsp** tamarind paste
- laksa spice paste **for 4** (quantity according to maker's instructions)
- **200ml** coconut milk
- **150g–200g** rice noodles (according to appetite)
- **200g** beansprouts
- To balance flavour of the broth, if necessary: juice of about ½ lime; 1–2 tsp fish sauce; 1–2 tsp jaggery, coconut palm sugar or other brown sugar

toppings:
- **100g** drained or fresh pineapple, *cut into 5mm chunks*
- ¼ cucumber, *cut into matchsticks*
- **2** spring onions, *finely chopped*
- **1 tbsp** *finely chopped mint*
- **2 tbsp** *finely chopped coriander leaf*

A bowlful of this golden Malaysian noodle dish is very cheering, both in looks and taste. I generally use bought spice paste livened up with fresh lemongrass and lime juice, but if you eat the dish often then it is worth finding a good recipe in an East Asian cookbook and making a batch of your own paste for the fridge or freezer, ready for use.

The best brands of coconut milk tend to be East Asian and do make a difference in this dish.

1. Take the shells off the prawns and put the meat in a small bowl, to be refrigerated until needed. Pour a little veg oil into a large pot and fry the prawn shells, heads and all, for 3 minutes or so over a medium-high heat, stirring a bit after a minute or so, to lightly toast the shells and bring out their flavour.

2. Add the water or stock and lemongrass and simmer, lid on, for 30 minutes. Strain off the shells and discard, then pour the stock back into the pot. Stir in the tamarind, laksa paste and coconut milk. Simmer for 10 minutes.

A CHEERING BOWLFUL OF MALAYSIAN NOODLES

3. While the laksa base is simmering away, soak the noodles in just-boiled water for 10 minutes, or according to packet instructions, and prepare the toppings as described in the ingredients list.

4. Drain the noodles and add to the simmering broth for 3 minutes, to soften. Stir in the beansprouts so they heat up. Taste the broth and adjust to make it more sour (with lime), sweet (with sugar) or fishy (with fish sauce) according to your tastes.

5. Spoon the laksa into four big bowls. Divide the toppings between them, ending with a scattering of the pale pink prawns over the tamarind-yellow broth.

PHO (VIETNAMESE BEEF NOODLE SOUP)

SERVES **4–6**

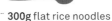

" **300g** flat rice noodles
" **1.5 litres** Vietmanese beef stock (see right)
" **3 tbsp** fish sauce
" **2 tbsp** Japanese soy sauce
" **2 tsp** caster sugar
" **1 tsp** olive or other vegetable oil
" **250g** rump steak
" **100g** beansprouts
" **1** lime

to serve:
" **1** red chilli, *deseeded & finely sliced*
" **8** spring onions, *finely sliced, including the green part*
" **a large handful** of *roughly chopped* coriander leaf
" **a large handful** of *roughly chopped* basil (ideally the stronger flavoured Thai basil)
" **a small handful** of *roughly chopped* mint
" **1** lime, *cut into wedges*

Slow-cooked stocks are the basis for many a fine noodle dish around the world, not least the pho that is sold at street cafes and food stalls in Vietnam. The deeply flavoursome beef broth is spiced with cinnamon and star anise and the dish is brightened with toppings, such as chilli, spring onions and strong-flavoured herbs. In Vietnam, these extras are put on the table for you to help yourself. Adopt self-service back at home, or put the extras on each bowlful yourself.

1. Put all the ingredients for the stock into a large pan and bring to the boil, skimming off any froth that rises to the top. Add ¾ tbsp flaky sea salt, turn down the heat and simmer for at least 3 hours, or up to 5 if possible. Strain off the broth. You can do this in advance, let it cool and leave in the fridge. This will be more than you need, but it is worth making more to freeze or refrigerate for another day.

2. Shortly before you want to eat, put the noodles into a pan of just-boiled water. Turn off the heat, stir them around and leave, with a lid on, for 10 minutes, or until tender.

3. Reheat the stock in a pan, adding the fish sauce, soy sauce and sugar. Rub the oil on both sides of the steak and season with salt and pepper.

Vietmanese beef stock (more than you need; freeze the rest or use in other dishes):
- **a big thumb** of root ginger, *cut into 2cm thick slices*
- **3** banana shallots, *peeled & sliced*
- **2** carrots, *roughly chopped*
- **2 stalks** celery, *roughly chopped*
- **3** star anise
- **1½** cinnamon sticks
- **2 tsp** black peppercorns
- **1kg** shin of beef, *cut into big chunks*
- **1kg** beef bones, (optional but good)
- **3.5 litres** water

4. Get a frying pan really hot then fry the steak on both sides until medium-rare on the inside and well-browned on the outside. How long this takes depends upon the thickness of the steak and the heat of your pan; about 2 minutes on each side for a steak 3cm thick should be enough. (Cut a thin slice off one end to check and keep cooking for longer if necessary.) Rest the meat for a minute or two, then cut into thin slices that will happily fit into a soup spoon.

5. Drain the noodles and place into 4 large bowls. Add the beansprouts and pour the stock over the noodles. Divide the beef between the bowls and finish each with a squeeze of lime.

6. You can either put the rest of the ingredients on the table for people to help themselves, or divide them between the bowls and serve.

For a more intense stock, toast the spices in a dry frying pan for a couple of minutes, and afterwards toast the ginger and shallots, shaking around so they brown but do not burn – a Vietmanese cooking tip from Rick Stein's excellent *Far Eastern Odyssey*.

SOUTHERN ITALIAN FISH PIE

SERVES **6**

- " **700g** mussels
- " **150ml** white wine
- " **juice of 1** lemon
- " **3 cloves** garlic, *finely chopped*
- " **80g** parmesan, *finely grated*
- " **6 tbsp** *roughly chopped* flat-leaf parsley
- " **½ tsp** chilli flakes
- " **¼ tsp** fennel seeds, *roughly ground*

- " **500–600g** mixed smoked fish & white fish skinned fillets: eg 200–300g smoked haddock & 300g haddock, coley, or cod
- " **900g** waxy potatoes, *peeled*
- " **50ml** olive oil
- " **700g** tomatoes, *cut into 2cm slices* (cherry or around 7 standard; whatever looks ripest)

Traditional fish pie with its mashed potato topping feels comforting, but I sometimes prefer a top layer with a more contrasting texture to the soft fish: either crispy breadcrumbs or, in this case, firm-textured potatoes that absorb the olive oil and the garlicky mussel cooking liquor. There is a certain amount of preparation involved in this dish but you can do much of this in advance and it is one of my most useful, straightforward and delightful dishes for entertaining. The recipe is an adaptation of a fish pie in *Entertaining All'Italiana* by foodwriter Anna del Conte, who has provided my table with many good meals for decades. Not only are her recipes delicious and full of the spirit of Italian food, but you also get a sense of her cooking in a real kitchen for family and friends. The recipe is related to the *tiella* dishes of Puglia, that are cooked in earthenware pots and are still taken to village ovens for communal cooking.

1. Preheat the oven to 200°C/Gas 6. Prepare the mussels by washing them in running cold water and pulling off the 'beards' that attached the mussel to its rope or rock. Discard any that are cracked or remain open when tapped.

2. Pour the wine and lemon juice into a wide, ovenproof and flameproof dish or sauté pan (mine is 30cm diameter and 8cm deep) with a lid and add the chopped garlic. Bring to the boil, then add the mussels and put the lid on. Cook over a high heat for 2 minutes, or until the mussels open, discarding any that don't. Turn off the heat, remove the lid and allow the mussels to cool slightly.

3. Mix together the grated parmesan, chopped parsley, chilli flakes and ground fennel seeds. Cut the skinned fish into chunks (the smoked fish into 2–3cm chunks and the white fish into 3–4cm chunks). Cut the potatoes as thinly as you can. Once cool enough, remove the mussels from the pan and take them out of their shell reserving the tasty cooking liquor.

4. Pour half the olive oil into the same pan. Place half the sliced potatoes in a layer over the base of the pot. Season with a small amount of sea salt (smoked fish can be salty, but the potatoes do need salt). Spoon over a third of the parmesan, parsley and spice mixture. Lay half the tomatoes on top. Scatter over the smoked fish, fresh fish and mussels, making sure they are evenly distributed. Put another third of the parmesan and parsley on top, then the rest of the potatoes. Pour over the mussel liquor. Put the rest of the tomatoes on top, then top with the rest of the parmesan and parsley. Drizzle over the other half of the olive oil.

5. Cook the pie on a baking tray in the preheated oven for 20 minutes, uncovered, then for about 55 minutes–1 hour, covered loosely with tin foil, or until the potatoes are tender. Leave to settle for 5 minutes, then serve with salad or greens.

Advance preparation for this dish can be done by cooking the mussels and making the parmesan mixture up to 1 day in advance, keeping them covered in the fridge. On the day, finely slice the potatoes and tomatoes and assemble the dish to get it into the oven just before guests arrive.

Cut the potatoes as finely as possible. This is best done on a mandoline, in a food processor or on the side of a box grater.

The fish fillets in this dish can be handily adapted to whatever is on hand. You do need the mussels, however. Miraculously, they don't become tough as they cook again in the pie.

Mussels vary and inevitably you will find some of them are dead (ie will not close when tapped or open when cooked) and you'll need to discard them. But it doesn't matter too much in this dish; just cook as many as you can. You are after the 'stock' you get from cooking them, as much as the meat. This is a useful dish for mussels that have plenty of unsightly barnacles as you discard the shells.

WILD BOAR
RAGÚ

SERVES **6–8**

- **a large knob** of butter
- **2 tbsp** olive oil
- **80g** pancetta, *chopped into smallish pieces*
- **2 onions,** *finely chopped*
- **2 cloves** garlic, *finely chopped*
- **2 stalks** celery, *finely chopped*
- **1 large** carrot, *peeled & finely chopped*
- **600g** wild boar or pork mince
- **500g** lean beef mince
- **300ml** red wine
- **3 tbsp** tomato purée
- **a good grating** of nutmeg
- **1** bay leaf
- **150ml** chicken stock (instant is ok; fresh better)
- **150ml** whole milk
- **600–800g** tagliatelle
- *freshly grated* parmesan

There's mince and then there's ragú, the slow-cooked Italian pasta sauce that is entirely distinct from bog standard 'spag bol'. What makes the difference is two-fold: the mix of meats and the liquid. Use two types of good mince along with pancetta. Then add more wine than you might think – this is important – and some milk as well as stock. This combination imparts richness, softness and flavour to the dish. Where I live in Sussex there are wild boar running around the woods, and so the farmer's market and butchers around Hastings sell the meat. Otherwise, good pork mince works well, too.

Lean beef mince is best for this dish and is worth the extra expense.

1. Melt the butter with the olive oil in a sauté pan over a medium heat, and add the pancetta, onions, garlic, celery and carrot. Cook slowly, stirring occasionally, for 10 minutes, or until softened.

2. Add the two types of mince, red wine, tomato purée and nutmeg. Mix these ingredients carefully into the softened vegetables and pancetta. Tuck in the bay leaf and pour in the stock and milk. Season with flaky sea salt and freshly ground black pepper.

3. Leave the sauce to cook slowly, uncovered, with the odd bubble coming up – blip, blip, blip – for 2 hours, stirring occasionally so that the meat cooks evenly. You shouldn't need to add any more liquid but add some more stock, wine or water if it looks to be getting too dry. Taste and adjust the seasoning if necessary.

4. Cook the tagliatelle in plenty of well-salted water until al dente. Drain briefly and serve the ragú with the pasta and parmesan for people to sprinkle over.

SPAGHETTI WITH BOTTARGA

SERVES **2** AS A LIGHT LUNCH
OR SUPPER

- **200g** spaghetti
- **100g** broccoli florets
- **4 tbsp** (60ml) good olive oil, plus a drizzle at the end
- **2 cloves** garlic, *finely sliced*
- **2** spring onions, *finely chopped, including the green part*
- **16** cherry tomatoes, *halved*
- **a large pinch** of chilli flakes
- **4 tbsp** *finely chopped* flat-leaf parsley
- **a squeeze** of lemon juice
- **40–60g** bottarga, *grated* (quantity depending on your generosity)

It is useful to have the odd special packet in your fridge that can produce an exceptional meal at a moment's notice. Bottarga is a slab of dried, cured fish roe that can be found in classy and authentic Italian delis or online. This artisanal product is expensive, but definitely worth a whirl for those who want a tastebud adventure that's an intense version of taramasalata. Bottarga is eaten in Southern Italy on pasta that is simply dressed with good olive oil and few other ingredients. I've added a few extras, but keep it reasonably simple; the eggs are the star.

Just a little bottarga transforms plain vegetables. I like it on Brussels sprouts or leeks that are lightly steamed then dressed in good olive oil and a splash of fancy vinegar. This is an economical way to use an expensive product and turns simplicity into something special.

1. Bring a large pan of salted water to the boil. Add the pasta and cook until al dente (about 12 minutes), steaming the broccoli over the top of the pan for the last 3 minutes. Drain the pasta into a colander and put the empty pan back on the stove.

2. Pour in the oil and cook the garlic and spring onions for a minute or 2 over a medium heat. Add the cherry tomatoes and chilli and cook for another minute, stirring occasionally. Stir the parsley into the mixture and squeeze in a good squirt of lemon juice.

3. Add the drained spaghetti back into the pan and stir around well in the sauce, so that every strand is coated.

4. Divide the pasta between two plates and briefly stir half the broccoli florets into each helping. Scatter over the grated bottarga and finish with a final drizzle of oil.

XINXIM DE GALHINA (BRAZILIAN CHICKEN & PRAWN STEW)

SERVES **6**

- " **12** chicken thighs & drumsticks, *with skin & bones*
- " **juice of 3** limes, plus juice of 1 more at end, if needed
- " **3 cloves** garlic, *crushed*
- " **1–2 tbsp** vegetable oil
- " **250ml** chicken stock (instant is fine)
- " **2** onions, *thinly sliced*
- " **3** green peppers, deseeded & cut into large chunks
- " **4 large** tomatoes, *cut into chunks*
- " **250g** peeled, raw prawns
- " **80g bunch** of coriander, leaves *roughly chopped*

coconut & prawn paste:
- " **30g** dried shrimp, or for a slightly different taste use 1 tbsp shrimp paste or 2 tbsp fish sauce
- " **30g** unroasted cashew nuts
- " **30g** unroasted peanuts
- " **1 thumb** of root ginger, *peeled & roughly chopped*
- " **400ml** coconut milk

Brazil has plenty of excellent One Pot dishes, including this colourful chicken and fresh prawn combo, thickened with ground nuts and fragrant with coconut and lime juice. My version has options for ingredients that are easy to get hold of, but you can also use the dish as a reason to explore the more exotic taste of dried shrimp, which can be found online or in shops and supermarkets for Brazilian, African and East Asian communities.

1. Put the chicken in a shallow container with the lime juice and garlic. Season with salt and pepper. Cover and leave in the fridge to marinate for at least 30 minutes, or overnight if possible.

2. To make the coconut and prawn paste, put the ingredients in a small liquidizer or grinder. Grind until the nuts and shrimps are finely ground. (If you don't have this kit, grate the ginger, chop the nuts as finely as possible and use shrimp paste not dried prawns, then mix everything together in a bowl.)

3. Scrape the garlic and lime juice off the chicken and reserve. Heat the oil in a large sauté pan with a lid over a high heat. Brown the chicken on both sides in 2 or 3 batches, so you don't overcrowd the pan.

EXPLORE EXOTIC TASTES IN ONE POT

4. Pour in the chicken stock, stirring hard to capture the nice brown bits on the base of the pan. Add the coconut paste, sliced onion, peppers and tomatoes, and the reserved marinade.

5. Cover with a lid, bring to the boil, then turn down the heat and simmer for around 50 minutes, stiring occasionally until the meat is tender through to the bone. Add the prawns and continue to cook for another minute or so, or until cooked. Stir in the chopped coriander.

6. Check the seasoning, adding more lime juice, salt or pepper as needed. Serve with steamed rice.

Dried shrimp are best when orangey-pink rather than brown, as these are fresher. Keep in a well-sealed container in the fridge and use within 1 month.

Other vegetables can be used in this dish, such as sliced okra, spring greens, and other colours of pepper. You can also add a finely sliced green or red chilli for some heat.

Ground-up nuts add flavour and also a thickening texture to the dish. Some recipes use peanut butter instead of freshly ground nuts, which is convenient, and others toast and coarsely chop the nuts or use just one type of nut. I like the mix of two kinds and freshly grind them for a more delicate flavour and texture. But this is an earthy kind of dish and all these approaches work fine.

GUMBO

SERVES **6**

- " **1 tbsp** olive or vegetable oil
- " **1** onion, *finely chopped*
- " **2 cloves** garlic, *finely chopped*
- " **2 stalks** celery, *finely sliced*
- " **2** green peppers, *deseeded & finely sliced*
- " **200g** spicy sausage (eg chorizo), *cut into 2cm chunks.*
- " **2** bay leaves
- " **¼ tsp** cayenne pepper
- " **2 tbsp** plain flour
- " **700ml** chicken stock (fresh is best or good instant)
- " **200g** okra, *trimmed & roughly chopped*
- " **6** skinned & boneless chicken thighs, *each cut into 4 pieces*
- " **300g** peeled, raw or cooked *peeled* tiger prawns
- " **2 tbsp** *finely chopped* flat-leaf parsley

Gumbo hails from Louisiana – I first ate it in New Orleans – and stirs together a spicy Creole mixture of flavours and ingredients to make a mighty fine One Pot.

1. Heat the oil in a sauté pan over a medium-low heat and gently cook the onion, garlic, celery and peppers with ¼ tsp flaky sea salt until soft (about 10 minutes), stirring occasionally. Stir in the sausage, bay leaves and cayenne and cook for another 5 minutes. Sprinkle over the flour and cook, stirring, for 1 minute.

2. Pour in the chicken stock, bring to the boil, then add the okra and chicken and stir well into the other ingredients. Turn the heat down and simmer, covered, for 40 minutes, or until the meat is tender.

3. Add the prawns to the pot and let them reheat or cook through. Taste and adjust the seasoning if necessary. Scatter over the parsley and serve.

You can adapt the dish by adding ingredients such as tomatoes, but don't be tempted to change the green peppers to other colours; their slight bitterness works well in this dish.

Gumbo is meant to have quite a thick texture. In the States, the mixture can be thickened with filé, the powdered leaves of the sassafras tree. It's a bother to track down and I don't personally rate the taste in any case. All you need is okra's gloopiness, along with some flour to thicken the stock.

TOMATO FONDUE

SERVES **6**

½ **clove** garlic
150ml white wine
500ml good-quality passata
1½ **tsp** cornflour
300g cheese, *grated* (ideally half hard cheese eg gruyère mixed with a softer & easily melted cheese such as emmental or raclette)
a good grinding of nutmeg

to serve:
1kg–1.5kg new, or small, potatoes (quantity depends if you've climbed a mountain or have a big appetite)
8 slices air-cured ham (optional) eg parma, serrano or a British variety
a bowl of cornichons
a large bowl of sharply dressed green salad

I came across this lighter version of fondue whilst staying at my friend Megan's home in the Vaucluse in south-west Switzerland. Her neighbours, Anna and René, kindly took us in after a long day of vertiginous mountain walking and fed us this dish as we sat, happy but exhausted, at their table. They poured it over home-grown spuds, just as you do for raclette, instead of dipping in pieces of bread as usual. Melted cheese can inspire an excess of greed and I've often enjoyed a fondue, but later regretted eating quite so much. This version is clever because the dish is more digestible yet still gloriously warming.

Kirsch is a traditional and delicious addition. If you have some, add ½ tbsp with the wine.

Cubes of a crusty bread such as sourdough can be dipped into the fondue on long forks, instead of pouring the sauce on top of the spuds.

To reheat any remaining fondue, just put it back on a gentle heat and keep stirring.

1. Put the potatoes in a large pan with ½ tsp flaky sea salt. Bring to the boil, turn down the heat and simmer for 10 minutes, or until tender.

2. Meanwhile, make the fondue. Rub the cut side of the garlic around the base and sides of a medium saucepan or fondue pot (I then chop the garlic and throw it back in the pot). Pour in the wine and bring to the boil for 30 seconds. Turn the heat down and add the passata and cornflour, then gradually add the cheese, stirring it around until it has melted. Season with plenty of black pepper and a good grating of nutmeg.

3. Divide the potatoes between the plates and pour the fondue over them.

4. Serve charcuterie and cornichons alongside and follow by a dressed green salad to provide a counterbalance to all that goo.

EASY
PUDS

ONE POT PUDS

ARE ABOUT

THE GENEROSITY

OF A TREAT

A One Pot pud can warm your kitchen and comfort you inside and out, or provide a fragrantly refreshing end to the meal. These recipes are about the generosity of a treat and how simple it is to make everyone happy just by putting a homemade pud on the table.

One Pot puddings can offer great flavour for very little effort. Simply add a few flavours to fruit then let warmth bring out their character. The chapter opens with a number of recipes to showing how this is done. Fruit is a key ingredient in many of my puddings, be it seasonal, fruit bowl standards such as apples and bananas, or storecupboard supplies.

Then there are the chocolate puddings and more substantial dishes based around sponge and pastry; easy comfort foods and crowd-pleasers, such as crumble and rice pudding; and recipes more suited for entertaining or family celebrations.

Whether they are light and bright or stick-to-your-ribs indulgences, this chapter should provide an 'after' to follow any main.

A good pud needs little embellishment. The colour code for this chapter is yellow – the colour of custard, cream and vanilla ice cream. I'm a fan of all three and recommend they provide the finishing flourish for these One Pot treats.

PLUMS BAKED WITH HONEY & STAR ANISE

" **12** plums
" **3 tbsp** honey
" **3** star anise
" **300ml** water

SERVES **6**

A bowl of baked plums is always handy for puddings. I make a potful of this when plums come in gluts and then use it in various ways: to top breakfast yoghurt and muesli, as the base of a crumble, or as a pud in its own right. This recipe improves all manner of plums, especially those that need a bit more flavour or aren't fully ripe.

Toasted whole almonds make this dish more substantial. Put the nuts on a baking tray in the oven alongside the plums for 8–10 minutes, shaking them around at least once and taking care they do not burn. Remove from the oven, leave to cool and roughly chop. Scatter over the cooked plums. If serving almonds with plums, do remove the stones as they look similar to the nuts.

Spices of many kinds work in this dish, such as a stick of cinnamon, the crushed seeds of 3 cardamom pods or a split vanilla pod.

The plums can be cooked alongside other dishes in the oven, and at different temperatures. Just cook them for longer or shorter: they are ready when the fruit has yielded its juices and the flesh has softened.

1. Preheat the oven to 190°C/Gas 5. Cut the plums in half and remove any stones that come away easily. Don't worry about the ones that stay put, you can remove them more easily from the cooked fruit.

2. Put the fruit in an ovenproof dish so they are in no more than a double layer. Drizzle over the honey and slip the star anise amongst the fruit. Add the water, then cover tightly with foil or a lid.

3. Cook the fruit in the oven for 40–45 minutes, or until tender (it'll be quicker with ripe plums). Stir the plums around once or twice, basting them in their juices.

4. Remove the spices and any remaining stones from the cooked plums – or leave them in if your guests aren't too fastidious or likely to choke on an unexpected inedible.

5. Serve the plums hot, warm or at room temperature with cream, ice cream or custard.

QUINCES POACHED WITH LEMON & BAY

SERVES **6–8**

" **4 large** quinces (about 1.5kg)
" **200ml** water
" **100g** caster or granulated sugar
" **1** lemon
" **4–6** bay leaves

The scent of quinces makes them effortlessly exotic and long, slow cooking turns their inedibly hard, pale flesh into a tender delight. As well as having a special flavour, the poached fruit is a beautiful colour: a soft pink that is on the right side of girly. Quinces are in season in the autumn and I get mine either from a friend's tree, or else from old-fashioned or Middle Eastern greengrocers. I love the fruit so much that we've now planted a tree in our garden and are rewarded not just with quinces, but also the tree's big, floppy leaves and beautiful white blossom.

Play around with the flavours. Pears can be substituted for half or more of the quinces. I made this with the first (and only) two quinces from my own tree in its first year and used pears to fill up the dish. Sometimes I add a pinch of saffron and a strip of orange peel in the dish instead of the lemon and bay. You can also substitute all or half of the water with pudding wine.

Make a quince syrup bellini by stirring some of the pink juices into prosecco.

1. Preheat the oven to 180°C/Gas 4. Wash the quinces, cut off the stalk and the end of the core. If you want to be more refined, peel the quinces. Usually I do; sometimes I don't. Cut each into quarters and use a small, sharp knife to cut out the woody core. If the quinces are large – or you are in that refined mood – then cut each quarter in half.

2. Put the quince pieces in a single layer, skin or curved side down, in a large, shallow pot with a lid. Pour over the water and sprinkle over the sugar. Use a vegetable peeler to cut away wide strips of peel from the lemon and tuck them, along with the bay leaves, among the quinces.

3. Bake the fruit in the oven for 2 hours, covered, until tender, fragrant and pink.

4. Eat the poached quinces warm or at room temperature with something plain, pale and rich, such as vanilla ice cream, greek yoghurt or cream.

PINEAPPLE & ROSES

SERVES **4–6**

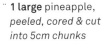

- **1 large** pineapple, *peeled, cored & cut into 5cm chunks*
- **1½ tbsp** kirsch or other liqueur
- **100ml** white wine or orange juice
- **1 tsp** rose water
- **2 tbsp** caster sugar

Pineapple has a great affinity with rose water, as I first discovered in a recipe for a pineapple and rose water ice by the great Victorian cook Agnes Marshall. The possibilities are endless and, with a recipe as easy as this, you can experiment to find the combinations that suit your taste.

1. Put the pineapple pieces in a serving bowl. Add the other ingredients. Stir. Leave for at least 1 hour, or up to 4 or 5.

2. Serve this dish as it is. For once, no cream – at least for me – though a lychee or mango sorbet might be nice.

Liqueurs are great for playing around with to flavour fruit. I like a distilled Cornish mead called Gwires, which gives a beautiful honeyed roundness to the dish. Such booze is potent. You don't need much to make a big difference.

Orange blossom water is a good alternative to the rose water.

APRICOTS WITH VANILLA

SERVES **6**

100g caster sugar
½ vanilla pod

16 small apricots
(about 650g stone-in
weight)

Classic One Pot cooking often involves a few well-chosen ingredients transformed by a simple yet intelligent technique. This recipe is a great example of that principle. Like most One Pot food, it can be made in advance and served at your convenience, either as a dessert or for a luxurious breakfast. Apricots are a beguiling blend of the sweet and the tart and this method brings out the best of this balance and their aromatic qualities. The idea for this came from Richard Olney's *Lulu's Provençal Table* and it is especially useful for the bargain apricots you find in a British supermarket or greengrocer, which undoubtedly need more help than those plucked off a tree in the South of France.

Vanilla pod pieces look good in the dish, alongside the speckled seeds. Afterwards, wipe them dry and put in a jar or bag of sugar where they will continue to spread their magic aroma.

If your apricots are on the firmish side (not fully ripe), add 20g more sugar and cook for a little longer.

Honey is an excellent alternative to the sugar, as suggested by my editor Madeleine. Use 3 tbsp light aromatic honey, such as acacia or orange blossom.

1. Weigh the sugar out into a large bowl. Use a small sharp knife to slit open the vanilla pod, then scrape the seeds into the sugar using the tip of the blade or – a better weapon – the end of a teaspoon handle. Chop the pod into three or four pieces and chuck these in the sugar as well for extra flavour.

2. Cut the apricots in half (or quarters if large) and remove the stones. Mix into the vanilla sugar and leave to macerate for 1–2 hours, so that the sugar draws the juice from the fruit. If you can leave the bowl in a sunny spot by a window, so much the better.

3. Put the fruit and its juices into a saucepan over a low heat, covered, and cook for 5–7 minutes, or until the apricots have softened slightly but still have their shape, and the sugary juices have turned to a syrup.

4. Eat the apricots at room temperature or chilled. These are best served with a good cream, such as clotted cream, thick yoghurt, or vanilla ice cream.

WINTER FRUIT SALAD WITH SPICED SYRUP

SERVES **6–8**

- " **6 small** pears
- " **3** clementines
- " **18** ready-to-eat prunes
- " **12** Brazil nuts

spiced honey-wine syrup:
- " **250ml** white wine
- " **3 tbsp** honey
- " **juice of 1** orange
- " **juice of 1** lemon
- " **½ tsp** *freshly grated* nutmeg
- " **¼ tsp** ground cinnamon
- " **a large pinch** of ground ginger

A bowl of winter fruit salad is useful to have in the fridge to add interest to weekday breakfast cereal, or to dress up for guests with crème fraîche and crisp biscuits. My formula is one type of fresh fruit, one type of citrus fruit, one type of dried fruit and one type of nut, but vary as you like, playing with textures, colours and tastes.

1. Put the wine, honey, orange and lemon juices in a medium-sized pan with the spices. Bring to the boil, then turn down the heat and simmer for 5 minutes.

2. Meanwhile, quarter the pears – I don't bother peeling them and, if in a rush, leave the cores in too. Peel the clementines and cut into 2cm slices, removing any pips.

3. Place the pears in the hot syrup and simmer gently for 15–20 minutes or so, until tender. Turn off the heat.

4. Add the clementines, prunes and nuts and stir together. Leave to cool, then put in the fridge for at least a day before serving.

If making for kids substitute the wine for water.

TROPICAL PEARLS WITH MANGO

SERVES **6−8**

- **400ml** coconut milk
- **400ml** whole milk
- **150ml** double cream
- **75g** soft brown or coconut palm sugar
- **120g** small pearl tapioca
- **a capful** of vanilla extract
- **juice of ½** lime
- **1** ripe mango, *flesh taken off stone & cubed*

Yes, this is tapioca. But not at all as people used to eat it at school, when it was called frogspawn (the smaller pearls, used here) or frog eyes (the larger pearls, which take longer to cook). Tapioca is processed cassava and has now come back into fashion as bubble tea. This fad made me rediscover the old-fashioned pudding. Its texture now seems interesting rather than weird, especially when combined with a lusciously rich and sweet coconut cream.

Tapioca pearls are sold in East Asian shops and online and keep well, as befits an island ingredient.

Coconut palm sugar is found in health food shops and online and has a superb flavour with a slight acidity. It's well worth finding, but light brown or muscovado sugar will do fine here too.

1. Pour the can of coconut milk into a medium pan. Use the tin to measure out the same quantity of milk into the pan. Add the cream and sugar. Bring slowly just to the boil, stirring occasionally so that the sugar melts.

2. Turn the heat down to low. Stir in the tapioca, vanilla extract and ¼ tsp flaky sea salt. Simmer for about 20 minutes, stirring occasionally for the first 10 minutes and then often towards the end as the mixture thickens, so it does not burn on the base. It is ready when the tapioca is soft and the liquid has reduced down to a nice creamy texture; the mixture should be firmish but not dry.

3. Squeeze the lime over the mango pieces and serve alongside the warm or room temperature tapioca.

LE GOOSEBERRY & HONEY CRUMBLE

SERVES **6–8**

" **500g** gooseberries
" **2½ tbsp** honey
" **3 tbsp** elderflower cordial
" **120ml** water

crumble topping:
" **100g** cold butter, *cut into small pieces*
" **150g** plain flour
" **75g** demerara sugar
" **75g** nuts (pecans, almonds or walnuts for preference), *roughly chopped*

Crumble is a homely sort of a pudding and it tickles me to see its high gastronomic status amongst the French. Chic versions of le crumble have graced white linen tablecloths for many years now. This Gallic gastronomic attention to detail has made me look again at the dish, to see how a little more care could make a difference. Elderflower cordial is a quintessential taste of the early British summer. I've put it with gooseberries for a summer crumble, but it's easily adapted to other times of year and other fruits.

1. Preheat the oven to 180°C/Gas 4. Make the crumble topping first. Put the pieces of butter into a large mixing bowl and add the flour. Use the tips of your fingers to rub the butter into the flour until you have a texture that's roughly like large breadcrumbs. You don't need the butter to be totally mixed in. Stir in the sugar and the chopped nuts. If you have time, put this in the fridge for 30 minutes or so to improve the texture.

2. Spread the fruit in a shallow ovenproof dish and try to make sure that the fruit is no more than a couple of berries deep. Drizzle over the honey, then pour in the cordial and water. Cover the fruit with the crumble topping, but do not press it down.

3. Put the crumble in the oven and bake for 45 minutes, or until the top is lightly brown and the liquid in the bottom is oozing up around the outside. Serve warm or hot with yoghurt, custard or, best of all, cold cream.

Alternative crumble fruits include 500g rhubarb, chopped into 2cm pieces; 3 Bramley apples, peeled, cored and cut into 1cm dice; or for a storecupboard emergency 1 x 400g tin of pears with syrup, mixed with 2 bananas cut into 2cm slices and 2 bulbs stem ginger, finely chopped.

Another version of a crumble topping is to swap some of the flour or chopped nuts with ground almonds.

To avoid a claggy crumble: do not pat down the topping; mix the crumbs with a light hand; leave the dish in the fridge for 30 minutes or so to let the butter firm up again; use demerara sugar, which adds crunch to the texture.

Have plenty of liquid in the base. Here I've added honey and elderflower cordial-flavoured water. You can also use citrus zest and juice; just make sure you have enough liquid. I love the sight of caramelizing juices bursting up around the edges of a crumble; one of those sights that says 'eat me now'.

CLAFOUTIS

SERVES **8**

" **450g** cherries, *pitted*
(half fresh, half tinned
is ok, or use defrosted
frozen)
" **3 tbsp** kirsch, or
another fragrant liqueur
(or elderflower cordial)
" **3 tbsp** caster sugar,
plus extra for the dish
" **a little** butter, for the
dish
" **2 tbsp** icing sugar,
to finish

batter:
" **3 medium** eggs
" **3 tbsp** caster sugar
" **1 tsp** vanilla extract
" **150ml** whipping cream,
plus extra to serve
" **3 tbsp** plain flour
" **3 tbsp** ground almonds

Like a number of French One
Pot classics, this dessert of fruit in
batter is easy to make and adapts to
whatever is in season. Details make a
difference in a dish as simple as this
and macerating the fruit in advance
(using sugar to help release the
juices) adds to the flavour, sweetness
and juiciness of the fruit. I don't like
kirsch as a drink, but find it adds an
indefinable extra to many kinds of
fruit, especially cherries, the fruit
from which it's made.

1. Put the cherries in a small dish and sprinkle over the kirsch and caster sugar. Leave to macerate for 2 hours to sweeten and flavour the fruit.

2. Preheat the oven to 180°C/Gas 4. Butter a shallow ovenproof dish, about 26cm in diameter or square, and sprinkle with a little caster sugar.

3. To make the batter, crack the eggs into a mixing bowl and whisk with the sugar until well combined. Whisk in the vanilla extract, cream, flour and groundx almonds.

4. Stir the fruit and its juices into the batter, then pour the mixture into the prepared dish. Bake for 30 minutes, turning the dish around once during cooking, if necessary, so it cooks evenly. The clafoutis is ready when it is lightly browned all over and the batter has set.

Other fruits for a clafoutis: 450g halved plums or apricots, or chunks of eating apples or pears.

5. Serve warm or at room temperature, with the icing sugar dusted over the top just before serving, and extra cream on the side.

EVE'S PUDDING

SERVES **5–6**

" **2 large** cooking apples
" **1 x 400g** tin of apricot halves or other fruit
" **1 tbsp** lemon juice
" **½** lemon, *finely grated zest*

topping:

" **100g** butter, *at room temperature*
" **80g** soft brown sugar
" **150g** self-raising flour
" **50g** ground almonds (or 50g more flour)
" **a scant capful** of almond extract (optional)
" **2 large** eggs
" **2–3 tbsp** milk

A cold day; a grey day; a slight feeling of mid-week slump, or just plain appetite: all can be fixed by Eve. Throw some fruit in a pot, top with a roughish sponge (made quickest of all in a food processor), put the pud in the oven and pour yourself a glass of wine.

Apples are the original base of Eve's pudding. Apples were never named as the fatal fruit in the Garden of Eden and scholars have put forward a number of other candidates, such as apricots or pomegranates. I've taken this as a cue to add a handy tin of apricots, not least because they go so well with apples and almonds, and make the dish more moist.

1. Set the oven to 200°C/Gas 6. Peel and core the apples and chop into small pieces. Place in a 1-litre dish with the apricot halves and their juice, plus the lemon juice and zest.

2. To make the topping, cream together the butter and sugar in a food processor, then add the rest of the ingredients, apart from the milk, and whizz briefly to mix. If making this by hand, cream the butter and sugar, then add one egg at a time, alternating with the dry ingredients. Add enough milk, pulsing or stirring as you go, to get a consistency that will fall off a spoon.

3. Spread the sponge mixture carefully on top of the fruit by dolloping it all over the top and then spreading it out into an even layer with the back of the spoon. Put the dish in the oven to bake for 40 minutes, or until the sponge is risen and golden and cooked all the way through.

4. Serve with cream, ice cream or, best of all, custard.

APPLE CHARLOTTE

SERVES **6**

6 eating apples (a sharpish variety such as Cox is best)

about **4 tbsp** caster sugar

½ **tsp** orange blossom water or ¼ tsp rose water

½ **tsp** vanilla extract

80g unsalted or lightly salted butter

9 thin slices white bread, *crusts removed* (about 160g, crustless weight)

Jane Grigson in her *Observer Guide to British Cookery* sings the praises of this classic pudding. She points out how, at its simplest, apple charlotte has just four ingredients: apples, bread, butter and sugar. This sort of 'good plain cooking' can be delicious, but only when the ingredients are totally tip-top. I generally add an ingredient or two to the apple purée, such as orange blossom water and vanilla. As well as adding to the overall flavour, these make the apple taste sweeter without adding too much sugar.

Another good flavour combination for the purée is a cinnamon stick and 2–3 cloves. Remember to fish both out before putting the purée in the charlotte.

Use eating apples rather than cooking apples for this dish, because you don't want too much liquid inside the crisp bread.

1. Preheat the oven to 200°C/Gas 6, with a baking tray inside to ensure the base crisps up nicely.

2. First make a stiffish apple purée. Peel, quarter and core the apples. Chop into small pieces and put in a medium pan with a little water (about 100ml). Cover with a lid and cook over a medium heat for around 10 minutes, stirring occasionally, until the apple pieces have softened. Take the lid off and keep cooking until most of the liquid has evaporated, pressing down occasionally on the apples with a wooden spoon to get a rough purée. Stir in the sugar, to taste, and then the orange blossom or rose water and vanilla extract.

3. Melt the butter in a small pan. Liberally brush the bottom and sides of a 1-litre soufflé dish (or oven proof bowl) with the butter.

AT ITS SIMPLEST, JUST FOUR INGREDIENTS

4. Cut 8 slices of the bread into two rectangles and the final slice into quarters. Use all but 4 of the rectangles of bread to line the outside of the dish, with about 4cm of each piece angled flat on the base of the dish to make an L-shape. Brush the bread on both sides with butter as you go, and slightly overlap the pieces and squidge them together to form joins. Lay three of the square pieces of bread in the base of the dish to cover it completely. If you need more to do this, just cut up another piece of bread into squares and butter them on both sides.

5. Spoon the apple purée into the dish and cover with the last 4 rectangles and final square of the butter-brushed bread. Reserve the remaining butter.

6. Bake the apple charlotte for 20 minutes, then reduce the heat to 190°C/Gas 5 and cook for another 20 minutes until the top has browned – you want the outside to be crisp.

7. Slide a knife around the outside of the pudding and carefully tip the charlotte out onto an ovenproof serving dish, wearing oven gloves when you invert it onto the plate. Brush the remaining butter on top and put back in the oven for 10 minutes. This can be done in advance of guests arriving and the charlotte kept warm in a low oven.

8. Serve hot or warm with cream; Jane Grigson recommends 'thick' cream and I tend to agree. Some may want a little more sugar to sprinkle over as well.

FITZHERBERT PUDDING

SERVES **8**

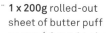

" **1 x 200g** rolled-out sheet of butter puff pastry (about A4 size)
" **75g** butter
" **400g** apple purée, homemade (see note) or bought
" **50–75g** caster sugar, to taste
" **4 medium** eggs
" **a good grating** of nutmeg
" **½** lemon, *finely grated zest*
" **75g** fine breadcrumbs
" **2–3 tsp** orange flower water, to taste
" milk or some beaten egg, to glaze (optional)

I found this eighteenth-century apple tart in the charming *Sussex Recipe Book (with a few excursions into Kent)*. This collection of recipes from homes and cookbooks was originally published in 1937 and I became absorbed by the book when writing an introduction for a republished edition, done by Ann Bagnall's Southover Press in 2005. Historic recipes are a good source of ideas when rediscovering seasonal cooking. The ingredients used in the book are still on my doorstep, cheap and tasty when their time comes around.

To make an apple purée, peel, quarter and core 2 Bramley or other cooking apples. Cut into small pieces and cook in a pan with the lid on with a small dash (20ml) of water for 8–10 minutes, stirring occasionally to ensure the mixture doesn't burn.

Ready-made puff pastry makes the tart quick to prepare. Make sure you get one made with butter.

1. Preheat the oven to 200°C/Gas 6. Place the pastry sheet on a baking tray and cook in the preheated oven for 10 minutes, until lightly brown and puffed up.

2. Meanwhile, melt the butter in a medium saucepan, then remove from the heat and stir in the rest of the ingredients, apart from the glaze, adding sugar, to taste, according to the sharpness or sweetness of your apple purée. Add the orange flower water, tasting after 2 tsp; it is stronger than you'd think.

3. Take the pastry out of the oven. Turn the heat down to 180°C/Gas 5. Score a rim around the pastry about 2cm wide. Push down the pastry in the middle and dollop the mixture into the centre of the case, spreading it out into an even layer with the back of the spoon. If you like, glaze the pastry rim with milk or beaten egg.

4. Put the dish back in the oven and cook for 20 minutes, or until the top is set. Serve hot or warm, with cream (it is also nice cold, but warm feels better).

LATE SUMMER PUDDING

SERVES **6**

¨ **450g** blackberries
¨ **2 medium** eating apples, *peeled & cut into small cubes*
¨ **3 tbsp** crème de cassis or blackcurrant cordial

¨ **4 tbsp** sugar (demerara for choice)
¨ **10 thin slices** white bread, *crusts removed*

This easy dish traditionally uses up stale bread and the glut of summer fruit. Here's a version with blackberries, ideally foraged from hedgerows, to go with windfall or scrumped apples: the food-for-free of late summer and early autumn that is cheap but not mean.

Bags of frozen berries, defrosted, are useful for this dish. They are cheap and can be good quality.

Blackberries arrive earlier than you think, especially in London's heat, where they could even be served at Wimbledon instead of strawberries. This wild fruit is there for the taking in most places in the lazy, late-summer days of August.

1. Put the fruit in a medium saucepan and add the crème de cassis or cordial and 3 tbsp of the sugar. Cover with a lid and bring to the boil. Turn down the heat and simmer for 5 minutes.

2. Drain the fruit in a colander set over a bowl, collecting the juice. Dip the bread into the juice and use it to line a 1-litre pudding basin: one piece on the bottom and six or seven around the sides. Slightly overlap the pieces of bread, squidging the edges together so there are no gaps.

3. Put the fruit into the centre of the basin and pour any remaining juice over. Cover with two last juice-dipped pieces of bread, so that the fruit is completely contained within its bready shell.

4. Cover a saucer with clingfilm and place on top of the pudding. Add a heavy weight (such as a tin of tomatoes) on top of the saucer and leave in the fridge overnight.

5. To turn out, run a knife around the outside of the pudding. Put a serving plate on top of the basin. Invert it quickly, giving the pudding a sharp shake to help ease it out.

6. Serve with cream and sprinkle over the last 1 tbsp of crunchy demerara (or other) sugar.

GIN COCKTAIL
JELLIES

SERVES **6**

" **10g** leaf gelatine (generally 5 small sheets, but check on packet)
" **100ml** gin (can be fruit flavoured, eg sloe or raspberry)
" **3 tbsp** caster sugar
" **500ml** good-quality apple juice
" **2 tbsp** elderflower cordial
" **juice of ½** lime

Cocktails are essentially alcoholic, drinkable desserts that mix flavours in a delightful way. Add enough gelatine and you make the liquid set into a spoonable, wibbly-wobbly jelly. These slip down as easily as cocktails and are a great way to savour the flavours of drinks without getting too tipsy.

1. Put the gelatine in a shallow bowl and cover with water. Leave to soak for 10 minutes, to soften.

2. Put the gin in a medium-sized pan with the sugar, heat gently – do not boil – and stir to dissolve. Turn off the heat.

3. Add half the apple juice to the sugary gin. Squeeze the water out of the gelatine leaves and stir into the pan until dissolved. The residual heat should be enough to do this. If not, heat very gently, stirring all the time.

4. Leave the mixture to cool slightly, then add the rest of the apple juice, the elderflower cordial and lime juice.

5. Pour into six glasses, each with a capacity of about 150ml – you want some space at the top. When completely cool, put in the fridge to set, covered. Allow 3 hours for it to set but it's best to give it a bit longer to be certain. Eat within 3 days.

Vary the mixture as you like and taste as you go. Remember that flavours lessen as they chill, so make sure your jelly has plenty of oomph.

The amount of gelatine is there to let the jelly set in a glass. If making one single jelly in a mould, add 4g more to ensure it holds its shape.

JAM
STEAMIE

SERVES **4–5**

110g unsalted butter at room temperature
100g caster sugar
2 large eggs
1 tsp vanilla extract

100g self-raising flour
100g jam (strawberry, blackcurrant & raspberry are especially good here)

Here's my ultimate nursery pudding. Everything about it makes me feel happy and loved, from the colourful hat of jam on top to the juicy, moist crumb of the sponge and the custard or cream sliding down onto the plate. What's more, this is a quick and easy pudding to make, even if it takes a while to cook. At the end comes the satisfaction of turning the pud out onto a serving plate. My inner 10-year-old feels one step further towards her Brownie hostess badge each and every time.

If you don't have a steamer, you can easily improvise your own. Put a large jar lid, a thick roll of tin foil curved into a round, or a large muffin ring, on the base of the saucepan and place the basin on top. Pour water so it comes about halfway up the pudding basin, bring to the boil and cook, at a slow boil, with the lid on. If the pan isn't big enough for the basin to fit under the lid, wrap foil tightly over the top and put a lid on top of that.

Jars of jam can accumulate, especially if you make your own, or are given pots by friends who do. This pud is a great way to show them off (and use them up) – you can even use a mixture of the remnants of different jars. If you have a glut of marmalade then use that and add the grated zest of 1 orange or lemon to the sponge mixture.

1. Use a food mixer, food processor, a hand-held beater, or a wooden spoon to cream together 100g of the butter and all of the sugar until fluffy. Beat in one of the eggs with the vanilla extract, then half the flour, then the other egg and then the rest of the flour and a pinch of salt.

2. Grease a 1-litre pudding basin with the remaining 10g of butter – you want it generously greased. Spoon the jam into the bottom, then dollop the batter on top.

3. You can cook this in a lidded pudding basin, or cover the top with foil, otherwise, tear off a piece of greaseproof paper large enough to cover the basin, with a little extra. Make a 3cm fold in the centre so the paper can expand as the pudding cooks. Place the paper over the basin and tie it down, just under the rim of the basin, with some string.

4. Put the basin in the top part of a steamer and steam for 2 hours, covered, taking care the steamer doesn't go dry.

5. Remove the covering and slide a knife around the edge of the pudding to loosen. Put a large plate on top and invert, so that the pudding turns out onto the plate. Serve with custard or cream.

PEAR &
CHOCOLATE
TRIFLE

SERVES **10**

This is a slightly adapted version of trifle belle hélène in the wonderful *Trifle*, by Alan Davidson and Helen Saberi. Helen told me it is one of her favourite trifles, and she is certainly spoilt for choice as the book runs from the sixteenth-century English kitchen to versions from Eritrea, Mexico, Laos and Trinidad.

¨ **3 x 410g** tins pear halves, *drained, juice reserved*
¨ **1 tbsp** caster sugar, if needed
¨ **200g** boudoir or amaretti biscuits
¨ **2 tbsp** amaretto or other liqueur (optional)
¨ **200g** dark chocolate
¨ **1 tsp** vanilla extract

¨ **2 x 250g** tubs mascarpone
¨ **100g** icing sugar
¨ **200ml** double cream

toppings according to your delight:
¨ toasted flaked almonds/angelica/ grated chocolate

1. Drain the pears and measure out the juice. You should have about 500ml, if not, top up with water and 1 tsp or so of caster sugar, to make the volume up. Put the biscuits in bottom of your trifle bowl. Sprinkle over the booze and 50ml of the juice from the pears. Slice the pears thickly and arrange on top of biscuits.

2. Break up the chocolate and put in pan with 250ml of the pear juice and the vanilla extract. Melt the chocolate over a low heat, then turn up the heat and boil the mixture for 1 minute, stirring continuously to let it slightly thicken. Allow to cool, then pour over the pears.

3. In another bowl, beat the mascarpone with the icing sugar and cream until smooth. Mix in enough of the remaining pear juice to keep it spreadable, but not sloppy (it should be about the rest of what's left). Dollop on top of the pears and spread out with the back of the spoon to get an even layer.

4. Decorate the top with grated chocolate or anything else you like.

You can poach your own pears but the tinned ones work fine here.

Toppings are dealt with in *Trifle* in an opening section called 'Trifle Architecture'. The trick is to ensure they don't sink and this can be about the wide 'footprint' of the topping, such as angelica, as well as the weight and the thickness of the cream.

CHOCOLATE
BEETROOT
BROWNIES

MAKES ABOUT 24
SMALL, RICH BROWNIES

- **200g** dark chocolate (around 70% cocoa solids)
- **220g** unsalted butter
- **100g** caster sugar
- **100g** light muscovado sugar
- **300g** pre-cooked beetroot, *peeled & roughly chopped*
- **3 medium** eggs
- **1 tsp** vanilla extract
- **2 tbsp** cocoa powder
- **4 tbsp** plain flour
- **100g** ground almonds

Grated beetroot combines with chocolate to make a dark, damp and rich version of brownies. These are slightly less sweet than many recipes, but still as sumptuously indulgent. A batch of brownies is useful for puddings as well as teatime and I make these often. The recipe is an adaptation from one in the excellent *Riverford Farm Cook Book* by Jane Baxter and Guy Watson. Their version is gluten-free. I've substituted ordinary plain flour for the original rice flour, but it's easy enough to revert back.

Additions include 100g roughly chopped nuts (pecans or macadamias for preference) or 4 tbsp mixed peel. Stir these in right at the end of mixing, just before baking. You can tip the mixture into a bowl or be lazy and do it carefully in the tin itself.

Cooked beetroot is easy to find in supermarkets and greengrocers. Just make sure it isn't the kind stored in vinegar.

Different size tins can be used. What matters is that the mixture is about 4cm deep, or else adjust the cooking time slightly to be longer or shorter.

Chocolate varies in its percentage of cocoa solids. If you use one with higher cocoa solids, cut down on the cocoa powder slightly. If the chocolate is less intense, add a bit more cocoa.

1. Preheat the oven to 180°C/Gas 4. Break the chocolate into squares and cut 200g of the butter into cubes. Place in a heat-resistant bowl and leave in the oven: the chocolate and butter will melt as the oven heats up in around 3 minutes. Give the mixture a couple of stirs as you go and then leave to cool slightly.

2. Meanwhile, get on with the rest of the preparation. Grease a shallow rectangular tin (about 30 x 20cm) with the remaining butter. Put the sugars into the bowl of a food processor along with the roughly chopped beetroot. Shmush together well to form a sugary, purple paste.

3. Crack in the eggs and add the vanilla extract, cocoa powder and a pinch of fine sea salt. Whizz to combine. Mix in the butter and chocolate mixture, then add the flour and ground almonds and pulse until the mixture is just combined.

4. Spoon the brownie mixture into the prepared tin and cook in the preheated oven for around 30 minutes, or until a skewer put into the centre comes out slightly smudged with dough – but not too much – and the top is firm to the touch.

5. Leave to cool and cut into squares. I like to cut 24 relatively small pieces as the brownies are quite intense. Store in an airtight container. Best eaten within a week.

CHOCOLATE CHIP
BREAD-&-BUTTER
PUDDING

SERVES **8–10**

˝ **4 medium** eggs,
plus 2 yolks
˝ **150g** caster sugar
˝ **400ml** double cream
˝ **200ml** whole milk
˝ **1 tsp** vanilla extract

˝ **10g** butter
˝ **400g** brioche with
chocolate chips
˝ icing sugar,
for dusting

This rich version of bread-and-butter pudding feeds a crowd and uses the handy short-cut of chocolate chip brioche. I got the idea from Borut Kozelj, a butcher at the renowned Ginger Pig in London. He served the pud at the end of a butchery class. We had already eaten a meat feast in the midst of the shop, yet his pudding inspired yet more greed and pleasure.

1. In a large bowl, whisk together the whole eggs and egg yolks with the sugar. Then beat in the cream, milk and vanilla until well combined, making the basis of your custard.

2. Butter a 30 x 20 x 7cm rectangular ovenproof dish (or similar capacity). Cut the brioche into 1cm-thick slices and dip them into custard, just like when you make eggy bread. Layer the dipped slices in the dish so that they overlap slightly. Pour the rest of the custard on top and leave to soak for 30 minutes.

3. Meanwhile, preheat the oven to 180°C/ Gas 4. Put the bread and butter pudding on a baking tray with at least 3cm sides and put in the oven. Pour a 2cm depth of just-boiled water from a kettle into the baking tray, to help create a soft and steamy bain-marie so the pudding cooks more gently. Cook for 30 minutes, or until lightly browning on top.

4. Take the pudding out of the oven and leave it to stand for 15–30 minutes. Dust lightly with icing sugar and serve warm or at room temperature.

Serve with more cream or ice cream. Indulgent, yes, but works well. The pud is also good with a fruit such as strawberries or the apricots with vanilla (see page 203).

RASPBERRY BREAD-&-BUTTER PUDDING

SERVES **6–8**

- **8 thin slices** white bread, *crusts removed* (standard sliced is fine)
- **40g** butter, *at room temperature*, plus more for the dish
- **4 tbsp** good raspberry jam
- **300ml** whole milk
- **150ml** double cream, plus more to serve
- **3 medium** eggs
- **1 tsp** vanilla extract
- **1 tsp** ground cinnamon (optional)
- **1–2 tbsp** rum (optional but good)
- **2–3 tbsp** caster sugar, plus 2 tbsp more for custard if necessary
- **125g** fresh or defrosted raspberries

Bread-and-butter pudding is such a classic One Pot that I couldn't resist including two. Out of season, frozen raspberries are a tasty bargain and work well here. Raspberry jam, a lovely dark pinky red, captures the flavour of the fruit and is one of my favourite preserves. I usually have a potful in the kitchen and like to use it in recipes as well as spreading it on toast, spooning it into rice pudding and using it in afters such as this.

You can prepare this a few hours in advance and cook it when guests arrive to eat warm, or make it the day before and reheat to warm or hot.

My homemade raspberry jam tends to be on the tart side. If your jam is sweet, adjust the sugar in the custard and on top of the pudding to get the right balance. Then again, sweet jam means a sweet tooth and you may want to keep the quantities as written. You can always take a quick taste before serving and sprinkle more sugar on at the end.

1. Spread the slices of bread with butter and then jam. Cut each slice into 4 triangles. Butter a gratin dish (about 20cm square and 8cm deep) and lay the bread slices into it in three lines, overlapping but in a single layer.

2. In a bowl, use a fork to whisk together the milk, double cream, eggs and vanilla, plus the cinnamon and rum, if using. If your raspberry jam is quite tart, add 2 tbsp caster sugar to this custard mix and leave to dissolve, stirring occasionally, for 5 minutes.

3. Scatter the raspberries evenly over the bread slices. Pour over the custard mixture. Leave the pudding to rest in a cool or cold place for at least 30 minutes and ideally 1 hour, for the bread to absorb the liquid.

4. Preheat the oven to 180°C/Gas 4. Sprinkle 2–3 tbsp (depending on your sweet tooth) of caster sugar evenly over the top of the dish.

5. Put the dish on a baking tray with at least 3cm sides and put them in the oven. Pour a 2cm depth of just-boiled water from a kettle into the baking tray, to help create a soft and steamy bain-marie so the pudding cooks more gently.

6. Cook the pudding for around 30 minutes, or until the top is firm and browning slightly. Serve warm or hot, with more cream.

CREAMY RICE PUDDING

SERVES 6–8

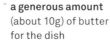

a generous amount (about 10g) of butter for the dish

100g short-grain rice

100g light brown sugar

1 litre whole milk & double cream (I favour half & half)

1 vanilla pod, *split*, or 1 tsp vanilla extract

1 tsp *freshly grated* nutmeg

Soothing yet treating, rice pudding transforms a dim winter day into a cosy treat. It even makes you look forward to staying indoors, warm by the oven and away from dripping grey. This is such an easy pudding but you do need decent ingredients. Jane Grigson nailed the common problem: 'Like so many other English dishes, it has been wrecked by meanness and lack of thought.' Sugar and spice and all things nice (not least butter and cream) are what's needed. There are lots of ways to play with rice pudding but I like the easy-to-remember proportions of this one.

The way a little rice absorbs so much liquid is one of the magical aspects of rice pudding. Don't lose your nerve and add more; it really does work.

A blob of jam is a traditional accompaniment, though you don't need it with this one. To make the dish go further, and be slightly less rich, I like to serve it alongside pears poached in heather honey syrup. My local pub, The First In, Last Out, in Hastings, serves their gorgeous rice pud with rosehip syrup; an excellent idea.

1. Preheat the oven to 150°C/Gas 2. Butter a gratin dish. Mine is 22cm square and 6cm deep and holds about 1.5 litres.

2. Mix all the other ingredients together in the dish, scraping out the vanilla seeds from the pod with the end of the teaspoon handle.

3. Cook for 2 hours, stirring once or twice. Serve hot, warm or chilled.

MARMALADE PARKIN

MAKES A TRAYFUL, FEEDS PLENTY

- **150g** unsalted butter
- **100g** treacle
- **100g** dark muscovado or molasses sugar
- **200g** thin-cut marmalade
- **150g** plain flour
- **200g** rolled porridge oats
- **1 tsp** mixed spice
- **3 tsp** ground ginger
- **½ tsp** bicarbonate of soda
- **2 globes** of stem ginger, *finely chopped*
- **1** orange, *finely grated* zest
- **2 medium** eggs
- **50ml** milk

Parkin is a traditional English bake that is eaten on Bonfire Night and at wintry teatimes. The original version should really be left for at least a week or so before eating. I love hardcore parkin, but also had a few goes at crossing it with easy-eating flapjacks and adding an orange tang. Here's the happy result – and you don't have to wait to tuck in.

You can eat this straight away or it keeps well (for months) if kept in one piece and wrapped in greaseproof paper in an airtight container.

Parkin is a great base for a pud. I love it with poached pears and clotted cream, macerated fruit such as apricots with vanilla (see page 203) or with a swirl of toffee sauce and vanilla ice cream.

1. Preheat the oven to 150°C/Gas 2. Line a baking tray (about 30 x 23cm) with baking parchment.

2. Put the butter, treacle, sugar and marmalade in a medium-sized pan. Heat gently, stirring occasionally, until melted together. Leave to cool slightly.

3. Meanwhile, measure out the flour, oats, spices and a pinch of salt into a mixing bowl. Stir together.

4. Add the bicarbonate of soda to the pan with the buttery treacle. Stir in the stem ginger and orange zest, then whisk in the eggs and milk. Pour into the bowl of dry ingredients and stir well to combine.

5. Tip the mixture into the baking tray and use the back of a spoon to spread it out evenly.

6. Put the tray into the oven to bake for 35–40 minutes, until firm to the touch. Leave to cool. Cut into thin strips, about 4cm thick, or small squares.

SUSSEX POND PUDDING

SERVES **6**

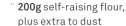

- **200g** self-raising flour, plus extra to dust
- **100g** ready-shredded or fresh suet, *grated*
- **120ml** cold water
- **100–150g** salted butter (according to greed), *cubed*, plus 15g for greasing
- **100–150g** demerara sugar (again, according to greed)
- **1 large** lemon

This particularly good suet pud is beloved by all, even those who don't normally like stodge. A whole lemon is surrounded by a suet crust and steamed. Cut it open at the table so a great buttery-lemony waft spreads around to all. There is some discussion whether Sussex Pond Pudding is a historic recipe or a more recent invention. Either way, I happen to eat it often in Sussex when I need an antidote to a certain kind of winter coastal weather.

I remember struggling along Hastings seafront on a dark and wild December night to watch football in the pub. The wind flung rain into our faces and tried to tip us over, but just a small bowlful of this suet pudding in our bellies was ballast enough to help us sail through any storm (or home defeat).

To scale up the recipe, up the quantities of suet pastry and cook the pud in a larger pudding basin, adding more butter and sugar to the filling. I once rolled out the smaller quantity of pastry to 5mm thick and put it in a larger basin. The lemon burst out of the thinner case when I turned the pud out but it still looked spectacular: a golden globe in the midst of the buttery pastry.

1. Grease a 1-litre pudding basin with 10–15g of butter, paying particular attention to the base. (If you are at all nervous, cut a small round of greaseproof paper to line the base and stop the pudding sticking when you turn it out; I don't find it necessary.)

2. Put the flour, suet and a pinch of salt into a mixing bowl and stir together with your hands. Add the water to the centre of the bowl and use a table knife to roughly mix it into the dry ingredients. Once the water is incorporated, use the splayed fingers of one hand, rather like a claw, to thoroughly combine and bring together the mixture into a ball of dough.

3. Dust the work surface with flour and knead the dough for 30 seconds or so to make it come together. Flour a rolling pin and roll the dough out to a round, scattering a little more flour on top of the dough before turning it over to roll it out some more. Turn the dough by a quarter every few rolls to help keep the thickness even. You want to end up with a 1cm-thick circle.

4. Cut a quarter out of your circle of dough and put to one side. Lower the rest into your buttered basin and press the two sides together to seal.

5. Put half the cubed butter and half the sugar in the bottom of the basin. The exact quantity of butter and sugar you use – 100g–150g – is up to you; the smaller amount is enough. What matters is that you should have the same weight of butter and sugar. Pierce the lemon all over with a skewer or the prongs of a fork and put in the basin. Put the rest of the butter and sugar on top.

6. Roll out the remaining quarter of pastry a little more to form a rough circle. Put this over the edge of the pastry in the basin and roll it over the top, pinching the two pieces together to make a seal.

7. Cover tightly with foil, or tear off a piece of greaseproof paper large enough to place over the top of the basin, with extra. Make a 3cm fold in the centre so the paper can expand. Place the paper over the basin and tie it down just under the rim of the basin with some string.

8. Put the basin in a steamer and steam for 3½ hours, taking care the steamer doesn't go dry. If you don't have a steamer, you can improvise (see note, page 231).

9. You can leave this in its steamer, bubbling away, until you are ready to eat.

10. To serve, remove the covering and slide a knife down between the pudding and the basin to loosen. Turn the pudding out onto a dish that you can put on the table. At the table, cut open the pud and serve each person with a small piece of pastry, soaked in the lemony buttery sauce. Cream alongside is essential.

TOFFEE BANANA
TARTE TATIN

SERVES **6**

- **3 large** bananas (firm; not too ripe)
- **125g** caster sugar
- **125g** unsalted butter, *cut into small pieces*
- **juice of ½** lemon
- **200g** ready-rolled butter puff pastry

The scent of this pudding cooking builds up anticipation, and it is a beautiful dish to set upon the table, worthy of a serving plate with a pedestal. Expect requests for seconds.

Small bananas, generally from the Caribbean, are sweeter and tastier than the larger fruit from South America and would be my choice for this dish, as well as my fruit bowl.

1. Preheat the oven to 220°C/Gas 7. Peel the bananas and cut them in half, lengthways, if small. If the bananas are large, cut in half down the middle and then these two pieces in half again, lengthways.

2. Dot the butter into an oven proof sauté pan (about 30cm in diameter) and sprinkle over the sugar. Heat over a lowish heat so that the sugar melts into the butter, drawing through the end of a wooden spoon occasionally to help this along.

EXPECT REQUESTS FOR SECONDS

3. Place the bananas around the pan like the spokes of a wheel, round side down and tips pointing into the centre. You can also place the banana pieces willy-nilly over the pan (especially if they break) and the dish still looks great.

4. Turn up the heat to medium and caramelize the butter-sugar mixture. This takes 8–10 minutes. Move the pan around over the heat every so often to encourage this to happen as evenly as possible.

5. When the caramel is bubbling and as brown as you dare (get it before it burns) take the pan off the heat and quickly sprinkle over the lemon juice to stop the cooking.

6. Roll out the pastry sheet so that it is a rough circle slightly bigger than the diameter of your pan. Cover the dish with pastry, tucking the sides in over the bananas, and put the tart in the oven for 15 minutes, or until brown on top.

7. This can be made shortly before your guests arrive and tipped onto a serving plate while still hot or warm. Some of the banana pieces may stick to the pan, but you can ease them off and put them back in place on the serving dish.

8. Serve with cream or ice cream.

HOT CHOCOLATE SOUFFLÉ

SERVES **6**

- **a little** butter (about 5g), *melted*
- **4 tbsp** caster sugar
- **150g** plain chocolate (70% cocoa solids or more), *broken into squares*
- **100ml** double cream, plus more to serve
- **2 tbsp** liqueur eg brandy, Cointreau, Grand Marnier
- **6 medium** egg whites

A soufflé feels like a show-off sort of a dish. But – shhhhh! – it is actually very easy to make and can even fit into supper entertaining without too much fuss. Really.

1. Shortly before your guests arrive, grease a 1-litre soufflé dish with a little melted butter and dust with 1 tbsp of the caster sugar, rolling the dish around in your hands so you get a sugary crust on the sides and base.

2. Put the chocolate with the cream in a small pan over a low heat and simmer, stirring occasionally, until the chocolate has melted. Stir in the liqueur.

3. Whisk the egg whites into stiff peaks, adding the remaining sugar in spoonfuls as it starts to stiffen. You can now leave these to one side until pudding time.

4. While eating the main course, put a baking sheet in the oven and preheat to 200°C/Gas 6.

5. After the main course, quickly warm up the chocolate by putting the bowl on top of a pan of steaming water. Rewhisk the whites briefly, then fold the chocolate mixture into the egg whites using a large metal spoon, keeping as much air in the mix as possible.

6. Spoon the mixture into the prepared soufflé dish and run a clean finger around the rim (this helps it rise higher).

7. Cook the soufflé in the preheated oven for 25 minutes. It is ready when risen and firm on top, but with a slight wobble remaining. Bring to the table with more cream to pour on top.

Timing in this recipe is geared towards a leisurely pause between courses. If your meal is at a faster pace, then just make 6 smaller soufflés in ramekins and cook them for 12–14 minutes at the same temperature. You could also cook a larger, single soufflé at the same time as you eat the main course, but that makes timing tighter and less relaxing.

Spare egg yolks can be used for an ice cream or the custard opposite.

SAUTERNES CUSTARD WITH ORANGES

SERVES **6**

150ml sauternes or other pudding wine
300ml whipping cream
2 medium eggs, plus 4 yolks
2–3 tbsp caster sugar
3 oranges

The addition of pudding wine brings an indefinable layer of luxury to a custard, and this subtle, silky dessert has become a modern classic. Use any kind of wine; sauternes just has the most glamorous name, as well as an exquisite taste. The custard is often paired with prunes plumped with armagnac. My version has oranges alongside, to make it a slightly lighter dish that's good to serve all year round.

For a posh crème caramel version, put 150g sugar and 75ml water in a small pan. Heat slowly so the sugar melts, then turn up the heat and cook until a dark brown, slightly swirling the pan around every 10 seconds or so to cook the caramel evenly. Watch it like a hawk: the difference between caramel and burnt is just 10 seconds. Add 2 tbsp more water to stop the caramel going darker – it will hiss and spit, so do this quickly and carefully. If necessary, stir around on a low heat to dissolve any lumps. Carefully pour the caramel into 6 x 100ml ramekins and then swirl each one around so the caramel coats the bottom. Pour the custard on top, place the ramekins in a roasting pan and cook as per the recipe. Shortly before serving, run a hot knife around the edge of each custard and turn out onto a serving plate where it will be surrounded by a moat of caramel.

1. Preheat the oven to 150°C/Gas 2. Put the pudding wine in a small pan and bring to the boil. Boil for 1 minute, then remove from the heat and leave to cool for 2 minutes. Add the cream and reheat until just boiling, taking care it does not boil over. Turn off the heat and leave to cool slightly.

2. In a mixing bowl, whisk together the eggs, yolks and sugar (use the larger amount if you have a sweet tooth). Pour in the cream and wine mixture from a height in a thin stream, still whisking (you do this to ensure the mixture doesn't cook the eggs instantly).

3. Pour the custard into 6 ramekins or a shallow ceramic dish (about 600ml in capacity) and place in a roasting pan. Put your custard in the preheated oven and carefully pour just-boiled water into the pan so it comes halfway up the side of the dish or ramekins.

4. Cook the custard for 20–30 minutes, or until set; gently touch the centre of the custard to see if it is firm; ramekins will take slightly less time than one dish, so check after 10 minutes. Leave the custard to cool.

5. Peel the oranges, removing as much of the white pith as possible, and cut into thin rounds, then cut these in half. Put in a serving dish along with any of the juice that comes out as you cut. Serve the oranges alongside the custard.

KITCHEN
BASICS

OVEN TEMPERATURE

Ovens vary and the temperature given in
the recipes may be slightly different to that
indicated by your oven dial. If your oven has
a fierce fan, take the temperatures down by
10°C (or one gas mark), or even a little more.
An oven thermometer is useful for gauging
how your oven works, but experience and
observation are even better.

TOP POTS

If pressed, I could narrow my kitchen down
to two pots. A large, deep casserole (or a big
saucepan) with a lid, is the most useful pot
of all. My other stalwart is a wide and shallow
ovenproof sauté pan. This is good for dishes
when you want to evaporate off much of the
moisture, such as a paella or roasted vegetables.
Beyond this, rectangular or circular ceramic
dishes – the kind you know feed roughly 4,
6 or 8 – are handy for gratins and other One
Pots cooked in the oven. An omelette pan
with sloping sides, about 15cm in diameter,
is a luxury, but helpful for tortillas as well as
omelettes, and when cooking for one or two.
Those with slow cookers and pressure cookers
will easily be able to adapt these recipes to
this specialist kit.

QUANTITIES

A number of these dishes feed more than a
standard table of four because it's always handy
to have leftovers. I now use my freezer much
more and find it helps the time-pressed household
cook to batch cook larger quantities.

COOKING FAT

Olive oil is delicious, infinitely varied and comes in a convenient bottle or tin that's quick to grab; it is my basic for cooking and dressing. I also use vegetable oil, especially when the taste of the oil won't come through, but concerns about the refining process and pesticides have made me veer towards olive oil and (mostly but not always) organic vegetable oil. Butter makes food delicious and, if a dish isn't based in the olive-oily Mediterranean region, I often fry in a combination of half butter and half olive oil, so you get flavour and a higher burning point. Animal fats such as dripping, lard and chicken fat are now thought to be ok for your health. I like to use them because they have distinctive flavours, and add another layer to your final dish.

SALT & SOY SAUCE

Flaky sea salt is my standard. If you are using fine salt or table salt then reduce the amount suggested. Salt varies more than you'd think; it's good to know your brand and to explore different kinds. I use Japanese soy sauce as another form of salt. Cut the quantity given if using stronger Chinese soy sauces.

MEAT & EGGS

I tend to use cheaper cuts to make high welfare meat more affordable. Organic eggs, or free-range from smaller flocks (generally sold in local shops and farmers' markets), are a notch up from mass-produced free-range. I use medium eggs and keep them out of the fridge because they cook better at room temperature.

COLOUR CODING

The recipes in the book are colour-coded:
red for meat, blue for seafood and green for
vegetarian (plus yellow for custard or cream,
to go with the puds). These categories are
not hard set. The red recipes may have just a
small amount of meat, and I give options for
how to make some vegetarian. Conversely,
the green recipes may have an option for using
meat stock or a tip on how to adapt them to
use fish or meat, should that be what you want.

DAIRY

I tend to use whole milk and dairy products,
but most of the recipes are generally adaptable
to lower-fat products if that's what you prefer.
Where the fat content makes a difference to
the chemistry of the dish, I've specified full-fat.
Butter is generally unsalted; cut down on the
seasoning if using salted.

LAST MINUTE TRICKS
& SEASONING

One Pots often benefit from some last minute
flourishes from the storecupboard and fridge,
be it a squeeze of lemon, a blob of Greek
yoghurt, a swirl of oil or a scatter of chopped
herbs. I've given tips throughout the book on
how to do this and also pointers for seasoning.

BEST
FOR

FAST FOOD

EASY ENTERTAINING

SLOW & EASY

FEED A CROWD

CHEAP & CHEERING

USING UP VEGETABLES

GETTING KIDS TO EAT VEG

AN ADVENTURE

FEW INGREDIENTS

ADVANCE COOKING FOR ENTERTAINING

FURTHER

COOKING

&

READING

There is much collective cooks' wisdom about One Pots to be found in cookbooks. Here's a selection of my favourite sources.

A BOOK OF MIDDLE EASTERN FOOD
by Claudia Roden
An exceptional achievement of gathering and sharing, this classic takes you to the heart of many kitchens, revealing their time-honoured recipes and One Pots.

A PLATTER OF FIGS / HEART OF THE ARTICHOKE
by David Tanis
Two books with the sort of evolved attention to detail that make food a joy to make and eat.

COOKED
by Michael Pollan
Each chapter of this fascinating book explores a different mode of cooking, including the chemistry and culture of braises and stews.

COOK SIMPLE
by Diana Henry
One Pot cooks will find much in this collection of truly easy and tasty recipes by a great food writer.

DUMPLINGS
by Barbara Gallani
From gnocchi to wontons: a social history that also shows how to add heft to your One Pot.

ENGLISH FOOD
by Jane Grigson
'Our classical tradition has been domestic, with the domestic virtues of quiet enjoyment and generosity,' writes Grigson in the introduction to English Food; a summation of the home cooking and One Pots that is at the heart of her books – all good companions in kitchen, study and armchair.

ENTERTAINING ALL'ITALIANA
by Anna del Conte
One of Anna del Conte's many great books, this focuses on how to cook for gatherings and gives ideas for cook-ahead One Pots.

THE ESSSENTIALS OF CLASSIC ITALIAN COOKING
by Marcella Hazan
Italian food is full of sensational One Pots and this classic is a top go-to for the Italian kitchen.

EUROPEAN PEASANT COOKERY
by Elisabeth Luard
Luard's inquiring mind and experience of living in rural Spain and the Languedoc make this an outstanding collection of time-honoured traditions from 25 countries.

FAR EASTERN ODYSSEY
by Rick Stein
Stein's culinary curiosity on his travels is infectious, and he skilfully translates his discoveries to the domestic kitchen.

FOOD IN ENGLAND
by Dorothy Hartley
From the medieval cauldron to a bargee's
pail and Cornish iron roasting-pot, Dorothy
Hartley describes and illustrates all aspects
of English food, including One Pots.

FRENCH COUNTRY COOKING
by Elizabeth David
Every recipe places you in a kitchen, glass of
wine in hand, having a conversation about the
sort of French food that is part of the soul of
One Pot cooking.

GOOD TEMPERED FOOD
by Tamasin Day-Lewis
The subtitle of this book, 'recipes to love, leave,
and linger over' could be a mantra for the One
Pot cook.

HOME COOKING
by Laurie Colwin
One of my favourite books on food; these
cookery essays are funny, honest and full of the
companionship and entertainment of the table.

HONEY FROM A WEED
by Patience Gray
Southern European cooking, from Tuscany
and Catalonia to the Cyclades and Apulia,
inspired Gray to write a beautiful book
of simple ingredients and equipment, partly
drawn from cooking in a pot over a wood fire.

HOW TO COOK BETTER
by Shaun Hill
Hill's wit, clear thinking and great experience
all combine in this book, which teaches some
of the key principals of cooking.

HOW TO EAT
by Nigella Lawson
A modern classic that brought the individual,
human voice back into the cookbook. Many
recipes have few ingredients but bags of taste.

JELLIES & THEIR MOULDS
by Peter Brears
A well illustrated book that is sheer delight,
as well as classy food history.

KITCHENELLA
by Rose Prince
A call to arms for home cooking with lots of
intelligent modern recipes and strategies for
making good fresh food.

MEDITERREAN CLAY POT COOKING / THE SLOW MEDITERRANEAN KITCHEN / MOROCCAN FOOD
by Paula Wolfert
American food writer Paula Wolfert shares
her explorations of clay cooking pots, be they
cazuelas, bean pots or crock-pots. These books
are for those who want to slow down and bring
ingredients together with care and pleasure.

NOSHE DJAN; AFGHAN FOOD AND COOKERY
by Helen Saberi
A cookbook that takes you into many homes and many stoves – and to a great soup made in reclaimed teapots.

PULSE
by Jenny Chandler
A most un-brown and vibrant book about beans, including their use in many famous One Pots, with a handy 'indentification parade' at the end.

RIVERFORD FARM COOK BOOK
by Jane Baxter & Guy Watson
Many vegetable-centred One Pots lie amongst these excellent and straightforward seasonal recipes.

ROALD DAHL'S COOKBOOK
by Felicity & Roald Dahl
The recipes of a family and of a place; like your fantasy home cookbook, yet real and approachable as well as charming. One Pots to be found amidst memories, anecdotes and family photographs.

SIMPLE FRENCH FOOD
By Richard Olney
Alongside much knowledge and taste, Olney's recipes dare to be simple when simplicity is all that is needed.

SUPERGRAINS
by Jenni Muir
A brilliant book to inspire and help the One Pot cook to explore the ever-wider variety of grains now available. (Book-lovers should seek out the original edition, *A Cook's Guide to Grains*, with its Angie Lewin illustrations.)

THE GOOD COOK
by Simon Hopkinson
Just one of Hopkinson's wonderful cookbooks, all with ideas that will add class to One Pots.

THE INDEPENDENT COOK
by Jeremy Round
One of my favourite cookbooks of all time for its sense of taste and fun, this is a seasonal cookbook full of the spirit of home cooking.

THE MAGIC OF FIRE
by William Rubel
A special book on hearth cooking that makes you look again at your fireplace and cooking in pots using embers.

THE MODERN PEASANT / AUNT LIZA HAD A CAT CALLED SQUEAKER
by Jojo Tulloh
How to bring skills back to the home and the hand, plus a great self-published appreciation of Elizabeth David, Queen of Le Creuset.

THE PAUPER'S COOKBOOK
by Jocasta Innes
Plenty of One Pots in a classic cookbook that proves necessity is the mother of creativity.

THE RIVER COTTAGE FAMILY COOKBOOK
by Hugh Fearnley-Whittingstall and Fizz Carr
One of the many excellent River Cottage books, this family cookbook makes food easy, tasty and accessible for anyone, including children. Shows how One Pots can be part of the joy and journey of learning to cook.

THE TRIFLE BOWL AND OTHER TALES / A CELBRATION OF SOUPS
by Lindsey Bareham
Connects dishes to kitchen kit, including the clay chicken-brick, pudding basins, paella pan and soufflé dishes. And her soup book is soup-erb.

TRIFLE
by Alan Davidson & Helen Saberi
Every whim-wham, jelly, sherry and oddity (eg Beef Trifle) are in this characterful and wide-ranging collection. Worth reading even if you detest trifle.

VEGETABLE SOUPS
by Deborah Madison
You'd never think that a book with such a plain title could be so enthralling, but this is a must for anyone interested in layering flavours in a pot.

YOU'RE ALL INVITED
by Margot Henderson
As well as family food, this book of excellent recipes has a chapter on Feeding the Masses: how to scale up One Pots to feed 10, 20 or 30.

INDEX

THANKS

Thanks to Petra Cramsie, Clare Moberly, Debbie Oates, Sue Reddish and Isabel Turner for welcome reading, road-testing and feedback; to George Bennell of Belazu, Booths and Robert Owen Brown (for mutton inspiration), Jared Brown of Sipsmith, Deborah Colman, Ivan Day, Anne Griffiths, Sylvain Jamois, Monika Linton of Brindisa, Marianne Lumb of Marianne's, Elaine Mason of Union of Genius, Josiah Meldrum of Hodmedod's and the Bungay Happy Mondays, Lori de Mori, James O'Brien (for books), Sophie Orloff, Levi Roots, Helen Saberi, WenLin Soh of Edible Experiences, Andrea Spencer, Hugh Thomson (for Tia Nena), Jojo Tulloh, Guy Tullberg of Tracklements and Megan Yates, for pots, talking to me about pots and for pots-related travel; to my agent Georgina Capel for leading me to Head of Zeus; to Laura Palmer and all at Head of Zeus for their skilful zest and love of books; to graphic designer Zoë Bather for her flair and commitment to creating the book's look and feel; to my superb editor Madeleine O'Shea, who caught the spirit of the idea and helped it come to fruition with such knowledge and steadfast care; to my friend and food companion, Emily Faccini, whose paintings embody the joy and generosity of cooking at home. And my love and thanks to my mother, Margaret Ellis for the pots that have shaped my food and cooking, and to Tim, Rupert, Theo and Brodie Neilson, for their mouths... and so much else.